THE
PROMISE
OF THE
COMING DARK AGE

THE
PROMISE
OF THE
COMING DARK AGE

L. S. STAVRIANOS

W. H. Freeman and Company
San Francisco

This book is for
Cynthia, Michael, and Christopher.

Library of Congress Cataloging in Publication Data

Stavrianos, Leften Stavros.
 The promise of the coming dark age.

 Includes bibliographical references and index.
  1. Civilization, Modern—1950–
 2. Civilization—History.   3. Regression
 (Civilization)
 I. Title.
 CB428.S8   909.82   76-8232
 ISBN 0-7167-0497-8
 ISBN 0-7167-0496-X pbk.

Printed in the United States of America

3 4 5 6 7 8 9

CONTENTS

PREFACE

This is an exhilarating moment in human history. Far from being an Age of Trouble, or Alienation, or Anxiety, this is rather the age in which man for the first time can turn from his age-old struggle for survival to a new struggle for self-fulfillment that will enable him to realize his humanity. *Homo sapiens* is on the way to becoming *Homo humanus.*

Such an interpretation of the state of our species may seem perverse at a time when people everywhere still suffer from war, hunger, racism, ignorance, and all the other scourges that have afflicted them throughout recorded history. But those who focus exclusively on these traditional ailments overlook the historic significance of our era. All the tumult and seeming chaos, when viewed in the light of historical perspective, can be seen to represent not only the death agonies of an old order but also the birth pangs of a new epoch—a new golden age which assuredly will outshine those of the past.

Three stages are discernible in the evolution of human civilization. Before 1500 the great civilizations—Chinese, Indian, Middle Eastern, European, African, and Amerindian—went their respective ways with little interaction. Together with numerous local cultures, these civilizations evolved in varying degrees of regional isolation.

After 1500 the globe was united for the first time by Columbus, da Gama, Magellan, and the other European discoverers, who brought hitherto isolated branches of the human race—West African agriculturists, Patagonian food gatherers, Chinese peasants and mandarins—in touch with a rapidly developing European technology. By the nineteenth century, Europe was the undisputed center of world power, and Europe's imprint was imposed on all peoples, with or without their consent.

During the twentieth century Europe's hegemony disintegrated and gave way to a new global pluralism. European, or Western, civilization no longer is the sole model. Several alternatives are now available—the modified capitalism of the United States, the mixed capitalist-socialist societies of Western Europe, the varieties of socialism in Eastern Europe and East Asia, and the still undifferentiated embryos of the emerging societies of the Third World. This pluralism is a healthy development, making possible world-wide interaction and mutual stimulation.

For example, when the Five Year Plans were introduced in the Soviet Union they were ridiculed in the West as inherently unworkable, or denounced as constituting the "road to serfdom." Recently, however, U.S. Senators Jacob Javits and Hubert Humphrey have introduced "The Balanced Growth and Economic Planning Act of 1975" providing for the establishment of a planning agency within the Executive Office of the President. And conversely, the Soviets have been persuaded by various difficulties with their Five Year Plans to experiment with the market mechanism in regulating their economy. Thus, economic planning and the market system no longer are viewed as mutually exclusive features of socialism and capitalism, and particular economic policies are coming to be judged more by their efficiency in attaining specific objectives than by their ideological purity.

Also the "growth Olympics" indulged in by capitalist and socialist societies in recent years are beginning to be impeded by queries such as "How much growth?", "For what purpose?", and "Does more GNP mean higher quality of life?" These questions assume a new urgency and significance as Western diplomats, businessmen, academicians, and journalists return from Maoist China with reports of a new type of society in which slogans such as "Fight Self" and "Serve the People" are apparently becoming the way of life for a quarter of the human race. Thus, we are living in a world that is experiencing unprecedented innovation and experimentation at the same time that it is shrinking into a global village. This juxtaposition of diversity and unity suggests that the law of hybrid vigor operates today in the realm of cultural evolution as well as that of biology, thereby facilitating a creative response to the scourges that have afflicted humanity throughout history.

This conclusion may seem hopelessly unreal when so many are already writing post-mortems on the human race. But the fact is that history offers examples of things seeming darkest before the dawn—of significant forces being unrecognized or ignored and passing difficulties exaggerated. This was the case with Europe's fourteenth-century slump when everything went wrong—a series of crop failures and famines, the devastating Black Death, and the Hundred Years' War between England and France as well as other conflicts in Germany and Italy. Yet the following fifteenth century witnessed a remarkable resurgence of civilization, which in retrospect was clearly the product of long-range trends. These included medieval technological advances that stimulated productivity in agriculture, mining, and handicrafts; provided the economic base for population increase; quickened local and interregional commerce; and together with concurrent intellectual movements furnished the material and human resources as well as the social dynamism for expansion into Eastern Europe, the Holy Land, and later to overseas continents and eventual global hegemony.

By the end of the fifteenth century Europe was bursting at the seams. Columbus' discovery of America was in a way a lucky fluke, since he persisted in believing the Caribbean islands to be the East Indies. However, the aftermath of Columbus' discovery was anything but a fluke. We need only contrast it with the aftermath of Leif Ericson's discovery five centuries earlier. When the Vikings stumbled on North America, they tried for about a hundred years to maintain settlements there but without success. The sequel to Columbus' expedition, however, was a massive and overwhelming penetration of both North and South America by emigrants from all parts of Europe. The explanation for this historic contrast is to be found in the growth of Europe during the intervening half millennium. By the late fifteenth century, Europe had the resources, the organization, and the dynamism essential for overseas expansion. If Columbus had not discovered America in 1492, then someone else assuredly would have done so in the next few decades. It was not a question whether some European would reach the New World but rather in what year he would do so and who he would be. Europe, in short, had reached the take-off stage, and the fact that Columbus led the actual take-off in 1492 is an incidental detail in a foregone conclusion.

The same situation prevails today, but with all humanity in place of the Europeans, and with the New World about to be reached being new in a social sense rather than a geographic one. Just as the Europeans were at the take-off stage in the late fifteenth century, so mankind is today in the late twentieth. Again the exact date and the precise personalities are incidental. What is important is to perceive the state of readiness and not be misled by our contemporary version of the fourteenth-century slump.

Today, as never before, we have the opportunity to take hold of our destiny. We are at last free for the task of growing up as a species. But growing up is not comfortable; it is accompanied by stresses and strains.

The purpose of this study is to set forth not only the demands and responsibilities, the perils and discomforts, but also the potentialities and achievements of mankind as it enters its adulthood.

December 1975   *L.S.S.*

ACKNOWLEDGEMENTS

The preparation of the material in this volume was supported by National Science Foundation Grant No. GI-29730 from the RANN (Research Applied to National Needs) Program of NSF to the Center for Advanced Study in the Behavioral Sciences. Any opinions, findings, conclusions, or recommendations contained herein are those of the author and do not necessarily reflect the view of NSF or of the Center. This disclaimer must be extended also to colleagues who read the manuscript in one of its several reincarnations, and who now may find the end product unrecognizable. Despite what must have seemed at the time as inordinate perversity on my part, I deeply appreciated then, as I do now, the generous help of the following scholars: Albert Bandura of Stanford University; John Buttrick of York University; Geoffrey Barraclough of Brandeis University; Eugene Genovese of Rochester University; Peter Lambropoulos of the University of Southern California; David MacMichael of the Stanford Research Institute; William Peters, author and television documentary producer; John R. Platt of the University of Michigan; and Frederic Wakeman of the University of California, Berkeley. I am indebted also to Joan Warmbrunn for her conscientiousness and skill in typing the manuscript and for her unfailing assistance with myriad details during my year at the Center.

THE
PROMISE
OF THE
COMING DARK AGE

1
DARK AGES: OLD AND NEW

See what has befallen Rome, once mistress of the world. She is worn down by great sorrows, by the disappearance of her citizens, by the attacks of her enemies, by numerous ruins. Thus we see brought to fulfillment what the prophet [Ezekiel] long ago pronounced on the city of Samaria.

—Pope Gregory I

The unleashed power of the atom has changed everything save our modes of thinking, and thus we drift to unparalleled catastrophe.

—Albert Einstein

The Dark Age after Rome

The Dark Age following the collapse of Rome was anything but dark. Rather, it was an age of epochal creativity, when values and institutions were evolved that constitute the bedrock foundation of modern civilization. It is true that this creativity was preceded by imperial disintegration—by the shrinkage of commerce and cities, the disappearance of bureaucracies and standing armies, and the crumbling of roads and aqueducts and palaces. This imperial wreckage explains, but scarcely justifies, the traditional characterization of the early medieval period as "dark." It was an age of birth as well as of death, and to concentrate on the latter is to miss the dynamism and significance of a seminal phase of human history.

Such myopia perhaps also explains the pessimism pervading current assessments of the condition and prospects of human civilization. Recall that, despite the volume of research and the sophistication of techniques in the social sciences, their practitioners failed almost without exception to foresee the fundamental trends of the decades since World War II. Their oversights include the dismantling of empires after 1945, the advent of the multinational corporations, the sudden shifts in the relative economic strengths of the United States, Japan, and Western Europe, and the viability of the Maoist experiment despite its reliance on the energies of communal service rather than those of personal gain—a sacrilegious departure that prompted both American and Soviet experts to prophesy inevitable disaster.

Present-mindedness appears to be responsible both for this failure to anticipate such major divergences of the past few decades and for the gloomy prognostications for the forthcoming decades. If one is living in an uncomfortable period of transition and in a country that militantly opposes movements and regimes favoring a speed-up of the transition process,

2

present-mindedness will project the anxieties and forebodings of the turbu-
lent present into the future—a future that consequently will be faced with
apprehension rather than welcomed with anticipation. But if present-
mindedness is cast aside in favor of a more dynamic analysis of the contemporary world, the prospect emerges of a new Dark Age that, like the
medieval original, will witness deterioration and demolition, but that will
also generate amidst the wreckage new values and new institutions herald-
ing a new epoch in human history.

Analyzing the significance of the barbarian invasions of Rome, the
historian Robert Lopez wrote: "All in all, the invasions gave the coup de
grace to a culture which had come to a standstill after reaching its apogee
and seemed doomed to wither away. We are reminded of the cruel bombings in our own day which destroyed ramshackle old buildings and so made
possible the reconstruction of towns on more modern lines."[1]* The analogy
is relevant for our age, for modern civilization is undergoing a disintegration-
reintegration experience similar to those precipitated by the barbarian
invasions and the World War II bombings.

The Roman Empire, like our contemporary global civilization, was
outwardly impressive and seemingly unassailable. The familiar phrase
"grandeur of Rome" conjures up images of monumental arches, ordered
government, judicious magistrates, conquering legions, and a magnificent
capital city of one million people provided with staples and luxuries from as
near as Gaul and as far as China. But the fatal defect in this imposing imperial structure was technological stagnation, deriving from the prevalence
of slavery. It was simpler and cheaper to put slaves to work than to design
and construct new machines. Inventors in imperial Rome usually devised
gadgets not to save labor but to wage war or to facilitate religious ritual.
For example, in the first century A.D., Hero of Alexandria used his knowledge of steam power to construct a device that opened temple doors.

Slavery also inhibited technology by fostering a negative attitude
toward work. Since labor was the lot of slaves, it came to be regarded as
demeaning for any free citizen. Thus Seneca expressed scorn for manual
labor and insisted that the "loftily enthroned" philosopher should keep aloof
from the artisan, with his "bowed body and lowered eyes." It was precisely
this isolation of the philosopher from the artisan that inhibited Roman technology. And, later, the interaction between the two—the ordered specula-
tion of the philosopher and the practical experience of the artisan—was to

---

*Superscript numbers refer to notes at the end of the book.

enable the West to achieve its great scientific and industrial revolutions in modern times.

Since few new inventions came about to increase the productivity of Roman labor, the Empire's wealth could be increased only by bringing new lands under cultivation or through conquest and exploitation. But virgin lands were not limitless; indeed, large-scale erosion was eliminating extensive fertile regions throughout the Mediterranean basin as sources of food. Likewise, the Empire could not expand indefinitely, for there were strict limits beyond which its military technology did not extend. Thus a point of diminishing returns was inescapable when the pressure of the burgeoning military and bureaucratic establishments became too much for the Empire's static productive capacity.

A vicious circle then set in. Rising taxes and the increasing impoverishment of ordinary citizens fomented uprisings in the cities and countryside, which invited barbarian incursions and led ultimately to successful internal revolts or external invasions, or a combination of the two. Thus political disintegration led to feudalism, a system of government in which those who possessed landed estates also possessed political power, with the result that state authority was replaced by contractual agreements between lords and vassals. Likewise, economic disintegration led to manorialism, a form of social organization within the fedual system, in which self-sufficient villages or manors were worked by serfs who were not free to leave, and who with their labor supported a hierarchy of lay and clerical lords.

Thus emerged a new world and a new era that, not unnaturally, came to be known as the Dark Age. Darkness indeed seemed to have fallen over the ruins of empire. Great cities had given way to obscure villages, bustling commerce to occasional Jewish or Syrian pack peddlers, and magistrates and proconsuls to petty feudal lords and their vassals. But in retrospect this imperial disintegration stands out not just as a process of fragmentation but also as a process of social change—the emergence of a new social order characterized by new relationships between man and man and between man and nature.

Interpersonal relationships were transformed by the replacement of slaves, who had no rights and who were considered subhuman, with serfs, who had very definite rights as well as duties. Whereas the slaves had toiled on large plantations owned by absentee landlords, the serfs, although they were bound to their lord's land, enjoyed communal autonomy on the manor. They elected their own officers, made their own regulations, and managed certain of their own affairs, such as deciding the time of plowing

4

or harvesting, designating the use of pastoral land, and policing the fields. The serfs were full members of their village communities, and they counted as individuals by virtue of the natural laws of conducting local business rather than by any theory or legislation imposed from above by large-scale government.

The manorial system also transformed the relations between man and nature. Frontier conditions stimulated the invention of labor-saving devices and also endowed manual labor with a status and respect unknown in the old slave-based civilizations. The traditional gulf between philosopher and artisan began to be bridged, and the resulting combination of brain power and sweat generated more technological progress in medieval Western Europe than had been made in the entire history of Classical Greece and Rome. The Dark Age's advances include the "three-field" system of rotation farming, the heavy wheeled plow that made possible the cultivation of rich bottom lands, a new harness that multiplied the tractive performance of the horse four to five times, and the all-important watermill and windmill. Both of these tools were known in Greco-Roman times but were little used because of the abundance of slave labor. By contrast, England's Domesday Book of 1086 revealed the existence of no fewer than 5000 mills, or one for every 50 households—a proportion sufficient to substantially raise living standards.

By the tenth century the Western European serf was enjoying a level of living significantly better than that of the proletarian during the height of Augustan Rome. Improving living conditions in turn stimulated further technological innovation—in contrast to the Roman period, in which the relative poverty of the domestic mass market (since slaves had no purchasing power) was a constant and unavoidable depressant on the imperial economy. Medieval Europe enjoyed, with a few interruptions, technological and economic growth that fostered the reappearance of trade and cities and, above all, an internal dynamism that was to culminate first in the Crusades to the Holy Land and later in the voyages of discovery and the control of oceanic trade routes. This expansion triggered a chain reaction: the profits from these overseas commercial enterprises provided some of the capital necessary for the Industrial Revolution, which in turn enhanced Europe's economic and military power to the point of unchallengeable global domination.

Thus the technological and economic stagnation that characterized premodern civilizations at last was overcome. For the first time, Western man could count on a constant increase in the volume of goods and services.

He had attained, as the economists put it, the "takeoff into self-sustained growth." Keep in mind that the roots of this significant achievement go back to the Dark Age, when Roman imperial disintegration freed Western Europeans to strike out in the new directions from which modern civilization evolved.

The circumstances of the fall of Rome and the advent of the Dark Age are very relevant to the present world. Especially significant are, first, the geographic location of the rejuvenating Dark Age and, second, the social behaviors that were nurtured by the manorial system.

The geographic location was in the most retarded, or "underdeveloped," region of the Eurasian land mass. This fact illustrates the principle that anthropologists call the Law of the Retarding Lead. This law holds that the best adapted and most successful countries have the greatest difficulty in adapting and in retaining their lead in world affairs, and, conversely, that the backward and less successful societies are more likely to be able to adapt and forge ahead. Thus Western Europe's great advantage was that Roman civilization in that region had been thoroughly and irrevocably plowed under by repeated and prolonged barbarian invasions.

Invasions were not peculiar to Europe during those centuries. The Han Empire of China fell before similar barbarian onslaughts. But the Han dynasty was followed by the Sui, and Chinese civilization continued to flourish relatively unchanged despite the rise and fall of successive dynasties. In Europe, however, Roman civilization did not survive the fall of the Empire because the barbarian incursions were repeated and protracted. The Merovingian attempt to restore the Roman Empire in the sixth century was shattered by the Avars, and the Carolingian attempt in the ninth century by the Magyars, Vikings, and Moslems. Because all efforts at imperial restoration failed, the end result in the West was the uprooting of the old order to a degree unparalleled in China or anywhere else in Eurasia. This devastation, ironically, was a principal reason for the primacy of the West in modern times, for a new civilization was able to emerge out of the ruins of the old—a civilization better adapted to the demands of a changing world. Thus Western Europe was freed from the burden of the Retarding Lead that was to hamper China through the Middle Ages and into modern times.

We shall return in the concluding chapter to the obvious implications of this Retarding Lead syndrome for the twentieth-century world, in which China and the West have exchanged their historic roles; China is now the underdeveloped society, while the West is balancing at the top, experiencing all the attendant perils of that position.

As for the distinguishing social characteristic of the Dark Age, it was an underlying participatory impulse that is distinctive of the present age as well. Medieval serfs engaged in more self-management than did the slaves of the Roman Empire, and this autonomy was to develop and blossom during the following centuries under the Western tendency toward pluralism in government. In fact, this popular participation was as integral a component of modern Western civilization as was its economic and technological sophistication. It lent social cohesion and dynamism to Western societies that contributed as much to their global expansionism as did their superior arms and factories. It explains why a handful of Spanish *conquistadores* were able to overthrow the Aztec and Inca Empires and why a handful of British merchants were able to conquer and rule the Indian subcontinent, which had a population many times that of their own country. It also explains the English, American, and French revolutions, which reflected the awakening and activation of the masses. The major result of these revolutions was that the people now not only participated in government but also considered it their inherent right to do so. This participatory impulse, which has been a distinguishing feature of Western civilization from its early medieval origins, is today a central feature of the emerging new Dark Age; the idea of popular participation is now worldwide in scope and has grown more pervasive in content, implying self-management in all phases of life and for all segments of society. Chapters 3, 4, 5, and 6 will explore in detail the ramifications of this idea.

Today's Dark Age

The Roman Empire was hobbled by technological stagnation, but the problem facing the world today is the exact opposite: how to make rational and humane use of a powerful and proliferating technology. Despite the diametrically opposite nature of these two situations, these periods were remarkably similar in their manifestations—in each case taking the form of (1) economic imperialism, (2) ecological degradation, (3) bureaucratic ossification, and (4) a flight from reason.

First, economic imperialism in both eras brought about the impoverishment of the provincial peripheries for the enrichment of the metropolitan centers. The Romans exploited their subjugated lands by outright confiscation of bullion and art objects, siphoning off of raw materials and foodstuffs, and wholesale enslavement of conquered peoples, who were sold in multitudes to plantation owners in Italy. Cicero warned his compatriots of the bitter alienation of the provincials in language that sounds uncomfortably familiar today:

> Words cannot express, gentlemen, how bitterly hated we are among foreign nations because of the wanton and outrageous conduct of the men whom in recent years we have sent to govern them. For in those countries what temple do you suppose has been held sacred by our officers, what state inviolable, what home sufficiently guarded by its closed doors? Why, they look about for rich and flourishing cities that they may find an occasion for a war against them to satisfy their lust for plunder.[2]

Roman imperialism was similar to that of the West as demonstrated by the Spanish conquerors of Mexico and Peru and by the British nabobs in India. Since Europe's economy was not adequately developed during that early stage to produce articles sufficient for obtaining the desired overseas commodities by trade, the Europeans, who did have superior weapons, helped themselves to what they wanted in the provinces of India, the slave forts of Africa, and the mines and plantations of the Americas. With the Industrial Revolution, the West acquired preponderant economic as well as military power. Thus plunder imperialism gave way to the free-trade imperialism of the nineteenth century and to the neocolonialism of today. Exploitation techniques have changed, but the end result remains the same in what is now termed the Third World. Roman subjects in Syria, Egypt, or Gaul would have comprehended the meaning, if not the specifics, of the following arraignment by the present-day Filipino lawyer, politician, and business executive Alejandro Lichauco:

> The massive and deepening poverty of our people, the rising unemployment, the inflation that has gone beyond control, the infantile state of our military and production capabilities, the disoriented state of our educational system, the remorseless exploitation to which our economy is being subjected, and the social anarchy which these conditions have bred are all traceable, directly and ultimately, to our status as neocolony. . . . Two superpowers, the United States and Japan, which waylaid us in the first half of this century as an outright colony, are now embarked on an aggressive drive to repeat, through neocolonization, what they once achieved through the direct colonization of our country.[3]

Second, economic imperialism inevitably degrades the ecosystems of the dependent areas through a process of what has been defined as ecological imperialism. Deforestation and subsequent erosion had become a problem in parts of the Mediterranean basin in pre-Roman times as a consequence of the advent of iron tools. But the process was greatly accelerated by the heavy lumbering necessary to build the vessels to ship 15 million bushels of grain annually from Egypt and North Africa to Italy. More serious was the large-scale slave hunting, leading to depopulation in many regions and thus to the neglect of terraced farmland, which consequently succumbed to erosion.

Present-day ecological imperialism takes a variety of forms. One is the disproportionate consumption of irreplaceable natural resources by the metropolitan centers. The familiar statistic is that six percent of the world's population, in the United States, consumes one-third of the world's energy and raw-material output. Unless prevailing trade patterns change drastically, this imbalance will increase, for the United States is rapidly exhausting its domestic reserves and becoming more dependent on foreign sources. This one-way flow prevails with foodstuffs as well as with energy and raw materials. It is the poor lands that are feeding the rich, and not the reverse, as is commonly inferred from the existence of aid programs and emergency grain shipments. The fact is that the rich nations—the United States, Europe, Russia, Japan, and the British Dominions—exchange most of their surplus food among themselves but receive a net protein import of one million tons each year from the poor countries. A specific example is the flow of high-protein seafood (shrimp, tuna, and fishmeal) from poor countries like India, Mexico, Peru, and Chile.

It cannot be rationalized that the poor soils and adverse climates of the poor countries are best suited for producing nonfoods like coffee and tea for the rest of the world. The choice of these crops was made centuries ago by early colonists and their European patrons, who were interested in producing what could be sold profitably in the mother country rather than what was needed by the native population. Hence the one-crop plantation system, which has left the poor countries vulnerable to the erratic fluctuations of world-market prices for their respective crops. Furthermore, plantation agriculture is often destructive of local soils, as well as precariously dependent on foreign fuel, pesticides, and fertilizers.

> It may not be improper [concludes an anthropologist] to characterize
> as ecological imperialism the elaboration of a world organization that
> is centered in industrial societies and degrades the ecosystems of the
> agrarian societies it absorbs. . . . We may ask if the chances for

human survival might not be enhanced by increasing the diversity and stability of local, regional and national ecosystems, even, if need be, at the expense of the complexity and interdependence of worldwide economic organization.[4]

A third feature common to both the Roman and the present eras is bureaucratic ossification. The rampant bureaucratization of the later Roman Empire was not the result of ideological preference. Emperors issued their regulatory decrees not because they believed in state intervention but because action was imperative to meet the urgent crises brought on by imperial decay. For example, it was in response to runaway inflation that the Edict of Prices (301) set maximum prices for thousands of commodities and services, with variations specified according to quality. Likewise, manpower shortages in certain crafts brought about a virtual caste system requiring sons to follow their fathers in those crafts. This legislation proved as futile as it was unpopular, for it was directed at the symptoms rather than the causes of imperial decline. And so the hapless subjects of Diocletian complained that soon "there will be more governors than governed."

Comparable bureaucratization plagues contemporary societies, although the roots of the disease are now different. Industrialization and urbanization produced mass dislocation and spawned social problems that, in an age of individualistic capitalism, could not be redressed by communal action. The state perforce intervened, and the scope of its intervention was vastly extended by the twin crises of the Great Depression and the two World Wars. In the United States between 1930 and 1970, the GNP multiplied nearly 11 times (from 90.4 to 976.4 billion dollars), but during the same period federal expenditures multiplied about 73 times (from 2.8 to 204.5 billion dollars)—nearly seven times as fast as the increase in GNP.

Implicit in this bureaucratic proliferation is the assumption that social and economic problems can be solved by federal programs and crusades. But the problems of the United States remain and have worsened despite the New Deal, the New Frontier, the Great Society, and the New Federalism. Not unnaturally, the American public now holds Washington mainly responsible for the national ills. A Harris Poll of September, 1973, reflected popular alienation and distrust as prevalent as in the days of Emperor Diocletian: 61 percent agreed that "what you think doesn't count any more," 71 percent that "the federal government made conditions worse, and 74 percent that "special interests get more from the government than the people do."

Finally, both the late Roman and the present eras are marked by widespread irrationality and mysticism. Between the early and late periods of the Roman Empire, a dramatic shift occurred in the mental atmosphere—a shift from knowledge to belief, from philosophy to theology, from astronomy to astrology, and from anticipation of the future to yearning for release from earthly miseries. Among intellectuals, this change in mental climate took the form of philosophies such as Epicureanism and Stoicism, which emphasized the pursuit of personal happiness and concerns rather than that of social welfare. The masses of the population found comfort in mystery cults of oriental origin that promised salvation in the afterlife. It is no accident that the earliest converts to Christianity were the lowly and dispossessed, who welcomed the assurances of a paradise to come.

A similar flight from reason is manifest in the contemporary world. Witness the Children of God, the "Jesus freaks," the Hare Krishnas, and the succession of glib gurus who have attracted millions of devoted followers in the West. Witness also the beliefs in faith healing and reincarnation, as well as the growing interest in the "old sciences" of numerology and astrology. An estimated ten million Americans are hard-core believers in astrology, and another 40 million are dabblers. Of the 1750 newspapers in the United States, 1200 carry daily thumbnail horoscopes, while dieting manuals instruct their readers in how to shed pounds by the light of the stars. The believers in astrology do not restrict themselves to the stars; most also have faith in numerology, palmistry, and tarot cards, and they are likely to be flirting with reincarnation. "Broadly speaking," says the London psychiatrist Dr. John Kelnar, "when the concrete day-to-day life becomes increasingly harder, people turn to the occult forces. Once a horoscope has been cast, the 'inner world' is settled for a while. Astrology takes the load off people. They are sharing their fate with an outside force."[5]

The similarity between conditions in late Roman times and those of today explains the corresponding similarity in disparaging self-appraisal. From the beginning of the Christian era, Roman writers were obsessed with a feeling of irreversible decline. The elder Seneca, in the first century B.C., asserted that under the emperors Rome had reached its old age and faced unavoidable death. By the third century A.D., Saint Cyprian was warning of impending doom in terms that sound very familiar today.

> The world has grown old and lost its former vigor. . . . Winter no longer gives rain enough to swell the seed, nor summer sun enough to toast the harvest. . . . The mountains are gutted and give less

marble, the mines are exhausted and give less silver and gold. . . .
The fields lack farmers, the sea sailors, the encampments soldiers.
. . . There is no longer any justice in judgments, competence in
trades, discipline in daily life. . . . Epidemics decimate mankind
. . . the Day of Judgment is at hand.[6]

Saint Cyprian has many counterparts today, especially in the countries
of the West. Most lugubrious are the scientists, of both physical and social
varieties, who stress the perils rather than the promise of science and technology. Many of them are virtually convinced that man is incapable of
adapting his values and practices to the incredibly powerful technology he
has created; they perceive this technology to be more a Pandora's box than
an Aladdin's lamp. Like Saint Cyprian they foresee climatic catastrophe,
soil and mineral depletion, and global famine. And to these familiar plagues
they add modern horrors: unbreathable air, unpotable water, lifeless oceans,
lakes, and rivers, and overhead the Damocles sword of the hydrogen bomb.

This cheerlessness of the scientists is matched by that of laymen. Those
of conservative persuasion resemble the Roman critics in lamenting the
lapse of time-honored traditions—in this case law and order, hard work,
rugged individualism, and orthodox values and life-styles. General Westmoreland, who led the American forces in Vietnam, expressed this attitude
when he announced that the American Revolution had ended the need for
any revolutions in the future. And the Soviet poet, Felix Chuyev, looks
backward with equally unshakable certitude.

What we learn in childhood is truth forever.
What was true for me in childhood—
Can never be interpreted to me in a new way.[7]

Such stalwart champions of the past are distressed by the accelerating
pace of change that characterizes modern societies. And so Joseph Alsop
writes that observing the course of events in the Western world "feels a bit
like watching the progress of a large and jolly party on the deck of the
Titanic, knowing all the while that icebergs lie ahead."[8]

On the other hand, there are the critics on the Left, who complain that
there is too little change rather than too much. They fear that the status quo
is frozen for the foreseeable future, both globally and domestically. They
see the fate of Dubček and Allende as pointing to a new age of reaction,
with the United States and the Soviet Union playing on a global stage the
nineteenth-century role of the Holy Alliance in Europe. On the domestic
scene, these critics on the Left warn that modern technology, with its un-

precedented productivity, "sells" itself to the people so pervasively that, in the words of Herbert Marcuse, they "recognize themselves in their commodities," thereby accepting "a comfortable, smooth, reasonable, democratic unfreedom." Thus contemporary man is viewed as the victim of his affluence, which persuades him to accept his servitude and even to hail it as freedom.

Between the chains of poverty in the Third World and the chains of affluence in the developed countries, the future seems a prison to many Western intellectuals. George Orwell, in his nightmarish novel *1984,* expressed his despair for the human prospect through his character O'Brien: "If you want a picture of the future, imagine a boot stamping on a human face—forever." I. F. Stone proposed this poignant inscription for a plaque commemorating the first moon landing;

> Here Men First Set Foot outside the Earth on Their Way to the Far Stars. They Speak of Peace but Wherever They Go They Bring War. The Rockets on Which They Arrived Were Developed to Carry Instant Death and Can within a Few Minutes Turn Their Green Planet into Another Lifeless Moon. Their Destructive Ingenuity Knows No Limits and Their Wanton Pollution No Restraint. Let the Rest of the Universe Beware.[9]

The New York Zoo has installed in the Great Apes House, between the gorilla and the orangutan compartments, an exhibit entitled "The Most Dangerous Animal in the World." The exhibit consists of a mirror with this text:

> YOU ARE LOOKING AT THE MOST DANGEROUS ANIMAL IN THE WORLD. IT ALONE, OF ALL THE ANIMALS THAT EVER LIVED, CAN EXTERMINATE (AND HAS) ENTIRE SPECIES OF ANIMALS. NOW IT HAS ACHIEVED THE POWER TO WIPE OUT ALL LIFE ON EARTH.

Visitors stop, stare at themselves in the mirror, and usually remark, "It's true!"

2
GRASS GROWING EVERYWHERE

Dawn on the somber sea brings on the sun,
Then passes the hill: look, darkness is lifting.

—From a tenth-century manuscript[1]

You know what I really think? I really think that one day the
world will be great. I really believe the world gonna be great
one day.

—Cesar Chavez

Myths of Our Times

The Western world today is reexperiencing the decay and despair of its early post-Roman centuries, but it is also reexperiencing their sense of creative renewal and anticipation. Just as green shoots took root amid the ruins of imperial Rome, they are growing now amid the wreckage of contemporary civilization. But to see today's green shoots we must discard the perspective of many modern observers who, like their Roman predecessors, perceive only darkness about them.

Among the Romans, the early Christians attributed imperial decline to moral decadence. Both Saint Jerome and Saint Augustine wrote that the ancient Roman virtues had deteriorated and that the only way to turn was toward the City of God. But later, when the deterioration of the Empire proceeded apace even after the acceptance of Christianity as the official state religion, the pagans in their turn laid the blame for Rome's decline on the hostility and disruptive practices of the Church. Whereupon the Christians, having become a part of the Establishment, now shifted their attitude in order to justify their support of it. The Roman Empire, they contended, represented the last of four world kingdoms—its predecessors being Babylon, Carthage, and Macedon—and was designed to be God's shield for the protection of the Christian world against chaos. Accordingly, all Christians should accept and support the Empire, for on it depended the fate of the universe. As the current saying went, "When Rome falls, the universe will fall with it."

This rationalization may seem to us today to be a quaint and unrealistic analysis of the problems of Rome. But will our own analysis of the problems now besetting us appear any less quaint and unrealistic to future

15

generations? Underlying today's pessimism are certain rationalizing myths as flimsy, on close examination, as those of the Church Fathers. These myths depict as inherently insoluble various problems that are basically sociopolitical in nature and for which solutions can be and are being found. Three of the most basic and widespread of these myths will be considered here: the perversity of human nature, uncontrollable population increase, and malignant technological growth.

In the eighteenth century, Samuel Johnson observed that patriotism is the last refuge of the scoundrel. Today, the last refuge of the reactionary is cynicism about "human nature." Any proposal for social change is branded by the stand-patter as being contrary to "human nature," by which statement is implied, although not usually spelled out, that humans are singularly disagreeable creatures—selfish, narrow-minded, covetous, and bellicose. But when we examine the record of our paleolithic ancestors, whose history comprises some 80 percent of the total human experience, we find the precise opposite of this "human nature" stereotype.

Consider the way of life of the few surviving food-gathering peoples of today, who are living under conditions essentially similar to those of the paleolithic hunters. The nineteenth-century anthropologist Lewis Morgan reported that "the law of hospitality as administered by the American aborigines tended to the final equalization of subsistence. Hunger and destitution could not exist at one end of an Indian village . . . while plenty prevailed elsewhere in the same village."[2] This testimony is supported by the recollections of a present-day descendent of Morgan's "American aborigines."

> Going back as far as I can remember as a child in an Indian community, I had no sense of knowing about the other people around me except that we were all somehow equal; the class structure in the community was horizontal. There was only one class. Nobody was interested in getting on top of anybody else.
>
> One of the very important things was the relationship we had with our families. We didn't always live at home. We lived wherever we happened to be at that particular time when it got dark. If you were two or three miles away from home, then that is where you slept. People would feed you even if they didn't know who you were. We'd spend an evening, perhaps, with an old couple, and they would tell us stories.[3]

This communality was not peculiar to the American Indians. It has been true of all peoples at the food-gathering stage throughout the world.

The most recent evidence of this fact was the dramatic discovery in 1971 of the Tasaday, a tribe of 27 Stone Age people who had been living in complete isolation in the southern part of Mindanao Island of the Philippines for at least six centuries. Their outstanding characteristic is a complete lack of aggressiveness. They have no word for weapon, hostility, anger, or war. They have eagerly adopted the long Filipino knife, the bolo, because it is much superior to their stone tools for gathering food, chopping wood, and slashing through jungle growth. But they have rejected the spear and the bow and arrow as inefficient for gathering food. All of the food they collect (yams, fruit, berries, flowers, fish, crabs, frogs) they divide equally with scrupulous care among all members of the band.

They are curious about objects from the outside world, but they are not acquisitive. After examining such objects carefully they will return them, saying "Thank you, we finished looking." Equally striking is their uninhibited expression of affection. They will unaffectedly throw their arms around a visitor they like, rub their cheeks against his, and sit quietly beside him with an arm around his shoulders. Living in a benevolent environment, with all of their needs satisfied by the resources of their food-gathering area of 25 square kilometers, they have no external enemies, and they have existed for centuries in complete peace with one another. In the words of a Filipino anthropologist, the Tasaday can help us identify "the qualities of humanity, the so-called universals which all men share . . . to better understand ourselves and the problems we have created. . . . We will never know how much we have gained until we learn how much we have lost."[4]

However, there is another side to the story. At the same time that the world was learning about the Tasaday, another band of 30 people, the Feutou, was being discovered in the New Guinea highlands. These tribesmen are fierce warriors who fight with bows and arrows and who cook and eat their slain enemies. Likewise, among the American Indians, the Comanches and Apaches raised their children to be warriors, whereas the Hopis and Zuñis reared theirs for peaceful living—and still do. The Semai of Malaya reflect these contradictory human behaviors within themselves. In their native hills, they are completely nonviolent. They rarely show anger, will not kill an animal they have raised, and are known in Malaya as extremely timid people. But these same gentle tribesmen, when drafted into the army and ordered to fight, become bloodthirsty killers reveling in butchery. And when these soldiers return to Semai society they again become as meek and averse to violence as their stay-at-home neighbors.

The obvious conclusion is that "human nature" is neither pacific nor violent, neither cooperative nor predatory. Human beings are not born, as the ethologist Konrad Lorenz maintains, with an inherited instinct of aggression that must be sublimated. They have no original sin; neither are they cursed by innate selfishness or perversity. One psychologist who specializes in this subject, Albert Bandura, has concluded that "from the social learning perspective, human nature is characterized as a vast potentiality that can be fashioned by social influences into a variety of forms. . . . Aggression is not an inevitable or unchangeable aspect of man but a product of aggression-promoting conditions within a society."[5]

The second great myth of our times is that population growth is out of control and has doomed the human race to decimation by mass starvation or war. But this myth has sprung from the misperception of an insoluble Malthusian predicament in a soluble sociopolitical problem.

The September 1974 issue of *Scientific American,* devoted exclusively to the population problem, estimated that less than half of the potentially arable land of the world is under cultivation, and that if all of this arable land were actually cultivated with modern techniques it would support over ten times the present world's population. Furthermore, birthrates and population growth, according to authors contributing to this issue, are not beyond human control. In demographic matters, as in others, people act according to their best interests as they perceive them. In societies with gross inequities in income distribution, few employment opportunities for women, and little social mobility or economic security, parents naturally resort to the only insurance available—a large number of children. Conversely, in more egalitarian societies that offer mass education, social mobility, and employment opportunities for women, the number of children per family tends to fall. Hence the substantial decline in birthrates in Taiwan, Sri Lanka, and China, as against the soaring rates in India, Indonesia, and South America.

South America has a far lower population density than the United States and possesses the largest amount of arable land among the continents, with 60 percent of this arable land lying fallow. And yet most of South America's food is imported at heavy cost to this poverty-stricken continent. The explanation is that most of the land is controlled by a few families who choose to grow profitable "cash crops" such as coffee and sugar for export rather than food crops to feed their own people. Furthermore, the large estates, though more productive per worker than the family farms, are less productive per acre because they use machinery rather than hand labor.

Machine farming is more profitable for the owner but socially disastrous for South America, with its high unemployment rate. The root cause of Latin America's economic ailments, then, is not the birthrate but the inequitable system of land ownership and the coalition of domestic and foreign vested interests that buttresses this system. Neither South America nor any other region is caught in an inescapable population-explosion trap, as is so often asserted. The basic problem is not some iron law of human perversity but the need for social and economic restructuring, which has already been undertaken in diverse forms by various governments around the world.

Dramatic proof of this proposition is to be found in China, the traditional "land of famine." The neo-Malthusian William Vogt wrote in 1948 in his popular book *Road to Survival:* "In China, it is estimated that 100,000,000 people have starved to death during the past century. There is little likelihood that we have seen the end of famine. . . . In 1950, according to the estimates of the U.S. State Department, China's population will reach 430,000,000. . . . China cannot feed the people she has. . . . The greatest tragedy that China could suffer, at the present time, would be a reduction in her death rate."

This same China today has a population of about 800 million, is self-supplying in its food needs (since wheat imports are balanced by rice exports), and enjoys health standards comparable to those of Western nations. In 1974 a team of American agricultural and social scientists made a four-week tour of China's communes. One member of the team was Dr. Norman E. Borlaug, the Iowa agronomist who was awarded the Nobel Prize for his work as the "father of the Green Revolution." "China's achievements in agriculture simply hit you in the eye," he reported after the visit. "The people everywhere, both in cities and the countryside, look well-fed. You don't see the abject poor and hungry that you see in other parts of the world."[6]

The "abject poor and hungry" are especially visible in India today, and yet the Irrigation Commission of the Government of India has estimated that the irrigated area of 43 million hectares on which grass crops were grown in 1973–1974 could be doubled during the next 30 years at a total cost of roughly 14 billion dollars, or less than one percent of India's current GNP. If these newly irrigated lands were cultivated using currently available agricultural techniques, concludes Professor Roger Revelle in the September 1974 issue of *Scientific American,* India could feed a population of 1.2 billion, or about double her present population of 580 million, and "the problem of India's food supply could recede into the background for the foreseeable future." Revelle adds that the socioeconomic changes resulting from such agricultural development would stimulate strong forces inhibiting the desire for large families, thereby bringing population growth gradually to a halt.

All of these facts point to the conclusion that to attribute hunger to population pressure is to confuse cause with effect. Rather, both hunger and population pressure are the unavoidable excrescences of a malfunctioning socioeconomic system—or, more precisely, a system that functions at the expense of the great majority of Third World peoples for the benefit of small native and foreign elites. This is the conclusion of the November 1974 United Nations World Food Conference Report, *Assessment of the World Food Situation—Present and Future:*

> Inadequate nutrition . . . results from socio-economic development patterns which in most of the poorer countries have been characterized by a high degree of concentration of power, wealth and incomes in the hands of relatively small elites of national or foreign individuals or groups. In the rural areas, land and water, capital, technical knowledge, credit and institutional assistance are distributed in a most uneven way. The majority of the rural population is either landless or has to make a living from the exploitation of meagre land and water resources. . . . Land tenure and production structures constitute therefore one of the basic reasons for rural poverty and malnutrition. . . . It will be necessary to break the vicious circle of unemployment, the low level of food production, low productivity-low income which is strangling such a high proportion of humanity. This, in its turn, could mean very profound transformation of the present socioeconomic structures.

The third myth distorting our view of the world concerns technology, which is widely regarded as an uncontrollable Frankenstein's monster forcing human beings to be the servants of a soulless machine. But the historical record shows that, on the contrary, each major technological breakthrough in the past has been accompanied by a corresponding breakthrough in mass assertiveness and participation rather than by mass subjugation and submissiveness.

Three early examples were the invention and diffusion in the second and first millenia B.C. of coinage, iron, and the alphabet. These three innovations have been described as "democratic inventions," and democratic they were indeed in their social impact. Coinage enabled the small farmer to sell his produce and to participate in the economic life of his community more efficiently than he had under the barter system. Likewise, the alphabet made the attainment of literacy a less time-consuming process than it had been under the earlier pictographic systems and hence accessible to a larger percentage of the population. Finally, iron, being plentiful and cheap in comparison with copper and bronze, which had been available previously, provided the masses with tools and weapons of a quality previously reserved for the aristocracy.

The seafaring Greeks, operating from their city-states, made exceptional use of these inventions and felt their social repercussions to a corresponding degree. This social growth contributed to the intellectual revolution that characterized the "Greek miracle" of the fifth century B.C. and that led the emancipated Greeks to look down on the inhabitants of neighboring Egypt and Persia as hopelessly subservient to their religious and political masters. The individual, stated Socrates, must refuse to be coerced by any illegitimate authority or to do or to think anything his mind condemns as wrong: "The unexamined life is not worth living."

Although the Classical Greek and Roman religions and philosophies allowed more freedom for human development than did those of the earlier civilizations of Mesopotamia and Egypt, nevertheless they were limited by two constraints felt by every premodern civilization, whether European, Middle Eastern, Indian, or Chinese. One was the class system. The Greek philosophers and statesmen had a plentiful supply of slaves to care for their creature comforts. The other constraint was technological backwardness, which meant low productivity and hence high incentive to acquire and employ slaves in the production process. Aristotle perceived the interrelationship between these two problems: "There is only one condition in which we can imagine managers not needing subordinates, and masters not needing slaves. This condition would be that each [inanimate] instrument could do its own work . . . as if a shuttle should weave of itself."[7]

Aristotle's observation points to the trap in which all premodern civilizations were caught: technological backwardness promoted slavery, and slavery perpetuated technological backwardness by reducing incentive for experimentation and invention. Thus these civilizations were inevitably based on the economic and psychological subjugation of the peasant and artisan masses, whether legally enslaved or not. The elites explained and justified the refinements of their life-styles as the products of their superior mental and moral qualities. In the course of the millenia the Eurasian peasantries adopted this view of the ruling classes as well, and thus became servile and obsequious. And for those who refused to bend the knee, force was always ready at hand—the physical violence of soldiers and the psychological violence of priests. In the words of Dostoyevsky's Grand Inquisitor, these were the millenia of "miracle, mystery, and authority," when "the universal and everlasting craving of humanity" was "to find someone to worship." Those who were worshipped in premodern times were the rulers of each civilization—Roman senators, Iranian warrior-nobles, Indian princes, and Chinese marquises and Grand Administrators—and its priests, the Indian Brahmans, Iranian magi, Christian priests, and Confucian literati.

The great historic contribution of the West was to spring this trap. Gradual technological and economic growth in the medieval West led to overseas expansion and the development of worldwide commerce, which in turn contributed to the ensuing Industrial Revolution. The latter finally produced what Aristotle had called for—the inanimate instrument that "could do its own work" and enable people to dispense with slaves. But relief was not immediate, for the slaves of old were replaced by new slaves who were tied to the new machines. "Miracle, mystery, and authority" continued in a new form. Kings, priests, and landlords gave way to a new triad of bosses, bureaucrats, and experts, the senior partners in the emerging corporate industrial society.

Yet during the nineteenth century the workers gradually won the rights to vote, to organize, and to mobilize political pressures to force social reforms. The Great Depression of the 1930s, the New Deal, and the aftermath of the Second World War speeded up this process, culminating in the United States in the "welfare state" that provides its citizens with basic needs "from the cradle to the grave." It is true that today this welfare state is racked by unrest and malaise—by the "white-collar blues" and the "blue-collar blues." The human liberation implied by Aristotle remains elusive. But for the first time in history it is now realizable, thanks to what amounts to a Second Industrial Revolution—a labor-*replacing* revolution, in contrast to the first, which was a labor-*saving* revolution.

Automation, nuclear power, computers, and rocketry; all of which led to space exploration and to the industrial uses of their technological spinoff, are the foundation of this Second Industrial Revolution. And again, as always in the past, a major technological advance is engendering a corresponding advance in mass assertiveness and participation. The British Labor Party leader Anthony Wedgwood Benn has emphasized the differences between the old subjects of the past and the new citizens of today.

> People today—these new citizens with this new power—have responded to the pressure of events by banding themselves together

with others of like mind to campaign vigorously for what they want; and thousands of such pressure groups or action groups have come into existence; consumer societies, educational campaigns, organizations to help the old, the homeless, the sick, the poor or underdeveloped societies, militant communal organizations, student power, noise abatement societies, and so on. These, like the early trade unions or political groups during the first industrial revolution, derive their causes, their influence and their power in some way from industrial change. . . .

The new citizen, despite his fears and doubts and lack of self-confidence, is a far more formidable person than his forebears. Increasingly he dislikes being ordered around by anyone, especially if he suspects that those who exercise authority under-estimate him.

A growing number of them—everywhere—are just not prepared to accept poverty, oppression, the denial of human equality, bureaucracy, secrecy in decision-making, or any other derogation from what they consider to be their basic rights—and are gradually acquiring the power to enforce that view upon the societies in which they live.[8]

"God Bless the Grass"

Benn's "new citizens" and their "new power" signify that the present meritocracy of bosses, bureaucrats, and experts is going the way of the earlier aristocracy of kings, priests, and landlords. This process is taking place not only in Britain and other Western nations, but also elsewhere in the world. Prior to the twentieth century, only an insignificant minority in the non-Western world had been affected by a knowledge of European languages, literatures, and ideologies. But today a rapidly growing proportion of the non-Western masses is actively and consciously in touch with global realities.

A partial explanation is to be found in the factories where they have found employment and in the highways that are ending their isolation. But equally important have been the new mass media of books, radio, and television. Loudspeakers blare out to illiterate yet responsive multitudes in village squares. New regimes and leaders have begun purposefully to exploit the mass media to the utmost in order to mobilize popular support for their revolutionary programs. "It is true," stated President Nasser of Egypt, "that most of our people are still illiterate. But politically that counts far less than it did twenty years ago. . . . Radio has changed everything. . . .

Today people in the most remote villages hear of what is happening everywhere and form their opinions. Leaders cannot govern as they once did. We live in a new world."[9]

Thus the current technological revolution, like the earlier ones, is leading not to a new age of the pharaohs but to greater self-knowledge on the part of humanity. The long historical process of popular awakening is now reaching its culmination with the twentieth-century demand for self-management in all phases of life. Thanks to modern mass-communications media, this tendency is appearing all over the globe, in varied forms reflecting local conditions and traditions.

With the perception of the artist, the folk singer Pete Seeger visualizes this self-management impulse—the distinguishing feature of contemporary history—as the struggle of sprouting green grass against smothering concrete.

> They roll the concrete over it
> To try to keep it back. . . .
> God bless the truth
> That fights towards the sun.
> They roll the lies over it
> And think that it is done.
> It moves through the ground,
> It reaches for the air,
> And after a while
> It's growing everywhere.
> And God bless the grass.[10]

The next four chapters deal with the sprouting of the grass in all regions of the world. They analyze the manifestations of self-management in various phases of human life: in the use made of technology ("From Aristo-Technology to Demo-Technology"), in the administration of the workplace ("From Boss Control to Worker Control"), in the relations between citizen and government ("From Representative Democracy to Participatory Democracy"), and in the perception of what it means to be human ("From Self-Subordination to Self-Actualization").

3

FROM ARISTO-TECHNOLOGY TO DEMO-TECHNOLOGY

Today it is true to say that "the economies of scale" was a 19th-century truth which, because of the advance of science and of technological skills, has become—if not all along the line, certainly over wide fields of application—a 20th-century myth. . . . We should now give some real thought to the possibility of reforming our technology in the directions of smallness, simplicity and nonviolence.

—E. F. Schumacher

Just as in the last century the forces unleashed by the Industrial Revolution metamorphosed the customs, ways of life and modes of thought in all countries, so today, the world is being swept by a tide of new technical and scientific discoveries which have the power to bring about still more radical changes. . . . We should make sure that the advance of pure and applied science is not led, under the influence of inflexible social and political structures (both national and international), into hampering the liberation of mankind.

—Dr. Salvador Allende,
President of the Republic of
Chile, 1970–1973

Technology is what humans and their hominid ancestors have been practicing for millions of years: using and modifying the physical objects surrounding them to satisfy their material needs. Starting with the use of a stone as a scraping and cutting tool, they progressed naturally to making a canoe by hollowing out a log with the stone; to harnessing the wind to propel the canoe with a sail; to constructing a steel ship driven by twin screws powered by a steam turbine; to assembling a spacecraft propelled by rockets, which enabled humans to leave the planet that bore and nurtured them.

Superficially, this technology appears to be an unalloyed blessing. Yet from the beginning man has felt ambivalent about his brainchild, and for understandable reasons. Pliny, in his *Natural History* (A.D. 77), referred to iron as "the most useful and the most fatal instrument in the hand of mankind. . . . It is by the aid of iron that we construct houses, cleave rocks, and perform so many other useful offices of life. But it is with iron also that wars, murders, and robberies are effected." Likewise, Francis Bacon observed in *The Wisdom of the Ancients* (1609) that the mechanical arts "have an ambiguous or double use, and serve as well to produce as to prevent mischief and destruction; so that their virtue almost destroys or unwinds itself."

Today there is greater concern than ever about this "unwinding" effect of technology, and for obvious reasons. But today there is also more comprehension of the causes of the "unwinding" and more ideas for the cure. In a perceptive essay written in 1947, C. S. Lewis asked "In what sense is Man the possessor of increasing power over Nature?" and concluded that "what we call Man's power over Nature turns out to be a power exercised by some men over other men with Nature as its instrument."[1] Herbert Marcuse observes that "man's struggle with Nature is increasingly a struggle with his society."[2] And along the same lines, William Leiss writes that "the liberation of science and technology . . . is a task that primarily involves the reconstruction of social institutions."[3]

In short, the social repercussions of science are determined not by the internal dynamics of science itself but rather by its external social environment. A change in the role of science requires a change in the structure of society.

Today, there is a detectable movement toward what has been termed demo-technology, as opposed to aristo-technology. The latter is so labeled because its great demands for capital, energy, and materials make it too expensive for all but a small minority of people. Conversely, demo-technology makes minimal demands on capital, energy, and materials and has a correspondingly small impact on the physical environment. Furthermore, it can be created and operated in small-scale units, thereby facilitating industrial or agricultural self-management rather than strengthening the inherent hierarchical nature of the large-scale industrial complex or of corporate agribusiness. Demo-technology should not be equated with primitiveness or low productivity. It can, and in most cases will, evolve from sophisticated scientific concepts, but these concepts will be adapted to human needs rather than to profit maximization by corporations.

In Industry

Technological self-management seems a quixotic concept in the face of the huge industrial complexes developed during the past century along the Great Lakes, in New England and Pennsylvania, in the Midlands of England, and in the Ruhr Valley of Germany. These concentrations of industry evolved where there were favorable combinations of abundant raw materials, cheap energy resources, and efficient transportation facilities. The cumulative investment, in successive stages, of large sums of money in these enterprises culminated in the mass-production empires of Krupp and Ford and Carnegie. Carnegie justifiably boasted that he transported four pounds of raw materials—iron ore, coal, lime, and manganese—hundreds of miles to his Pittsburgh steel mills, "and these four pounds of materials I manufactured into one pound of steel, for which the consumer pays one cent."[4] It is understandable that size became equated with efficiency, and that any deleterious effects that this type of industry had on the labor force or the physical environment were accepted as the unavoidable price of modern productivity and affluence.

Today this assumption is beginning to be challenged, in light of the availability of what is termed "centrifugal" industrial technology. This technology uses new sources of power, new types of materials, new methods of fabrication, and new means of transport. The combination of these innovations allows for a decentralized technology that is knowledge intensive rather than capital intensive, relatively simple to use, and inexpensive to operate.

Highly versatile multipurpose machines are reversing a century-old trend in machine design. This older trend, reflecting the increasing division of labor in industry, was toward single-purpose devices. The inevitable consequence of this technological specialization was that the machine had to be discarded when demand for its product ended. The newer multipurpose machines make possible the production of a wide range of products in a single plant. A small community can use these machines to meet its needs for a limited number of a variety of goods, thus avoiding underemploying its industrial facilities. This trend toward decentralization is also facilitated by the increasing substitution of electrical power for steam. Whereas steam confined industrial plants to the location of their source of power, electricity can be transmitted over great distances, allowing plants to be situated according to considerations other than the availability of power.

Equally important to decentralization are the numerous materials now available for fabrication as alternatives to the traditional wood and steel. The most important are plastics, fiberglass, "high performance" composites, and new forms of concrete, such as prestressed concrete. It is expected that within 20 years more new products will be made of plastics than of all other materials combined. Most of the plastic materials are manufactured by a few large chemical and oil companies. But the more expensive and labor-consuming later fabrication of the plastic materials into finished products can be done in small plants with about 50 workers, because of the simplicity and low cost of the machinery involved. As a result, plastics-fabrication plants are scattered throughout the country to a degree that would be out of the question for steel mills.

Miniaturization is another recent technological innovation with significant social repercussions. It has improved mechanical performance and at the same time has reduced the size and cost of capital equipment. One example of the trend toward miniaturization can be seen in the field of data processing. The first digital computer ENIAC, unveiled at the University of Pennsylvania in 1945, occupied 1500 square feet of floor space, weighed over 30 tons, and contained 18,000 vacuum tubes with 500,000 soldered connections, a vast network of resistors, and miles of wiring. Today small firms can purchase, for a few thousand dollars, a desk-size computer capable of performing 100 times more computations per second than ENIAC. In addition, data-processing centers operating throughout the United States provide, for a fee, processing services to the smallest concerns. Thus such companies can now secure types of services and information that formerly were available only to a few large corporations.

These new technological developments are making it possible to adapt technology to society's needs rather than society to technology's needs. Modern industrial archeology is revealing, in many areas, the remains of long-deserted farms, mines, and small factories that were snuffed out by large industries based on steam power and mass-production techniques and by commercial farms with national markets. The local resources on which these old enterprises rested are often still available for use, and the plants can be resurrected in many cases, serving as part of the solution to the mounting problems of living and working in the urban centers. Thus a material possibility now exists for ameliorating the crowding of 75 percent of America's population into 1.5 percent of America's space. Industrial decentralization and local self-management are becoming viable alternatives rather than utopian dreams. "There appears to be a-borning a second industrial revolution," concludes one authority on this subject, "which, among its other features, contains within itself the seeds of destruction for concentrated industrial structures."[5]

In Community

Centrifugal industrial technology is paralleled by a centrifugal community technology that extends decentralization and self-management to the rural or urban individual. This community technology has been greatly stimulated during the 1970s by the pressures of rising food prices, energy shortages, and environmental deterioration. The scope and nature of this centrifugal movement in community technology are exemplified by a house constructed by a Cambridge University research team of engineers, biologists, chemists, and architects. This house runs entirely by the sun, the wind, the rain, and the wastes of its occupants, so that it is entirely independent of outside electrical, gas, oil, water, and sewage systems. The objective, as explained by the head of the research team, was not to "create a house for a 'dropout society or for ecology freaks" but to maintain present living standards despite the energy shortages expected in forthcoming decades. To attain this objective, the team has combined into one integrated system many principles hitherto used in isolation: solar energy to provide heat, wind to provide power, rainfall to provide water, human excrement and food and garden wastes to provide gas for cooking, and new devices to recapture and recycle lost heat and water.

Similar work is being done in the United States by the New Alchemy Institute, a band of young scientists who seek not to turn lead into gold but to apply the insights of science on a human scale, so that people "may learn to live more gently upon the Earth." On a 12-acre farm near Falmouth, Massachusetts, these scientists are experimenting with wind power, solar power, fish culture, and less energy intensive and more ecologically sound farming practices. "We aren't antiscience or antitechnology," explains John Todd, one of the Institute's founders. "I think it's essential to *save* science and technology—but it must be done on a human scale. We believe that the quality of the whole depends on the quality of the smallest parts, so we concern ourselves with what we hope are microsolutions."[6]

The redirection of modern technology toward society's critical needs is also the objective of the New Rural Society (NRS), funded by the United States Department of Housing and Urban Development and operating in ten townships in northeastern Connecticut. The rationale of the NRS is that communications technology can be used to improve the quality of rural life in America and thereby to create a viable alternative to urban and suburban living. Jobs can be created in rural areas by applying existing communications technology to decentralize business and government operations and direct them into the countryside, where they can still function efficiently. Improved health care can be provided to rural communities through the use of computers, television links, and data-transmission and voice-transmission devices. In education, satellite technology can convert the "little red schoolhouse" into the kind of educational experience that only affluent suburbs offer today. Likewise, as various public broadcasting agencies have demonstrated, cultural activities hitherto confined to metropolitan centers—concerts, operas, plays, ballets, museum visits—can be carried by satellite and cable television to rural audiences.

The basic goal of the NRS, according to its leader, Dr. Peter Goldmark (former head of CBS laboratories), is to make it possible and desirable for people to work and live in the same rural community. If this goal can be achieved, some 4000 existing American communities with populations ranging from 2500 to 150,000 will become viable growth centers rather than the decaying anachronisms most are today.

Most of the redirecting of modern technology has taken the form of equipping rural projects or individual urban houses with solar devices, wind turbines, and heat pumps (for example, experimental buildings at the Massachusetts Institute of Technology and the Thomason houses in Washington, D.C.). It has been assumed that the large urban centers must remain completely dependent on outside supplies of energy, foodstuffs, and raw materials. This assumption is being challenged by the Adams Morgan neighborhood of 30,000 people in the northwest section of Washington, D.C. The Adams Morgan Organization (AMO) is striving for administrative and economic self-management and for technological autonomy. For this last purpose Community Technology, Inc., with a staff of craftsmen, technologists, scientists, and professionals with social-action experience, has been established. These people contend that centrifugal or low-impact technology is needed most urgently in the cities, where 75 percent of America now lives, and that the human and material resources of these cities enable them to apply the new technology more effectively than the rural areas can.

Several current AMO projects are attempting to prove the cities' ability to use low-impact technology. One is a machine and tool shop that repairs or redesigns into useful items broken or unwanted "junk" materials. It repairs household goods and appliances without charge if the owners work with the staff and learn from the experience.

A wind-energy project involves the investigation of various aspects of wind-generated energy: high- and low-speed mills for electrical generation and pumping, the speed-up effect of shrouded mills and natural urban wind tunnels, the effects of placement of units, and the effects of wind-generator fields (for example, what is the environmental effect of a large number of units in a small field?). The research results will be used in the construction of one- and two-kilowatt units that will generate power at cost rates that are competitive, if environmental pollution costs and the future increase in the costs of traditional forms of energy are taken into account.

A solar-energy project is planning two types of solar units. The first, a solar kitchen, can provide high-grade heat for household uses such as cooking, baking, and ironing. The second is a solar water heater, based on existing designs but adapted to specific Adams Morgan needs. After the initial trial period, the experience acquired will be applied to community-scale food processing, power generation, steam generation, chemical-process heating, and the development of inexpensive, "engineless" solar water pumps.

A sewage-disposal project is planned to replace conventional sewage systems, which waste water and contaminate waterways. The amount of money needed to modernize the overloaded and inadequate sewage system most American cities have would pay for "an inhouse, non-water-carrying disposal system" for each home. Such a system is now available; the Swedish engineer Rikard Lindstrom has developed the Clivus Multrum, a combined toilet and garbage disposal that uses no water. After a couple of years' use, the door at the end of the tank is opened to remove a few buckets full of humus, which may be used as fertilizer.

A plan to achieve decentralized food production utilizes unused basement and rooftop space for hydroponic greenhouses and high-density fish culture. Hydroponic greenhouses dispense with soil and thus eliminate the possibility of soil infestation and the need for fungicides. With temperature, carbon-dioxide concentration, and humidity levels maintained to produce optimum growth, greenhouses produce yields dramatically higher than those from conventional agriculture, and on a continuous year-round basis. Correspondingly high yields of fish are obtained from aquaculture utilizing the most advanced technology. Four tanks, each $10 \times 4 \times 3$ feet, give a steady supply of about 400 pounds of fish per month.

Finally, the AMO considers itself a pioneer in developing innovative technology for urban use, and therefore maintains an information service for gathering, cataloguing, and disseminating throughout the United States and the world the available existing information on centrifugal technology and their own research results. Future projects include an annual conference to bring together people from all over the world who are working on practical aspects of centrifugal technology, and a newsletter covering subjects such as alternative sources of energy, new construction materials and technical developments in hydroponics and accquaculture, and new forms of community transportation. Two AMO leaders, David Morris and Karl Hess, have written *Neighborhood Power: The New Localism* (Beacon Press, 1975), which analyzes the current state of community technology and how it can be utilized by the individual neighborhood—how to compile an inventory of human and natural resources (soil space, rooftop space, recreation space, sunlight and rainfall availability, human and organic wastes) and how to use these resources to produce energy, grow vegetables, and raise fish and other protein sources.

Such experimentation and innovation are not limited to members of the alternative culture. No less a pillar of the Establishment than Harold

Geneen, Chairman of I.T.T., has speculated about the economic and social implications of single-cell microorganisms that double their weight every few hours. A structure one mile square in which these yeast-like, protein-rich microorganisms could grow freely would supply all of the world's protein needs indefinitely. Since these microorganisms are potential producers of fats and carbohydrates as well as protein, such an approach to food production, concludes Geneen, "could bring about a nutritional revolution as significant as the Industrial Revolution."[7] The implications of such a food source for community technology and self-sufficiency are manifest.

In Agriculture

Self-management in agriculture appears to be almost as quixotic a goal as self-management in industry. The "factories in the field" of the United States seem to be as unassailably entrenched as factories in Detroit or Pittsburgh or Birmingham. Since World War II the number of American farms has fallen from 5.9 million to 2.9 million, and Secretary of Agriculture Earl L. Butz has forecast the disappearance of another 1 million farms by 1980. Of the 2.9 million now extant, 50,000 grow one-third of the country's food supply and 200,000 produce over one-half. The degree of corporation control exercised over the new "agribusiness" type of farming has been analyzed by a witness at a Senate hearing, describing a Thanksgiving dinner of 1971: "The Smithfield ham comes from I.T.T., the turkey is a product of Greyhound Corporation, the lettuce comes from Dow Chemical Company, the potatoes are provided by the Boeing Company, and Tenneco brought the fresh fruits and vegetables. The applesauce is made available by American Brands, while both Coca-Cola and Royal Crown Cola have provided the fruit juices."[8] The impression that agribusiness is the wave of the future is supported by Eric Thor, director of the Agriculture Department's Farmer Cooperative Service: "Farming is moving with full speed toward becoming part of an integrated market-production system. This system, once it is developed, will be the same as industrialized systems in other U.S. industries."[9]

Although these predictions by Butz and Thor now seem incontrovertible, before long they may sound as bizarre as the assurance of September 1929 by Secretary of the Treasury Andrew W. Mellon that "there is no cause for worry. The high tide of prosperity will continue."[10] The predominance of agribusiness over family farming is of very recent origin. Prior to World War II, American farms were small-scale family affairs, operating without the use of migratory workers or compounds such as

DDT and parathion. They employed horses, mules, and human labor abundantly. Yet they were highly productive units, producing more food and fiber than the nation could absorb. "The experiences of the 1920s and 1930s," declared Agricultural Act administrator H. R. Tolley in a 1938 radio address, "taught us that it is necessary to be able to put the brakes on farm production."[11] But then came World War II, and the demand and prices for farm products soared. Farmers expanded their holdings, and corporate farming spread rapidly, along with absentee farm management. Within a few years American agriculture changed in character from a vast agglomeration of family units to an enterprise dominated by corporate agribusiness.

Two principal factors explain this sudden transformation. One was the availability of cheap oil for operating the increasingly complex and expensive farm machinery and for manufacturing the chemical fertilizers, insecticides, and herbicides now being used in enormous quantities. The willingness of Middle Eastern and South American rulers during the 1950s and 1960s to sell their oil for paltry royalties suggested that this supply of cheap oil was assured and inexhaustible. The other reason for the change in American agriculture was federal support of agribusiness—to an extent that is little realized. This support takes the forms of direct government subsidies, preferential tax treatment, and billion-dollar research programs designed specifically to aid agribusiness rather than family farming.

Government subsidies, consisting primarily of farm-price supports and soil-bank payments, have made up 30 to 40 percent of farm income for the years since 1955. The express purpose of these subsidies was to strengthen the family farm, but today they are doing the exact opposite. In 1971, 34.5 percent of all direct government payments went to farms with sales of $40,000 and over, compared with 24.8 percent to those with sales of $20,000 to $39,000, 18.1 percent to those making $10,000 to $19,999, 9.5 percent to those making $5000 to $9999, 6.5 percent to those making $2500 to $4999, and 6.6 percent to those making less than $2500.[12] The same federal partiality toward agribusiness is evident in the capital-gains provisions and other tax loopholes. In 1963, Secretary of the Treasury Douglas Dillon told the House Ways and Means Committee that nonfarm corporations and wealthy individuals buy farms and cattle ranches for tax-benefit reasons and "create unfair competition for farmers who may be competitors and who do not pay costs and expenses out of tax dollars but who must make an economic profit in order to carry on their farming activity."[13] This practice persists to the present day.

Large corporations are also virtually the sole beneficiaries of agricultural research financed by the federal, state, and county governments. Research oriented toward benefiting family farms would devise cooperative-ownership systems and credit schemes; develop low-cost simple machinery; provide information on the purchase, operation, and maintenance of machinery; and promote biological control of insect pests. Instead, scientists with research grants develop complicated and tremendously expensive machines. They breed new food varieties better adapted to mechanical cultivation—tomatoes hard enough to survive the grip of mechanical "fingers," grapes that ripen all at the same time for the convenience of mechanical harvesters, strawberries that grow year round (but are pulpy and tasteless), and similar tailor-made varieties of broccoli, cauliflower, cucumbers, carrots, and asparagus. They develop chemical pesticides and herbicides with uncertain long-range effects. The end product is sometimes less nutritious, less tasty, or even harmful because of added chemicals. But Senate hearings have ignored, or simply not considered, these facts. Paramount has been the vision of rural America as a factory producing food, fiber, and profits for vertical monopolies extending from the fields to the supermarket checkout counter.

Agribusiness's ultimate justification for its predominance is superior productivity. One oft-quoted statistic is that one American farmer now feeds 48 other persons—a result of the decline in the farm population from 30.1 percent of the total population in 1920 to 15.3 percent in 1950 and to 4.8 percent in 1970. Yet these figures are basically misleading, for they reflect high manpower efficiency but ignore equally high energy consumption and wastefulness—the Achilles heel of the entire agribusiness system.

Even the assumption of manpower efficiency is open to question. The one farmer who feeds 48 other persons actually is supported by so many other workers, who produce machinery, fertilizers, and pesticides and who transport, can, freeze, or bake the farmer's produce, that it is estimated that about 20 percent of the nation's work force is involved in one way or another in supplying food. Some scientists raise the question of whether "the idea of a reduction of labor input [in agribusiness] is a myth when the food system is viewed as a whole, instead of from the point of view of the farm worker alone. . . . Yesterday's farmer is today's canner, tractor mechanic, and fast food carhop. . . . One must ask if the change was worthwhile."[14]

Although the degree of labor efficiency may be in dispute, the high cost of enormous energy expenditures by agribusiness definitely is not.

Agriculture experts of Cornell University and New York State College of Agriculture and Life Science have calculated the relationship of energy inputs to corn production in the United States.[15] They found that the corn yield per acre between 1945 and 1970 increased 240 percent, while labor input decreased more than 60 percent. The introduction of hybrid corn accounted for 20 to 40 percent of the greater yield, and the remainder was due to increased energy input. The latter took the form of a jump in fuel consumption by farm machines from an average of 15 gallons per acre in 1945 to 22 gallons per acre in 1970. Much more marked was the rise in consumption of fertilizers, whose main ingredient is petroleum. Between 1945 and 1970 the use of phosphorus increased 3.5 times, that of potassium 12 times, and that of nitrogen 16 times. Corresponding increases in energy input occurred with the rising use of insecticides and herbicides and of a drying process that reduces the moisture content of corn from 26.5 percent to the 13 percent necessary for storage purposes.

The net result is that the equivalent of 80 gallons of gasoline is expended to produce an acre of corn. This energy-production ratio makes the high-energy agriculture system of the industrialized world one of the least efficient in history. "Primitive" cultures obtain 5 to 50 food calories for each calorie of energy invested. Some Asian civilizations based on wet rice cultivation have done as well and occasionally better. The Western high-energy food system, by contrast, requires 5 to 10 energy calories to obtain one food calorie. It is hundreds of times less efficient than Asian wet rice cultivation.[16]

Regardless of its efficiency, the intensive use of petroleum cannot continue at current levels because of petroleum's recent steep rise in price, which is expected to continue. More expensive petroleum will automatically make increased labor input and correspondingly decreased energy input profitable. Another reason for the declining use of fossil fuels is environmental pollution, which is reaching unacceptable proportions. Nitrogen insecticide and herbicide runoff into lakes and rivers, disruption of natural plant and animal populations, and depletion of natural resources all call for the use of more labor and less energy. Finally, the social disruption that has been produced by the substitution of energy for labor is as serious as the ecological disruption. It has forced the migration of large numbers of white and black rural families to the cities, thus depopulating the countryside and adding to the crowding, the tensions, and the crime of the urban centers. For this reason, two-thirds of the Department of Agriculture's 1975 budget was allocated for food programs to support the urban poor, many of whom have been driven off the land by the Department's own pro-agribusiness policies.

In short, energy-intensive agriculture is becoming economically, ecologically, and socially nonviable. But its very nonviability offers hope for the future. Professor Barry Commoner, director of the Center for the Biology of Natural Systems at Washington University, has made the most comprehensive study of the functioning and implications of agribusiness in America. In an address before the National Conference on Rural America (Washington, D.C., April 17, 1975), he concluded that "we can be optimistic that the necessary changes will take place, because the new production technologies—to use a classical, old-fashioned phrase—contain within themselves the seeds of their own destruction."[17]

Some alternative technological methods have been proposed by the agricultural scientists who calculated the relationships of energy input to food production cited above. One is the substitution of animal manure for chemical fertilizer, which would alleviate not only the pollution problem of nitrogen runoff but also the polluting runoff from animal feedlots. Another alternative is to reduce the use of chemical fertilizers by rotating clover or vetch, or other nitrogen-fixing crops, to produce "green manure." If rotation is not feasible, legumes can be planted between corn rows in late August and plowed under as green manure in early spring. Fuel consumption can be reduced by avoiding the use of extremely large tractors and other machinery, which can do more work per unit of time but which have heavy fuel requirements. The need is to use machinery precisely scaled to the job it is doing and to make fuller use of machinery through cooperative arrangements. Likewise, spot-spraying of herbicides with a hand sprayer involves one-sixteenth as much energy input as the currently popular blanket spraying with tractor and mechanical sprayer. Although the labor cost of hand application is four times that of tractor application, it could still become economically profitable as fuel costs rise, especially in view of the greater effectiveness of spot treatment. Plant breeders could pay more attention to factors such as hardiness, disease and pest resistance, reduced moisture content (to end the wasteful use of natural gas in drying crops), and increased protein content—even at the cost of some reduction in overall yield. Finally, energy can be saved by producing methane gas from manure and by reviving the use of wind power, especially with the efficient modern windmills being developed in Australia.

These various alternatives add up to a return to the earlier American family-farm type of agriculture, although supplemented by the knowledge and techniques of recent decades. Such a shift would *not* represent a step backward in efficiency. The Economic Research Service of the U.S. Department of Agriculture issued in August 1973 a study entitled *The One-Man Farm*. It concludes:

> The fully mechanized one-man farm, producing the maximum acreage of crops of which the man and his machines are capable, is generally a technically efficient farm. From the standpoint of costs per unit of production, this size farm captures most of the economies associated with size. . . . Beyond that range there may be diseconomies due to the increasing burden of supervision and communication between supervisor and workers. . . . The incentive for increasing farm size beyond the technically optimum one-man farm is not to reduce costs per unit of production, but to increase the volume of business, output, and total income.[18]

The size of a technically optimum farm varies with the nature of the crop and the geographic location. Thus the size of a technically optimum wheat and barley farm in Montana is 1960 acres; of a corn and soybeans farm in Indiana, 800 acres; of a cotton and soybeans farm in the Mississippi Delta, 600 acres; and of a vegetable farm in California, 200 acres.

A small farmer in California, Berge Bulbulian, was more specific and emphatic about the advantages of the family farm in the course of testifying before a Senate subcommittee.

> Probably the biggest obstacle we face in our struggle to save the family farm is the attitude of many Americans, including some farm people, that the family farm is obsolete, it is inefficient, and therefore, unable to compete with the efficient and well-financed conglomerates. Well-financed they are, but efficient they are not. I challenge any giant agribusiness corporation to match my efficiency. There is no way a large concern with various levels of bureaucracy and managed by absentee owners can compete in terms of true efficiency with a small, owner-operated concern. I cannot hire anyone to perform with the level of competence and efficiency that I perform. I seldom do one job at a time, but often two and three jobs simultaneously. While driving the tractor, I watch for other things that need to be done. I watch for pests, for nutrient or water deficiency, and generally consider management problems while doing a purely physical job. I work long hours each day and seldom have even a Sunday completely without work.
>
> I am the manager, personnel director, equipment operator, maintenance man, bookkeeper, laborer, welder, and so on. When I

do hire labor, I usually work with them. I can afford to buy any equipment ever built which will lower my cost of operation. I have never failed to secure the capital needed to make purchases of land or equipment. With 150 acres of vineyard, I believe that we are at or near the optimum level of operation for our type of farming. No, I can't sell for a loss and make it up in taxes, nor can I lose on the farming end of the business and make it up at another level as a vertically integrated operation can, and I happen to market many of my crops, too, through a cooperative, so to some extent I have attempted to cash in on integration, but certainly not to the extent giant farmers do.

I have no political clout and lobbying to me means writing a letter to my Congressman or Senator. But that is not what efficiency is all about.

Efficiency has to do with the relation between input and output. No, the big agribusiness firms are not efficient except in farming the government.[19]

A leading champion in Washington of embattled family farmers like Berge Bulbulian is Senator James Abourezk of South Dakota. Addressing the annual assembly of the Consumer Federation of America (Washington, D.C., January 30, 1975), he urged consumers and farmers to form a "winning coalition." On April 17, 1975, Senator Abourezk introduced the Family Farm Anti-Trust Act prohibiting corporations with more than 3 million dollars in nonfarm assets from engaging in farming. Senator Abourezk has also tackled the petrochemical industries, which, in the words of Professor Barry Commoner, have "colonized U.S. agriculture,"[20] and has introduced legislation banning horizontal energy monopolies (coal, petroleum, uranium, geothermal, and solar) and vertical energy monopolies (oil fields, pipelines, refineries, and service stations). The fact that this legislation almost won majority support in the Senate reflects the degree to which these drastic reform proposals are gaining public backing.

Another response to the looming crisis in American agriculture is the movement supporting the abandonment of chemical fertilizers, pesticides, and herbicides. Since this change would drastically reduce yields per acre, most land in the soil bank would need to be put back into farming. Those who favor the change argue that final output would fall only five percent, that farm income would rise 25 percent because of the savings in energy input, and that nearly all subsidy programs could be ended. A similar argument was supported by a study at Iowa State University, using linear-programming techniques.[21]

The results of an experiment testing this argument have been reported by Colin Fisher, director of the Pye Research Center in Suffolk, England. Careful records of all expenditures and yields from two adjoining wheat fields, one farmed with chemical fertilizers and the other using nonchemical methods, showed that the somewhat higher labor costs of nonchemical farming were more than outweighed by savings on fertilizer. The "organically" grown field averaged 1.75 tons per acre during the experimental period; the chemically fortified and pest-cleared field averaged 2.50 tons. "But that was the maximum we ever got from the chemical field," Fisher explained. "Experience has shown that such fields are prone to sudden drops in productivity when the natural nutrients in the soil are exhausted. By contrast, the constantly replenished supply of organic waste and bacteria in the natural field produces a living soil that acts as a factory churning out nutrients in steady reliable quantities." Fisher warned that fertilizers and pesticides cannot be eliminated entirely—that they will always have a place in emergencies. But Fisher concludes that, with the price of fertilizer spiraling so rapidly, "organic farming will soon be the only way food can be grown economically."[22]

Professor Barry Commoner's researches bear out the grass-roots observation among farmers that the ground can become addicted to chemical fertilizers "like an alcoholic." "In U.S. agriculture as a whole," reports Commoner, "we now use about five times as much fertilizer as we did in 1947 to produce the same amount of crop. In other words, the efficiency with which nitrogen is converted into crop has decreased by 80 percent in that time."[23]

Ralph Engelken is one of about a dozen organic farmers around Greeley in eastern Iowa. His yields are considerably higher than those of his "chemical neighbors," who laughed at him when he began organic farming in 1960. "The whole mood has changed now. Three years ago the press wouldn't print nothing bad about those sprays. Now, some farmers are learning more about what the sprays have done and want to know what I'm doing." The man who led Engelken and others into organic farming is a 73-year-old Roman Catholic priest, Louis White. Each year since 1946 Father White has cultivated a two-acre organic garden, and some of his parishioners began to follow his example after they tasted the produce. "We had to go through hard times. The press made fun of the organic farmer, agribusiness made fun of him, but now he's in the driver's seat. His costs are lower. The organic farmers are the only farmers in my parish who are making money."[24]

The significance of these experiences is that organic agricultural methods lend themselves to the family style of farming better than to the mammoth corporate agribusiness operations. And family farming means a healthier society, as revealed by a 1947 study of two communities in California's Central Valley. One was dominated by large corporation holdings, and the other was a community of small farms. The latter enjoyed a higher living standard, more parks, more stores with more retail trade, superior physical facilities, such as streets and sidewalks, twice the number of organizations for civic improvement and social recreation, and two newspapers, whereas the other community had one. In short, the small-farm community appeared to be a better place to live.

This conclusion may explain the rural revival apparently under way in America for the first time in 100 years. Census estimates for 1970 through 1973 indicate a net growth in the population of 300,000 to 500,000 in the nation's 2500 rural counties, as against zero population growth, or even net losses, for some metropolitan areas. These figures contrast with the gain of 2.2 million for the cities and suburbs between 1960 and 1970. "This is a real turnaround," states Calvin Beale, head of the U.S. Agriculture Department Population Studies Group. The cause for this unprecedented "turnaround" is evident in the findings of a Gallup Poll in August, 1972, which asked the residents of 300 scientifically selected localities where they would prefer to live if they had a choice—in a city, in a suburb, in a small town, or on a farm. The results were: city, 13 percent; suburb, 31 percent; small town, 32 percent; farm, 23 percent.

In the Third World

Technological self-management in the Third World, as in the industrialized West, appears on first consideration to be a remote possibility. The predominance of the great industrial complexes and agribusiness operations seems to stand unchallenged on the national stage. So does the subordination, on the global stage, of the economies of the peripheral regions to the interests of the metropolitan centers. But surface appearances may again prove misleading because of the inherent nonviability of existing institutions and practices.

It is undeniable that global economic relationships are generally determined by global political relationships. A multinational corporation, which uses its influence at home to obtain favorable dispensations, can and does use its global resources, backed by the power of its parent state, to make and enforce key decisions regarding Third World economies. The higher functions of management, research and development, enterpreneurship, and finance operate in the metropolitan centers, along with their supporting computers and data banks. As a result, Western models of economic development are adopted by the peripheral regions—and not necessarily under coercion, since in the prevailing circumstances the Western models seem to be the only feasible ones. Yet the end result has been the unceasing flow of wealth and benefits from the underdeveloped peripheries to the centers of financial and political power—a hierarchical world economic order that has generated affluent development for a minority of mankind and dependent underdevelopment for the large majority.

Although this pattern has prevailed in the past, its prospects for the future are uncertain because of two factors. One is the basic change now occurring in the global political configuration—the relative decline in U.S. power, the increasing relative strength and assertiveness of Western Europe and Japan, the growing military forces of the Soviet Union, the emergence of China as a major power, and the resulting changing relationships among Washington, Moscow, and Peking and, correspondingly, among Washington, Tokyo, and the European capitals. This new global fluidity provides more room to maneuver to the Third World states, or at least to the few that are coalescing into centers of regional power—such as Brazil, Nigeria, Iran, and the Arab oil states.

As important as these political realignments is the inescapable fact that Western models for economic development have not worked in the Third World as a whole. This contention can be illustrated with two examples: the vast Volta River power project and the much-heralded Green Revolution. The Volta project in Ghana was built with American money borrowed at high interest rates. It provides Kaiser Aluminum with enormous amounts of electricity, contracted at a long-term low price. But none of Ghana's bauxite is used by Kaiser, and no aluminum plants have been built in the country. Instead, Kaiser imports its aluminum for processing and sends it to Germany for finishing. Thus a great natural resource is being exploited in return for a meager contribution to the overall development of Ghana and the benefit of its people.

Equally disappointing has been the Green Revolution, which is essentially an overseas extension of the energy-intensive American agricultural system. In the course of the exportation of the Green Revolution, the interests of Third World peasants have been disregarded as completely as have the interests of American family farmers. In Mexico, for example, 97.7 percent of the land planted in corn and the overwhelming percentage of wheat lands were nonirrigated. A Mexican research group, the Institute for Agricultural Investigation, started a program to improve corn and wheat seeds for the small nonirrigated farms, but their efforts were superseded by those of Rockefeller Foundation scientists, who concentrated on increasing yields through genetic changes that require irrigation and fertilizer. The resulting new "miracle" strains enabled Mexico to become self-sufficient in wheat, but the beneficiaries were the wealthy landowners, who could afford the fertilizers and irrigation. The mass of the Mexican peasants have experienced increased unemployment or underemployment with the growing mechanization of the large estates.

Nevertheless, the Rockefeller Foundation was delighted with its "successful" Mexican test project. It established the International Center for Improvement of Maize and Wheat, with eight regional research organizations. This organization has benefited American corporations by opening up new global markets for their machines and chemicals at a time when the United States market is saturated and when concern about environmental abuse is mounting. In the Philippines, for example, the Esso Standard Fertilizer and Agricultural Company staffed and ran 400 agroservice stores in the early 1960s. The Philippine government supplied credit to farmers for purchases of seeds, fertilizers, and chemicals and also introduced a sales force of government agents. The profitability of the Esso venture into agricultural development was guaranteed by government assurances of subsidies to farmers who desired to purchase the Esso products.

But in the Philippines, as in India and Pakistan—these three countries forming the vanguard of the Green Revolution—the final results have been disappointing. The basic problem is the same one that arose in Mexico: 70 to 90 percent of the farmers of these countries have no irrigation and little money to purchase fertilizers. India's Minister of Agriculture, Mohan Ram, summarized the situation in 1969:

> The beneficiaries of the Green Revolution are the privileged minority of medium and large scale farmers. . . . Three to four percent of the biggest farmers exert all the political power, wield their influence, make all the decisions in collaboration with the State administration and take all the resources and the technical knowledge of government experts for themselves, while the poor receive very little. . . . The economic and political position of the rich peasantry has been

strengthened and consolidated. . . . Large landowners are attempting to get rid—if necessary by force—of their sharecroppers and former tenant farmers, with the objective of exploiting the land themselves or with the help of agricultural laborers.[25]

The overall effect of the Green Revolution has been to create conditions in the countryside precisely the opposite of the general prosperity and tranquillity that was anticipated. It has caused land reform, which is the prerequisite for any substantive and lasting improvement, to be shunted aside as a goal and forgotten. It is inducing the few farmers who can afford the new agricultural technology to introduce labor-saving mechanization. This mechanization in turn forces the already underemployed rural lower classes to flee to the slums in the cities, where they find themselves as superfluous as they had been in the countryside. This new urban lower class is now becoming the majority of the populations of the Third World cities. The net effect is to accentuate economic inequality and social tensions, leading some observers to predict that the Green Revolution will prove to be the prelude to Red Revolution.

The inadequacy of past efforts toward worldwide economic development is evident in the disappointing outcome of the First Development Decade of the 1960s and the Second Development Decade of the 1970s, launched by the United Nations. The income gap between developed and underdeveloped countries, which stood at a ratio of one to ten in 1960, increased to one to 14 by 1971. The foreign debt of the underdeveloped countries amounted to 21.6 billion dollars in 1961, but it rose to 75 billion by 1970—an increase of 3.5 times. Unemployment in the Third World, according to United Nations estimates, amounted to 27 percent of the labor force in 1960 and 30 percent in 1970. Thus M. M. Mehta of the International Labour Organization has warned that "the marginal men, the wretched strugglers for survival on the fringes of farm and city, may already number more than half a billion. By 1980 they will surpass a billion, by 1990 two billion. Can we imagine any human order surviving with so gross a mass of misery piling up at its base?"[26]

It is this misery that is basically responsible for Third World turbulence—for the thirty-second military coup in Africa since World War II, which occurred in Niger in April of 1974, and for the disappearance of constitutional regimes in all but a half dozen or fewer of the Latin American countries. But military dictatorships offer no way out; they only paper over the cracks. The way out is to achieve economic development rather than mere economic growth—that is, to plan purposefully for the comprehensive development of human and material resources rather than growth in GNP figures. Brazil and Nigeria and Indonesia boast of booming growth statistics, but the real incomes of Brazilians and Nigerians and Indonesians are anything but booming. To spread the benefits beyond a few foreign shareholders and a small local elite, genuine decolonization must be effected in all phases of national life.

Economic and political decolonization will be considered in following chapters. As far as technological decolonization is concerned, the underlying problem is not money. If it were, the Brazilians and Nigerians and Indonesians would now be in the clear. Rather, the problem is to achieve mass participation and self-management in the technological process. In the past, technology has relied heavily on Western experts and on an indigenous elite, neither of whom have had any meaningful contact with the masses in the cities or the countryside. As Mansur Hoda, the Indian economist, points out:

> Development does not only mean increased production of goods—but also the development of people—the stimulation of their innate abilities, giving them a feeling of self-determination and enthusiasm, self-respect, self-reliance. . . . Unless people are involved in the process of development and are given a chance to do something worthwhile, to grasp new ideas, acquire new skills and develop a sense of their own worth, no society can move out of misery and poverty. Indeed, development is almost a meaningless word when a large percentage of the population can neither contribute to the nation's progress nor benefit from it.[27]

The way out, then, is through the subordination of technology and the market economy to human needs. In the Third World, this means a technology that is designed for the villages rather than for the cities, that is cheap and suitable for application on a small scale, that is labor intensive rather than energy or capital intensive, and that uses local materials and makes products for local use.

Some successful revolutionary regimes in Africa and Southeast Asia have recently turned their backs on the world's market economy and opted for primitive but independent self-sufficiency. Their decisions have been based partly on ideological principles and partly on the knowledge that old trade connections and foreign-aid arrangements are usually no longer available to revolutionary governments. Such economic restructuring took place in Somalia after the Marxist-oriented army coup in 1969, in Mozambique and Guinea-Bissau after the ousting of the Portugese in 1974, and in Vietnam, Cambodia, and Laos after the expulsion of the Americans in 1975.

In Cambodia, for example, the economic reorientation began in spectacular fashion with the forced evacuation of all of the 1.5 million inhabitants of the capital, Phnom Penh. At the time the Western press sensationalized the evacuation as a "death march." But according to William Goodfellow, an associate of the Institute for International Policy, who left Cambodia with the final American evacuation in April 1975, the evacuation "was a journey *away* from certain death by starvation." Under the former government the capital had become dependent on American rice imports; furthermore, states Goodfellow, "starvation was already a reality in the urban centers, and widespread famine only a matter of weeks away."[28]

Later accounts by Cambodian refugees depict the hundreds of thousands of uprooted urbanites being directed to rural areas, where they were assigned shrub land or jungle to clear and plant with rice. According to these accounts, the refugees received a daily ration of rice and salt and were told to supplement this with whatever edible roots they could find. Two or three times per week they attended political-instruction sessions, where the basic theme was that all Cambodians are equal and all must therefore grow their own food. In case of illness, they were to use roots found in the forest to prepare traditional medicines. For clothing, they were instructed to grow cotton and mulberry trees to feed silkworms. What they produced they could exchange with others. Later the government would purchase their surplus and thus again put money into circulation. The middlemen, who disappeared with the evacuation of the cities, would not be allowed to reappear; life in the future would be organized along cooperative lines. Meanwhile, small groups of soldiers in the empty cities planted banana trees in front of government buildings, in villa gardens, and in any other available plots of arable land. And the few factories that remained in operation began turning out essentials such as soap, batteries, and canned milk.

In addition to these new revolutionary regimes, there is the example of Tanzania, one of the few Third World countries that for several years has been striving to evolve an independent technology based on mass participation and self-management. Tanzania's commitment was spelled out by President Julius Nyerere in the Arusha Declaration of February 1967. It sets forth a program of self-reliant rural socialism designed to avoid the pitfalls into which other African societies have fallen—runaway urbanization and exploitation by foreign interests and an indigenous elite of merchants and officeholders. Nyerere implemented his declaration by nationalizing all foreign banks, insurance firms, and import-export and wholesale businesses, also taking majority control in important manufacturing enterprises. His basic objective is to deemphasize the capital, Dar es Salaam, and to focus on development of the villages, where 80 percent of the people live. This development, Nyerere insists, must be achieved with as little foreign aid as possible. He has warned repeatedly of the dangers of foreign aid—how it could sap local initiative, induce undesirable capital-intensive types of economic growth, and compromise his foreign policy of nonalignment.

The instrument for rural development is the *ujamaa* (familyhood), a village organized as a producers' cooperative. Some 1500 of these villages have been organized; a typical one is Mbambara, founded in 1964 by members of the Youth League of Nyerere's party, TANU (Tanganyika Africa National Union). They cleared new land and planted it with sisal, which fetched a high price at the time. When sisal subsequently dropped in price, the settlers grew more food crops, supplemented by chickens and fish. Each member has his own private plot, but he can work it only after completing a full day's work in the communal fields. The members collectively decide what proportion of the cash income (mostly from sisal) should be divided among themselves and what proportion should be allocated for development projects such as granaries, poultry houses, cattle herds, or buildings for the school, nursery, or dispensary.

A principal concern of the government is to raise the technological level of such villages. "We've got to change," insists Nyerere. "We must mechanize, we must have better tools. But what are better tools? Not the combine harvester. If I were given enough combine harvesters for every family in Tanzania, what would I do with them? No mechanics. . . . Americans, when they speak of better tools, are talking about something quite different. We are using hoes. If two million farmers in Tanzania could jump from the hoe to the oxen plow, it would be a revolution. It would double our living standard, triple our product."[29]

In line with this kind of thinking, the Tanzania Agricultural Machinery Testing Unit (TAMTU) strives to develop village technology by using local talent and resources to meet local needs. It is necessary to begin with what is available, which is usually very meager—an occasional carpenter and blacksmith, and very few tools. Villagers are first taught to make simple tools like the axe and adze, using locally built stone anvils and goatskin bellows. Then they retrieve discarded local materials such as planks, bolts, nails, old rubber tires, and scraps from abandoned vehicles, and go on to construct wheelbarrows, handcarts, oxcarts, bicycle trailers, and weeding machines and other agricultural equipment. One of the most useful items is the "vegetable express," a cart the size of six vegetable crates of the type used by most Tanzanian farmers. The vegetable express can carry 18 crates, stacked on top of one another, at once—a boon for the farmer in transporting his produce. Over a period of years, an enterprising village can progress from constructing a goatskin bellows and a stone anvil to building portable welding equipment and a well-equipped workshop. Farmers are encouraged to visit the more progressive villages, receive training along these lines, and then return to their own villages to set up workshops.

Obviously, the specifics of the Tanzanian program cannot be applied to a Third World country with a relatively large and complex economy, such as Nigeria or Brazil. Yet the underlying issue, regardless of the country's material wealth or level of development, remains economic growth versus economic development—encapsulated islands of rapid, foreign-directed, capital-intensive growth versus comprehensive and autonomous development of human and material resources. The encapsulated islands are at first impressive and convincing, but they have repeatedly engendered social polarization and political disintegration. Iraq, for example, used large oil revenues to construct huge water-control projects during the 1940s and 1950s. These projects dramatically increased the acreage of cultivated land and the total national GNP. But this economic growth was superimposed upon an archaic social structure, so that the rising productivity benefited the two percent of the population that controlled over two-thirds of the arable land. Ninety percent of the peasants were landless, and in the process of this sudden and uneven growth they became saddled with such onerous tenancy terms that they flocked to Baghdad. The capital became a nightmarish slum, and it was these displaced peasants who took to the streets during the revolution of July 1958, exterminated the Hashimite royal family, and established a republic.

The Iraqi experience brings to mind the similar situation developing in Nigeria, with its soaring oil revenues and provocative display of wealth by the nouveaux riches juxtaposed against mass misery in Lagos and the countryside. The implications are self-evident in the following report from an American newspaperman in Lagos.

> "Lagos is horrible," an expatriate businessman said at a recent cocktail party. "I wake up to the warm, moist aroma of open sewers,

the water, electricity and telephones don't work, the traffic jam begins
at my garage."

"By eight in the morning," he continued a well-practiced mono-
logue, "I'm sweating profusely from the heat, trapped in the traffic
jam blocks from my office and besieged by hordes of beggars pushing
their crippled bodies at the car window with cries of 'Mercy, master—
master, mercy.' Lagos is horrible."

Only a recent arrival was naive enough to ask: "Why do you
stay here?"

The businessman laughed.

"You can make money here," he said. "There's money to be
made in Lagos."[30]

Why money can be made in Lagos was spelled out in detail in the
following advertisement of the Electricity Corporation of Nigeria, published in the same 1973 issue of the *New York Times.*

There is a huge domestic market of 55 million people and an external
market of 300 million at the doorstep.

Abundant manpower is available at a rate as low as 7 U.S. cents per
man-hour.

Raw materials are plentiful and agricultural products are in abundance.

Good land is everywhere and is easily accessible to electricity, water
and good roads.

There is stable environment.

Business is booming.

Pioneer industry enjoys substantial amenities.

It is possible to get your investment back in less than three years.

Electric power is plentiful and can be as low as anywhere if you are
on bulk supply rate.

People are earning huge profits in NIGERIA,

why don't

YOU!

For detailed information write to:

The General Manager and Chief Executive Officer, Electricity
Corporation of Nigeria.[31]

What these "huge profits" have meant for the people of Nigeria has been noted by the Chancellor of the University of Ife, addressing the graduating class: "In spite of the fortuitous boom in oil, resulting in rapid economic growth, we have achieved very little in the way of economic development." Likewise, Chief Awolowo has warned that "our per capita real income remains as low as ever. Poverty, ignorance, and disease are in evidence everywhere, more particularly in the rural areas. It is pertinent to remind ourselves that a situation such as we now have, under which the good things of life are assured to a small minority of Nigerians, and almost totally denied to the vast majority of our countrymen, is pregnant with unpredictable dangers for all of us, if allowed to continue for much longer."[32] The military coup of July 1975, which followed protracted labor and student unrest, suggests that this analysis had merit.

Chief Awolowo's warning is as pertinent for Iran, Brazil, Venezuela and Indonesia as it is for Nigeria. All of these countries indubitably show more bustle and outward glamor, and more impressive economic statistics, than does Tanzania. Yet the past record and present signs argue against their representing the developmental model for the Third World of the future.

This proposition seems particularly accurate if the problem of population control is taken into account. It is considered axiomatic that the current global population explosion hinders the development efforts of the Third World and widens the prevailing economic chasm between rich nations and poor. The solution has long been assumed to be the dissemination of birth-control information and devices. But recent experiences throughout the world suggest that families must be provided with the *motivation,* as well as the *means,* to limit births. It is now realized that substantial and enduring birthrate decline cannot be expected until the living conditions of the majority of the population improve enough that they no longer consider large families an economic necessity. The prerequisite for such a change in attitude is not a high *average* income but rather the availability of economic and social benefits to a substantial majority of the population rather than just to a small minority. Thus high birthrates persist in Mexico and Venezuela, despite their relatively high and rising GNPs, because the benefits of national economic growth have not been widely distributed. Conversely, birthrates have dropped sharply in Ceylon and China, despite their much lower per capita income levels, because social services and economic opportunities have been distributed more equitably. "'Growth with justice,'" concludes a recent study of world population trends, "may well be an indispensable key to the reduction and eventual stabilization of population."[33] This conclusion has obvious implications for the future prospects of the competing models for Third World development—Tanzanian versus Nigerian, Cuban versus Brazilian, Chinese versus Indian.

In China

Prior to the 1949 Communist revolution, China's technology and economy were typical of an underdeveloped semicolonial society. Eighty percent of the population were engaged in agriculture, and fewer than ten percent owned 70 percent of the land. The few modern industrial plants, concentrated along the eastern seaboard, were devoted to the production of consumer goods—textiles, cigarettes, processed foods, and the like. The industrial base and infrastructure were smaller than Russia's in 1914 or India's when it became independent in 1947.

After four years of postwar rehabilitation, the chinese Communists adopted in 1953 the first of a series of Soviet-type Five Year Plans. These plans gave priority to large-scale, capital-intensive heavy industry and neglected agriculture and consumer-goods industries. After the Cultural Revolution of 1966 to 1969, this Stalinist strategy was reversed. Heavy industry, however, was not to be neglected. Rather, the Chinese saw that there were two options open: one was to build heavy industry at the expense of the development of light industry and agriculture, and the other to build heavy industry through the expanded development of light industry and agriculture. According to official spokesmen, if the first option were chosen, "the people would not be satisfied and heavy industry would not run well"; if the second, "a large quantity of agricultural byproducts and light industrial products could be produced to satisfy the daily requirements of the people and more capital could be accumulated for the build-up of a powerful heavy industry."[34] This simultaneous development of capital-intensive heavy industry and labor-intensive agriculture and light industry was termed the policy of "walking on two legs."

Essentially, this policy meant the substitution of abundant labor for scarce capital—in other words, the transformation of labor into capital through vast public-works projects (reforestation, land reclamation, water conservation, irrigation) and the nationwide development of small rural industries and urban neighborhood workshops. This mobilization of labor was stimulated by a pervasive decentralization movement designed to release "the spontaneous initiative of the masses." The corollary to decentralization was self-sufficiency; each metropolitan area, each commune, and each province strove to be as self-contained as possible in all aspects of life. This combination of decentralization and autonomy had the additional advantages of minimizing vulnerability to foreign attack and easing the strain on the overburdened railway system.

This new developmental strategy is molding the Maoist China of today. The salient features are mass participation and self-management, which, as will be noted in the following chapter, are manifested in the elected Revolutionary Committees for every organization, in the collectively owned and operated communes, and in the factories, with their "three-in-one" combinations of workers, technicians, and administrators. Grass-roots initiative is most strikingly evident in the proliferating rural industries and urban neighborhood workshops, which are producing a rising percentage of China's industrial output.

The rural industries are small, labor-intensive enterprises, using local raw materials and manpower and supplying local markets with farm tools, insecticides, fertilizers, and consumer goods. They have grown so rapidly that 60 percent of China's chemical fertilizer and 40 percent of her cement now come from rural plants, and 90 percent of China's 2000 counties are manufacturing some type of farm machinery. In compliance with the stress on self-sufficiency and self-reliance, the communes depend as little as possible on outside experts, and wherever feasible they obtain necessary metals from primitive local iron mines and foundries. In southern China, so many small peasant-operated coal mines have been opened that the traditional dependence on coal from the North has almost ended.

The economist Roland Berger, who has visited China almost annually in his capacity as U.N. Secretariat official and as trade consultant, observed at first hand the development of local industry in Tunghua County of Hopei Province. This county of 485,000 people had formerly been a wholly agricultural area. Responding to the call for self-sufficiency, it constructed a total of 31 medium and small enterprises between 1969 and 1971. These included a coal mine, a liquid-ammonia plant for fertilizer production, a cement works, a repair shop for farm machinery, an iron and steel plant producing 3000 tons of iron and 1700 tons of steel annually from local ore, a miscellaneous-engineering factory (207 workers) making compressors, electric motors, and bearings, a small metal factory (84 workers) for wire drawing and straightening and the production of nails, and a ceramic plant producing irrigation pipes and insulators. Light industrial enterprises included a cotton mill, a paper factory (producing 600 tons a year), a tire-reconditioning shop, factories producing knitwear, and a plant that prepares medicines for animal and human use, mostly from locally collected herbs. Concludes Berger:

> The Chinese see [the commune industries] as serving a social as well as economic purpose, in that they help to lower the barriers between industry and agriculture, while developing local skills and stimulating workers unaccustomed to industrial processes to find simple technological solutions. Perhaps most important, in explaining the rapid growth rates, is the speed of commissioning and the quick return on investment made possible by the relative simplicity of construction and of the equipment utilized. Frequently, as I saw in Tunghua, machines disposed of as obsolete by the big factories are reconditioned and adapted by the local workers.[35]

Berger's observations and conclusions are borne out by those of a delegation of economists, sociologists, and engineers from the American Academy of Sciences that visited China in June and July of 1975. They examined over 50 small-scale commune industries, instead of the larger factories in major cities that visitors usually see. According to the delegation's leader, Professor Dwight H. Perkins of Harvard University, all were surprised at the scale, technological level, and extensive spread of these commune industries, which some Western economists have tended to belittle as primitive and inconsequential. "We came away with the impression," Professor Perkins reported, "that the population of China is becoming very skilled."[36]

The same mass initiative and participation is evident in the urban neighborhood enterprises. The city of Nanking (population 1.5 million) has more than 500 workshops and producers' cooperatives with 20,000 workers, 75 percent of whom are women. The total output value of these enterprises in 1972 was equal to the city's total industrial output value in 1949. The workshops turn out over 1000 different products, including precision instruments and meters, radio parts, hardened glass, lathes, and planing machines, as well as the daily necessities found in the notions departments of Western stores. Rewi Alley, a New Zealander who has lived in China for 35 years, describes these urban street factories in terms of the human struggle to get the factories started and the people's own transformation in the process. In the following account of two such factories in Chengtu, capital of Szechuan Province, Alley depicts the "street committees" as the urban counterpart to the commune brigades and work teams in the countryside.

The Wang Ja Kwai street committee decided to set up its first factory here in December, 1965. It consisted of some six housewives, an old retired metal worker, and two lower-middle-school graduates, too young to be sent out to country assignments. Their first product was screws for general use, made with the simplest of hand tools. The boys were too short to work at the bench so they stood on boxes. For lubrication, they used cooking oil from their homes. For the first three months none took wages, only a few yuan for food money. The leader, Tseng Chen-fang, smiled as she discussed the early struggles. Every day new difficulties had to be overcome. The first vices for bench work were very hard to get, as street factories received no allocation of this sort. Everything had to be foraged for amongst heaps of scrap in factory yards.

Tseng Chen-fang, now 55, is as capable as they are made. The two boys have grown up to be able technical leaders. The group has built its own workshops, which at the time of my visit were still being extended. From making screws with simple equipment, they have gone on to build their own lathes and other machine tools; they now turn out a line of medium and heavy punch presses which is sold to industry. The Lan Ho factory, as it is called, now has 197 workers, a hundred of whom are local housewives, the remainder mainly school leavers, the youngest aged sixteen. The old retired worker is still with them, and the oldest member, one of the original women, is now an agile seventy.

In 1972 the value of the factory's production was 340,000 yuan. Planned production that year was 34 presses of 65 kg. rating, but in fact they turned out 43. The 1973 target is for 72 of the heavier 150 kg. type. Most of their machine tools were discards from modern plants when re-tooling, rebuilt and adapted by the Lan Ho factory. The technical innovations they have improvised to machine the heavy castings are impressive. The factory is going all out now to modernise its machine tools, while producing its quota of machines and maintaining their quality.

Next door to the punch press factory is another also set up by the Wang Ja Kwai street committee. It was started in March, 1966, under the leadership of a young woman called Teng Fu-hwei, who brought in eight other women. Like the Lan Ho factory, they started by making screws, but soon went on to truck and factory parts. They expanded rapidly, and in 1972 their production reached 500,000 yuan. In 1973 they expect the total to be about the same; they are putting a great deal of energy into complete re-tooling, which will enable them to get a really big increase in production by 1974. Of the

184 workers now employed, 121 are women, mostly over 35. All are from homes near the factory.

When Teng Fu-hwei and her first group came to the site, just inside the old city wall, it was a stagnant water pool with a broken-down pigsty beside it. Some of the building bricks were obtained from the wall, but most were brought by the women from the country four kilometres away. So that work could go on in rain, plastic sheets were used as a temporary awning. But by 1974 they will have roomy new workshops and 33 modern machine tools.

The people who built them and brought these factories into production are no longer the same people as they were. Their quality of life has changed, their outlook has changed. Living and working together has created new people out of them, thoughtful and very self-reliant.[37]

4
FROM BOSS CONTROL TO WORKER CONTROL

There can be no real freedom or democracy until the men who do work in a business also control its management.

—*Bertrand Russell*

Certainly there is no more reason why industrial power at plant or office level should be exclusively linked to ownership of shares, than that political power should have been exclusively linked to the ownership of land and other property as it was in Britain until the "voters' control" movement won its battle.

—*Anthony Wedgwood Benn*

Ever-Growing GNP and Ever-Present Boss

In the realm of economics, the impulse toward self-management takes the form of a striving to substitute worker control for boss control over what goes on in the workplace. For most citizens, what happens in the workplace is the most important single factor in their lives. Their jobs shape their sense of identity. They describe themselves through their occupations: "I'm a housewife," or "teacher," or "farmer," or "lawyer." In short, the individual tends to become what he does. The importance of the workplace was revealed by an impressive 15-year longitudinal study of aging that showed job satisfaction to be the most important single factor determining the longevity of the individual American.[1] It is more important than his genetic inheritance, his style of living, or his drinking, smoking, or eating habits.

But job satisfaction today is often prevented by two major assumptions, which, like the concrete in Pete Seeger's song, are smothering the workplace and its workers: (1) that an ever-growing GNP is the cure-all for social problems, and (2) that an ever-present boss is the prerequisite for growth in GNP. The fallacy of the GNP assumption is becoming evident in all types of societies, underdeveloped as well as developed. Two prominent American economists, Irma Adelman and Cynthia Taft Morris, who published in 1973 the results of their meticulous quantitative investigation of the interaction among economic growth, political participation, and distribution of income in noncommunist developing nations, wrote that the results of their analyses "came as a shock" to them.[2] They found that the development programs of the 1950s and 1960s did not alleviate human misery. On the contrary, the programs decreased both popular participation in political life and the relative share poor people had in the national income. Brazil's per capita GNP, for example, rose in real terms during the 1960s by 2.5 percent annually, but the relative share of the national income received by the poorest 40 percent of the population fell from ten percent in 1960 to eight percent in 1970, while the share of the richest five percent rose from 29 percent to 38 percent. During the same decade, popular political participation was steadily repressed in a process that culminated in the outright military dictatorship of the 1970s.

Increasing the GNP has proved equally unbeneficial in developed societies. The prime example is the United States, whose annual GNP has now surpassed 1 trillion dollars. But the cost of this unprecedented economic achievement is the consumption of about 35 percent of the world's energy and material output by the U.S. population, which constitutes only 5.6 percent of the world's population. This imbalance has created two serious ecological problems: the rapid depletion of finite global resources and the need to dispose of mounting waste products. These problems alone make it impossible for the American consumer society to become a model for the rest of the world. The present inequitable distribution of the world's raw materials could perhaps be justified if it resulted in a model society, in terms of human welfare and happiness. Unfortunately, the unprecedented American affluence has been accompanied by unprecedented social unrest and disruption, including alcoholism, drug abuse, urban crowding, a soaring crime rate, environmental deterioration, and inadequate government services—all the familiar symptoms of public squalor amid private affluence.

Even those who are in a position to enjoy the private affluence have found it to be a mixed blessing. Consider this graffito on an American university campus: "Ask not what your country can do for you, ask what your country is doing to you." What it is doing is suggested in the comment by a member of the first Nixon cabinet on the difficulty of recruiting personnel for top federal posts: "I never realized what a toll the fierce competition of American business and professional life has taken on many of our most talented and successful men. Many of them have simply been worked out in the struggle. Many more have all kinds of family problems they cannot leave. In a great many cases they have taken to drink to such an extent that the risk is too great."[3]

The fallaciousness of the second major assumption mentioned earlier, that the boss is indispensable, is also becoming evident. A high official of the National Association of Manufacturers commented "Democracy is all right for politics, but in business, we have to be sure things get done."[4] But the fact is that both theoretical studies and workshop experience indicate that it is under democracy that "things get done," and under hierarchical management that they do *not* get done—or at least not so efficiently. Chris Argyris, an industrial psychologist, explains that the individual's social growth from infancy to mature adulthood is a progression from a subordinate role to an equal role in family and society, and from the infant's state of dependence to the adult's control of and responsibility for his own behavior. This vital growth toward adult independence is usually blocked when a worker takes a wage-paying job. In return for wages, workers normally have to accept what is euphemistically termed the "employer-employee relationship," which means employer control over the work process, the work purpose, and the work output. The resulting frustration of human creativity is the root cause of the widespread and growing worker unrest and alienation we see now in the United States, Western Europe, and the U.S.S.R.

This proposition is borne out by the results of more than 100 studies done in the past 20 years, which show that the worker's chief desire is to become master of his or her own immediate environment. Workers want responsibility and a sense of achievement, so that they can feel that their work and they themselves are important—the twin ingredients of self-esteem. Workers are realistic enough to recognize that certain jobs are inherently dirty and arduous, yet it is not these features of such jobs that they find so oppressive; it is rather the constant supervision and coercion that accompany them—the generally servile relationship that management demands of workers. The reality of this servility is stressed by Senator Charles H. Percy, former president of Bell and Howell Company:

> Outside the plant gate or office door is the new American: A future-oriented, demanding, expectant, educated, freedom-loving individual. Inside that gate or door this interesting, creative, inventive American is expected to conform to a past-oriented, authoritarian, hierarchical, class-based, freedom-fearing social system. Is there any wonder then that, in the past two years, the national media have given us example after example of the grinding effects of old-style jobs on new workers? . . . In spite of more pay and benefits than ever before, all kinds of working men and women, "blue collar" and "white collar," are unhappy in their work, and thus unhappy and unfulfilled in a large and very important part of their lives.[5]

The reality of this frustration of the work force and its results are made clear in numerous studies by American behavioral scientists in the field of "organizational science." After surveying these studies, the sociologist Paul Blumberg concludes "There is hardly a study in the entire literature which fails to demonstrate that satisfaction is enhanced or that other generally acknowledged beneficial consequences accrue from a genuine increase in workers' decision-making power. Such consistency of findings, I submit, is rare in social research."[6]

As will be noted later in this chapter, the findings of the behavioral scientists have been borne out by workshop experience in various societies. Thus Adelman and Morris conclude from their study of the performance of Third World economies that, "in our opinion, the only acceptable strategy for the decades ahead is development of the people, by the people, and for the people."[7] The same judgment is reached in the 1973 study *Work in America,* commissioned by former Secretary of Health, Education and Welfare Elliot L. Richardson: "The main conclusion is that the very high personal and social costs of unsatisfying work *should* be avoided through the redesign of work. . . . Not only can work be redesigned to make it more satisfying but . . . significant increases in productivity can also be obtained."[8]

Such findings are gradually exposing the traditional myths regarding GNP growth and managerial elitism. The problem now is to find viable alternatives—the goal of a great variety of experiments being conducted throughout the world. These experiments, which we will now explore, are the harbingers of the future; they are the grass that is "growing everywhere" in the workplaces of the world.

Industrial Democracy in the West

A 1974 opinion survey in France asked citizens to name the single most important reform they wanted from the new government of Giscard d'Estaing. Thirty percent said "democratization of the company." Reacting to this public sentiment, d'Estaing a year later introduced legislation giving workers more rights and more control over their jobs. Referring to the 1867 laws that still governed the operation of French enterprises, a government spokesman explained, "We cannot manage modern industry within the juridical structure of the Second Empire."[9]

There is no comparable interest in worker self-management in the United States, on the part of either the government or the public. The difference stems partly from the strength and the Marxist orientation of European labor parties and trade unions; the United States has no strong prolabor party, and its trade unions, although sometimes strong, do not have the clout of the European unions. In addition, the discrediting of some European big businessmen for collaborationism during World War II made them much more submissive to the demands of both government and labor than their American counterparts. In fact, this submissiveness on the part of management explains the advent of one of the three chief forms of worker self-management currently operating in Europe—the "codetermination" (*Mitbestimmung*) of Germany.

In order to prevent the resurgence of Nazism in the postwar years, British occupation authorities decreed in 1951 that German workers should have equal representation with capital on the supervisory boards of the coal and steel industries, and one-to-three representation in other industries. The supervisory board in Germany corresponds roughly to the board of directors in the United States; it is the seat of final authority. It appoints management personnel but does not interfere in day-to-day management business. Unfortunately, this separation of supreme formal power from the actual management process made codetermination ineffective as an instrument for promoting meaningful worker self-management. A handful of labor representatives on a high-level board, meeting infrequently to decide on matters of little concern to the average employee, can have little influence on what goes on in the workplace. Some managers claim that codetermination has promoted understanding of company problems among employees and thereby has contributed to the remarkable industrial peace of postwar Germany. But regardless of its role in facilitating communication within German industries, codetermination has in fact proven of little value in furthering genuine industrial democracy.

More significant is a second form of worker self-management, the works councils, which are legally obligatory in most Western European industries. Established by legislation or collective agreement in the early postwar years, these councils are elected and controlled by rank-and-file workers. Although regarded at first merely as forums used by management to announce decisions already made, the councils have acquired more power and significance since the mid-1960s. With variations from country to country, they now have the right to demand certain information from management, and they also enjoy consultative, veto, and/or decision-making rights in specified areas. Workers generally welcome the councils as a means of keeping informed and of protecting their rights; some managers like the works councils because they assume responsibilities and contribute to the solving of problems. "We don't really mind having workers on the supervisory board," explained one German manager, "though it's a nuisance. They come to the meeting, eat a free lunch, collect their fee, and go home. But it's the works council that gets things done."[10]

The third major form of worker self-management has been pioneered in Norway by the social psychologist Einar Thosrud. His researchers demonstrated that man is an "active animal" who likes to work, provided that the job affords an outlet for his ideas and inventions within the context of a collective effort. This definition of rewarding work requires the abolition of repetitive assembly-line jobs, ritualized and inflexible office routines, and other types of fragmented, hierarchically organized work in favor of "whole work," in which the individual or group makes a complete product, assuming responsibility for the work process and for the quantity and quality of output.

This reorganization of work, sometimes called "job enrichment," has usually proven quite successful where it has been implemented in Western Europe and the United States. Phillips in Holland has applied "job enrichment" to the assembly and adjustment of color TV sets. Work that formerly had been fragmented into a hundred operations, each lasting less than one minute, is now performed by groups of seven workers who arrange the details and the speed of the assembly process to suit themselves. Preliminary results showed a five-percent increase in output, a 25-percent decrease in absenteeism, and a virtual disappearance of defective sets. Imperial Chemical Industry in Britain has introduced "workers' control" in several factories employing a total of 5000 men. In one of the plants, a synthetic-fiber factory in Gloucester, former assembly-line workers increased productivity by 30 percent when freed from the supervision of foremen and technical experts. In the process the workers learned to adjust, maintain, and repair machines that were previously assumed to require the attention of experts. American Telephone and Telegraph Corporation redesigned its claims and invoices department. Instead of assigning workers to repetitive specialized tasks (such as answering phones, recording data, or checking), the workers were granted total job responsibility for a given neighborhood and were permitted to vary their working hours within set limits. The result was a 27-percent increase in productivity.

A few companies have carried this trend further by instituting "open systems" or "total systems" designed to serve human needs as well as corporate. An example of such a system in the United States is that of the Procter & Gamble plant in Lima, Ohio. Time clocks and job classifications have been eliminated; workers are encouraged to add to their skills and handle a variety of jobs; the manager serves as a resource and has little decision-making power, and the workers control hiring and firing; everybody is on a straight salary; the workers set the pay scales, and all salaries are common knowledge because the workers keep the books. The result is a virtually perfect quality record, with overall costs approximately half those of a conventional plant, and workers' salaries, as well as company profits, are considerably higher than average. But more significant than productivity and profits has been the impact of the new work conditions on human lives. When asked whether worker administration of the budget was not dangerous for the company, the manager responded "Sure, they could hold us up and say, 'you're not paying enough.' But by now you could almost say that those employees have less interest in their pay than the management people do, who think the Lima people are not being paid enough."[11] Along the same lines, Neil McWhinney, a University of California psychologist who has worked as a consultant with Procter & Gamble, has written:

> One of the striking features in our "pure" open systems plant is that workers take on more activities outside the workplace. The most visible involvements had to do with community racial troubles. Following major disturbances in the small city where they lived, a number of workers organized the black community to deal directly with the leaders of the city and of industry. . . . Blue collar workers won elections to the school board majority office and other local positions. Nearly ten percent of the work force of our plant holds elective offices currently. . . . We have noted that open systems workers join more social clubs and political organizations.[12]

The very success of this radical experiment suggests the solution to the problem of the resistance of the continuing hierarchical organization of American and European business enterprises to change, despite the striking advantages of the democratic alternative. The Lima experience shows how thin the line is between worker participation and worker control. The rationale of industrial democracy is that worker self-management creates more meaningful and satisfying work, more contentment among workers, greater productivity, and higher profits. But how far should self-management be allowed to go? Changes in the work process at the shop level do not threaten traditional employer-employee relationships. But what if self-management did not stop at the shop level? What if it were expanded from the work process to work purpose and to decision making regarding work product? If the extension of worker self-management that occurred at the Procter & Gamble Lima plant were implemented nationally, would not the *raison d'être* of supervisors, managers, and owners come into question? From the owner-manager viewpoint, the self-management concept is a dangerous two-edged sword. Carried to a certain point it generates good labor relations and higher profits. But beyond that point it infringes progressively on vested interests until eventually it undermines the capitalist system itself.

The real issue, then, behind worker self-management is not efficiency but power. It is power that gives the Soviet bureaucrat or the Western capitalist control over the means of production and the distribution of output. It is power that enabled General Motors management at Lordstown, Ohio, to give the unchallengeable response "Well, it's our plant" to justify their rejection of a successful doubling-up technique introduced spontaneously by assembly-line workers in order to gain extra time off the line. Indeed, recent research indicates that from the beginning of the Industrial Revolution it was the drive for power and profits, rather than technological considerations, that engendered the hierarchical factory system.

It is not just atavistic myopia that prompts American business executives to perceive worker participation only as a "management technique," to refuse to release information on their "radical" experiments, to keep a tight rein on their more innovative managers, and to bristle when they hear the term "industrial democracy." Consciously or subconsciously, they sense that the implied parallel between political and industrial democracy will stimulate demands that democracy be implemented in the workplace just as it has been implemented in the voting booth.

The parallel between political democracy and industrial democracy is compelling. The British Tories passionately opposed the first Reform Bill of 1832, which increased the number of voters only from 500,000 to 813,000, because they feared that "the more you give them, the more they want." Their fears proved perfectly justified, for not only was the franchise extended by successive reform bills to encompass the entire population, but today the demand (as we shall see in the following chapter) is for a much more revolutionary leap—from indirect representative democracy to direct participatory democracy. It seems reasonable to expect a parallel development in the economic world, under which employees who have won control of the work process may then begin to question the validity of producing polluting detergents, or unsafe automobiles, or appliances with built-in obsolescence. Why continue raising the GNP, and thereby polluting the environment and wasting scarce raw materials, when it may be possible to live better by producing less under a different economic value system?

This potential threat to management control may soon materialize in Sweden, according to certain proposals presented at a conference sponsored by the Swedish government and the Institute of Industrial Relations of the University of California, Los Angeles. Ingemund Bengtsson, Sweden's Minister of Labor, informed the conference of two plans being considered by his government. The first, a long-range scheme, would require employers to put 20 percent of their profits into a fund to enable workers to buy stock in the Swedish corporations. In time this practice would lead to ownership of private industry by workers, through their unions. The other plan, more immediate but equally revolutionary, would give unions equal decision-making power with management in solving every corporate problem.

Swedish corporate managers, like their American counterparts, have hitherto enjoyed the right to decide where raw materials should be purchased, the nature of the product to be manufactured, the prices at which it should be sold, and a host of other such matters. But under the proposed new law, management must delay a decision until negotiations with the unions have culminated in an agreement. If management can prove that a delay would involve "serious risk" to the company while negotiations are being conducted with the union, management can make a unilateral instant decision. But the government will impose "heavy damages" on companies, warned Bengtsson, if they "abuse this safety valve." Since workers spend such a large part of their lives on the job, added Bengtsson, they have "an interest in seeing to it that the enterprise is run in a sensible manner. Drastic changes must be made, because the work place is the last bastion of totalitarianism."[13]

Worker control threatens the status and privileges not only of bosses but also of labor-union leaders. The latter generally recognize the legitimacy of the prevailing hierarchical business structure and are interested only in negotiating seniority rights, higher wage scales, and better working conditions. They suspect that job enrichment is a management trick to persuade workers to produce more for the same pay, and to be more satisfied with their jobs and less interested in unions. William Winpisinger, General Vice President of the International Association of Machinists, dismisses job enrichment as "a stopwatch in sheep's clothing." "The better the wage," he insists, "the greater the job satisfaction. There is no better cure for the 'blue collar blues.'"[14]

This assumption is contradicted by the findings of a 1972 University of Michigan survey based on interviews with 1533 employed adults. It showed that the better-educated workers of today are concerned with work quality as well as with remuneration, and that this concern involves young and old, skilled and unskilled, white-collar and blue-collar, and high-income and low-income types. "It is grossly in error," concludes the study, "to remain fixed on the idea that the blues syndrome is the exclusive property of the hardhat. He shares it about equally with his neighbors of disparate personal backgrounds, occupations, and incomes."[15]

Mobilization of this pervasive sentiment is the objective of the organization called People for Self-Management, which held its first annual conference at the Massachusetts Institute of Technology in January 1974. Professor Jaroslav Vanek of Cornell University set forth the rationale of the meeting:

> The main idea is . . . that something should be done about the underdeveloped state of self-management in the United States. . . . The comparative lack of success of self-management in the past is not a demonstration of its intrinsic impossibility but rather the result of some special conditions not inherent in the basic nature of self-management. On the contrary, we now know from the facts as well as theory that self-management is a highly efficient form of economic organization. . . . The American economy, as the most advanced in the world, shows most clearly the crises and contradictions of advanced capitalism and by implication the need for placing the working man, instead of the capital owner, at the center of the world of work.

To realize this goal of worker self-management, the 300 delegates at the conference agreed to promote a research and educational program, to publish a newsletter or journal, and to provide technical assistance to any firm that wished to try self-management.

Although this conference was attended by many more "intellectuals" than "workers," a 1974 survey by pollster Daniel Yankelovich suggests that the imbalance may be temporary. He found that the counterculture values of the college campuses were spreading to noncollege youth, who are now adopting goals beyond good pay and economic security.

> Today's generation of young people are less fearful of economic insecurity than in the past. They want interesting and challenging work but they assume that their employers cannot—or will not—provide it.
>
> By their own say-so, they are inclined to take less guff than older workers. They are not as automatically loyal to the organization as their fathers, and they are far more cognizant of their own needs and rights.

Nor are they awed by organization and hierarchical authority. Being less fearful of "discipline" and the threat of losing their jobs, they feel free to express their discontent in myriad ways, from fooling around on the job to sabotage.[16]

Worker independence naturally varies with economic conditions and employment opportunities. The recession and the high unemployment rates of the mid-1970s forced American workers to temper their militancy. "It changes your outlook quite a bit when you have those mortgage payments, car payments, and kids to feed," explained Martin Ford, 33-year-old president of Local 1112 of the United Automobile Workers, which earlier had closed down the giant General Motors assembly plant in Lordstown, Ohio. And yet various employees of that plant repeatedly stated, when interviewed in March 1975, that their basic complaint against high-speed assembly-line work remained unsatisfied and that future eruptions were inevitable. "Basically, I'm the same guy. If I think I'm right, I'm going to fight for it. I still believe a lot of things have to be changed. . . . If they raised the flag and said, 'We're gonna go at this again,' we'd do it."[17]

High unemployment and inflation affect the attitudes of the general American public as well as those of American workers. A national poll conducted in the summer of 1975 by Hart Research Associates revealed the following:

- Of the 1209 people polled, [13 percent said that they would definitely support a candidate for President who favored worker control of the nation's businesses, 43 percent said they would probably support such a candidate, 26 percent said they would not support such a candidate, and 18 percent were undecided.]
- Sixty-six percent said that they would prefer to work for an employee-owned and -controlled company, if given a choice; 20 percent would prefer an investor-owned company and eight percent a company owned by the government.
- Forty-one percent favored making major adjustments in the economy to try things that had not been tried before; 37 percent favored minor adjustments, and 17 percent preferred to keep the economy as it is and allow it to straighten itself out.[18]

Worker Control in Yugoslavia

The industrial democracy sought after by reformers in Western Europe and the United States is the law of the land in Yugoslavia. Its emergence in that country was unique in that it was developed and implemented from above rather than forced by mass pressure from below. Until 1948

Yugoslavia followed Soviet ideology and political strategy faithfully. The clashes that occurred between Stalin and Tito during World War II and immediately thereafter were power struggles, pure and simple. But when Stalin persisted in intervening in Yugoslavia's domestic and foreign affairs, and when the Cominform expelled Yugoslavia from its ranks, Tito and his comrades reluctantly and hesitantly began to formulate an ideological rationalization for their defiance of the Kremlin.

The basic thesis they evolved was that revolution and expropriation of private property do not guarantee a socialist society free of exploitation. The danger is always present not only of a counterrevolution and a capitalist restoration but also of the rise of a Party and state bureaucratic elite that, through its control of state power, would enjoy as much privilege and luxury as did the old capitalists. This, claimed the Yugoslavs, is what had happened in the Soviet Union, where a "new class" had emerged in what had become a society based on "state capitalism" rather than socialism.

To avoid such a regression at home, the Yugoslav leaders introduced in 1950 and elaborated in the following years a system of worker control of industry. This system provides that all enterprises belong not to the state but to the workers, who formulate policy and also elect the managers responsible for implementing policy. The Yugoslavs refer to this system as "social control," rather than state control, of the means of production. Power is vested in the workers themselves rather than in state bureaucrats. More specifically, all members of an enterprise constitute the workers' collective, which decides by direct vote basic policy issues such as relocating the plant or merging it with other enterprises. The members also elect by secret ballot a workers' council, which meets approximately once a month and is charged with making decisions on important technical matters such as setting prices on its products and preparing production and financial plans.

In distributing profits, the company first pays its taxes and debts and allocates a certain fixed amount for depreciation, and then transfers the remaining capital to the workers' council. This body decides how much to distribute among various business funds, such as those for workers' welfare and emergency reserve, and how much to allocate to new investments. What is left is divided among the workers, who are guaranteed a certain minimum wage fixed by law. The amount the individual worker receives above that minimum depends upon his education, seniority, and responsibility. Pay differentials are modest; the wage of a director may not be more than five times that of the lowest-paid worker. This ratio may be compared to wage differentials of about 18 to 1 in the Soviet Union and of about 40 to 1 in the United States.

On paper these arrangements seem ideal, meeting the requirements of worker self-management as spelled out by social scientists in the West. In practice, however, there is considerable discrepancy between theory and reality. The actual functioning of institutions depends on the qualifications of the people involved. Unfortunately, the workers who run the factories in Yugoslavia have many handicaps to overcome. Being citizens of what was until recently a decidedly underdeveloped country, many are poorly educated first-generation industrial workers. They lack self-confidence as well as expertise, and they are most interested in matters of direct relevance to them, such as housing, pay schedules, and working conditions. On issues of great significance for the future of the enterprise itself, they tend to defer to the technicians, who have more education and experience. Another complication is the wide differences in levels of education and general development within Yugoslavia between the relatively advanced republics of Slovenia, Croatia, and Serbia, and the relatively retarded republics of Macedonia, Montenegro, and Bosnia-Herzogovina. Another problem is the exaggerated influence of consumerism, stemming from the large number of tourists who visit Yugoslavia and the equally large number of Yugoslavs who go to Western Europe to work and who return with Western consumption habits and aspirations. These factors create tendencies to allocate capital in ways that, although immediately profitable, may be frivolous and contrary to long-term goals. Perhaps most serious are certain contradictions in governmental policies. For example, Yugoslavia's dependence on market mechanisms has led to advertising and marketing campaigns that raise consumer expectations beyond reasonable levels. Also, official ideology has tended to transform self-management from the ultimate societal goal to the most efficient means of attaining another goal: economic growth through industrialization. As a result, the stress is on individual gain rather than social transformation.

All this adds up to a system quite different from the ideal envisaged by the champions of worker control. Technocrats and bureaucrats are in the saddle, and the resulting technobureaucracy, as it is called, is described in the following account by a Zagreb worker of a typical Communist meeting in his plant:

> The secretary sits at the table, in the first row is the [plant] director, the deputy director, etc. The secretary opens the meeting of the basic

[Party] organization, and looks at the director like he sees a holy object in him. And how is the secretary elected? Everything's carried out real fast and they regularly elect the one who suits the higher-ups.[19]

It is not surprising that the most common worker response to a survey conducted by the League of Communists of Croatia was "The working class doesn't decide; others decide in its name, but everyone swears in its interest."[20] Professor Josip Obradović of Zagreb University observed for three years the functioning of 20 Yugoslav firms in four of the six republics and found that

> participation of rank-and-file employees in the most important policy-making areas was almost nil, the discussions of the meetings being preempted by the executives and staff experts. Somewhat greater employee participation was registered in the "labor relations" areas (especially in the area of human relations); however, even in those areas the amount of participation was not impressive.[21]

Likewise, Professor Josip Zupanov of Zagreb University reported that his studies during the 1960s of the power structure in Yugoslav enterprises

> showed no difference in the distribution of "executive power" in the surveyed Yugoslav organizations as compared with the American organizations: an oligarchic pattern was found in both of them. . . . Summarizing the results of the studies in social power one may conclude that the hierarchical organization has survived within the new institutional shell of democratic organization.[22]

The Yugoslav experiment, however, cannot be dismissed as a lost cause. By the early 1960s, the limitation on consecutive terms in office had enabled one-fourth of the total industrial labor force to obtain experience serving on workers' councils and managing boards. The Yugoslav sociologist Stipe Suvar declared in January 1971 that "there are more than a million and a half skilled workers who have knowledge and education for performing any political function in our society."[23] Also noteworthy are the findings of the sociologist Jiri Kolaja, who observed the operation of both Yugoslav and Polish factories. When he asked the workers if they felt that the factory belonged to them, a substantial majority of the Yugoslavs answered affirmatively, whereas a typical Polish response was "This factory mine? What a queer idea" or "What an idea! Only the plant director can have a feeling of ownership. This is his factory."[24] Furthermore, whatever the dysfunctions of the Yugoslav system, the fact remains that it has been an outstanding success in terms of economic performance, thus demonstrating the practical feasibility, at least, of worker control. During the 1960s Yugoslavia's rate of GNP increase was one of the highest in Europe, barely lower than Japan's.

Finally, we need to remember that the Yugoslav experiment is of recent origin and is still in the formative stage. It was introduced in 1950 after the 1948 break with Stalin, but it did not really get under way until the reforms of 1953, and since then its legal framework and organizational forms have been constantly reviewed and altered; the latest instance was Yugoslavia's adoption of a new national constitution in 1974. It is not without significance that Professor Joze Goricar, after describing the division of Yugoslav society into two major social classes—workers and technobureaucrats—nevertheless concludes:

> No matter how limited is the participation of workers in the managing process within the Yugoslav enterprises, no matter how the tiring work in production is hindering the workers in their efforts to engage more fundamentally in solving the global problems of their enterprises, no matter how much lacking self-government is in other respects, it is nevertheless a great educative experience for the working class. As is true of every other educative experience, its positive effects will become manifest only after a longer period of time.[25]

Worker Control in the Kibbutzim Factories

The Yugoslav experiment demonstrates the problems as well as the promise of self-management, showing that worker control is not a cure-all that materializes automatically out of political reform, even after a successful revolution such as that led by Tito. The social milieu is a crucial factor, for an underdeveloped society means an underdeveloped labor force, accustomed to obeying orders rather than making decisions. This is strikingly evident when the results of worker control in Yugoslavia are compared with those of worker control in Israel, where traditions and social conditions are altogether different.

Kibbutz factories are part of the larger social system of the Israeli kibbutzim, or rural communal settlements varying in size from 40 to 1000 members. The kibbutz economy comprises several autonomous branches, mostly agricultural, but recently including a variety of industries as well. All workers in kibbutz industries are co-owners rather than salaried employees. The entire communal income goes into the industry's common treasury; each member's needs are provided for by communal institutions on an equal basis, and each member, regardless of the value of his services, gets only a small annual cash income for personal expenses, in addition to meals in the communal dining room. Between 1960 and 1970 the total number of kibbutzim industries rose from 108 to 170, and their contribution to the total Israeli industrial output grew from 3.1 percent in 1955 to 6.2 percent in 1961. The majority of these kibbutzim plants are engaged in four industries: in order of importance—metal works, plastics, food, and wooden furniture.

Kibbutzim industrial plants operate along more communal lines than do those of Yugoslavia. Another critical difference is that the educational and general cultural levels of kibbutzim members are substantially higher than prevailing levels among workers in Yugoslav factories. Most kibbutz industrial workers have had secondary education and vocational training, since the kibbutz agriculture in which most have been trained operates on a high technological level.

The industrial management expert Professor Seymour Melman of Columbia University has compared the performance of Israeli plants operating under egalitarian cooperative lines within the kibbutzim with that of plants under hierarchical managerial controls outside the kibbutzim. He selected six enterprises of each variety and matched them regarding capital investment, product they manufactured, technology they utilized, and markets for which they produced. He found that the cooperative enterprises showed 26 percent higher productivity of labor, 24 percent higher productivity of capital, 115 percent larger net profit per production worker, and 13 percent lower administrative costs.[26]

The significance of these results is apparent. Under effectively controlled conditions, the kibbutzim industries, which have no material incentives, are proving to be decisively more productive than the outside enterprises, which depend on traditional hierarchical management and income differentiation. The kibbutzim are challenging the assumption held for two centuries—since the days of the first machine-powered factories—that industrialization and the boss are inseparable, and that humans consequently must adapt to the machine and allow its imperatives to mold their lives.

Socialized Factories in Chile

As noteworthy as the kibbutzim industries are the 275 enterprises that passed under worker control during Salvador Allende's 34 months as

President of Chile. In theory, each firm was managed by an administrative council comprising an equal number of workers and state representatives and headed by a state-appointed administrator. In practice, only a few of the largest enterprises followed this plan. The great majority of these socialized firms were run by administrative councils in which the workers formed a majority and frequently selected the administrator. The counterpart of the councils at the shop-floor level were the worker-run production committees, which were responsible for maintaining output in their sections. Suggestions and information were channeled from the shop floor to the administrative council through a coordinating committee run by the president of the union with the largest membership in the factory.

Economist Andrew Zimbalist of Smith College, who spent a year surveying 40 randomly selected socialized Chilean factories,[27] found that workers quickly comprehended and participated in union-related issues such as safety, security, work rules, and wage schedules. They also soon grasped and managed related matters such as hiring, firing, scheduling, and organizing training courses. Next they moved into the actual production process—quality control, machinery maintenance, supplying of raw materials and spare parts, and selection and modification of technology. Employers had hitherto discouraged foremen from accepting any such initiative on the part of the workers, thus reinforcing the uneducated workers' sense of inferiority: "How can I, poor laborer with no education, ever understand any of that?"[28] But the worker response to the loosening of the bonds under Allende was precisely the opposite of their customary passivity and apprehension. Free for the first time to apply their talents to their jobs, they did so with extraordinary exuberance and effectiveness. A Spaniard who spent seven months in Chile under the Allende regime wrote:

> Best of all, paradoxically perhaps, is what I have seen in the way of the liberating capacity of human beings, the inventiveness of the workers in the intervened factories, who built new machine parts when the old no longer functioned. To see a factory of 2000 workers with a twenty-seven-year-old manager, who completed elementary school only, resolving problems by telephone, with no documents in triplicate and no red tape in general, to see buses requisitioned by the masses so that they could go to work is a stirring experience.[29]

Zimbalist reports that, despite the shortages of raw materials and other problems plaguing Chilean industry at this time, 32 of the 40 socialized factories he surveyed either maintained or increased their worker productivity. Fourteen firms were able to sustain an increase of over 6 percent annually. Overall industrial output rose between 11 and 15 percent during 1971 and between 2.5 and 3 percent during 1972. The slowdown in 1972 was due largely to the work stoppage called by the Truck Owners' Association (since disclosed to have been CIA-financed). The socialized factories also expanded their social services dramatically without diverting resources from production. The new or enlarged services included medical facilities, day-care centers, cafeterias, consumer cooperatives, athletic fields, libraries, theater troupes, and folk-singing groups.

At the same time, wage differentials were sharply reduced from a ratio of 30 or 40 to 1 to ratios between 5 to 1 and 11 to 1. This reduction contradicts the common assumption that differential incentives are a prerequisite for optimum productivity. "To the contrary," concludes Zimbalist, "the reduced wage disparities in Chile's political context produced less invidious division and more solidarity within the working class. The resulting cooperative spirit motivated the productivity gains."[30] More specifically, Zimbalist found production to be positively correlated with degree of worker participation, rather than with technical factors such as capital-labor ratio, size of firm, or type of technology. In turn, he found the extent of participation to be dependent not on the workers' formal education but on their understanding of political issues and on their political activity. In the factories where the parties of the Left had the most following, there was more worker control and correspondingly greater rise in productivity.

Communes and Factories in China

More significant, today, than Yugoslavia's worker control or the structure governing Israel's kibbutzim plants are the communes and factories of China, which have been transformed by Mao's Cultural Revolution. This transformation is more significant quantitatively because it involves one-fourth of the human race; it is more significant qualitatively because its avowed aim is not only a new society but a new people—the new Maoist men and women. And Mao now has the resources and the favorable social conditions that enable him to actually implement his ideology to a degree that is impossible for other world leaders. Tito has been dependent on foreign tourists for much of his capital and has had to deal with the disruptive influences of emigration by many Yugoslavs to Western Europe; the kibbutzim are declining in importance in an increasingly consumption-oriented Israeli society. By contrast, China, today as throughout her history, is a world unto herself, but a world no longer so isolated as it was in the days of Marco Polo or even of John Foster Dulles. In this era of the global village, what goes on in the Chinese quarter of the village cannot fail to affect what goes on in the other three-quarters.

The Cultural Revolution will be analyzed here in its economic manifestations and implications; other aspects will be considered in the following chapters. Contrary to general belief, the Cultural Revolution was not a campaign designed to cope with economic difficulties. Following the 1950 Sino-Soviet Treaty, a series of Five Year Plans had strengthened China's economy substantially. GNP growth between 1950 and 1966 was almost six percent per annum, or roughly equal to that of the Soviet Union between 1928 and 1938 and between 1950 and 1966. Yet Mao became progressively disenchanted with the Soviet-type Five Year Plans. One reason was economic—the irrationality of slighting agriculture, and the peasants who comprised 80 percent of the total population, in favor of developing heavy industry, and the policy of stressing capital-intensive technology amid capital scarcity and labor surplus. Even more of a problem for Mao was the incompatibility of Soviet developmental strategy with the basic egalitarian and participatory principles that were evolved during the years when he led the revolution from the remote northwest outpost of Yenan.

Populism has always been prominent in Mao's thought and strategy. He has emphasized the indispensable role of the masses as well as that of their leaders. The latter are doomed to failure unless they are responsive to, and capable of learning from, the former. Nothing permanent can be achieved without mass participation, which requires continual interaction between Party and people, between cadres and masses. This is the essence of Mao's famous "mass line," the basis of his operational strategy, and the essence of what has come to be known as the "Yenan Way."

Mao views the "mass line" as a permanent guide for action, valid not only during the years of revolutionary armed struggle but also during the ensuing period of economic development and social transformation. Hence his concern that the Five Year Plans were generating a Party and state elite that was becoming powerful, affluent, and estranged from the masses. He warned repeatedly that this emerging bureaucracy, unless curbed, would effect a peaceful transition from socialism to "state capitalism" in China just as those in the Soviet Union and Eastern Europe already had. His apprehension was not unwarranted—the American historian A. Doak Barnett, writing in the mid-1960s, was describing precisely such a trend:

One of the most significant trends in recent years has been the seemingly irresistible growth of complex bureaucratic patterns of social
stratification even within the ranks of the Party cadres in Communist
China. The Party has tried in many ways to resist these trends—for
example, by promoting physical labor by cadres, sending personnel
to work in rural areas, and taking such drastic steps as abolishing
ranks within the army—but as the egalitarian heritage of active revolutionary struggle has tended to recede into the background, deep-
rooted authoritarian and bureaucratic predispositions, especially the
tendency to differentiate people by rank, have reasserted themselves.[31]

In the winter of 1966 and 1967 Mao launched his Cultural Revolution,
a vast housecleaning with no precedent in history. He waged the revolution
by calling on the students, organized in the Red Guards, "to struggle
against and crush those persons in authority who are taking the capitalist
road." Thus Mao unleashed the students to smash the Party and state Establishment. By the summer of 1967 the demolition job was done, and Mao
began the second stage of the Cultural Revolution. He used the People's
Liberation Army to bring the rampaging Red Guards under control, sending them back to school or to rural areas to work. The third and final stage
was the restoration of power to a rectified Communist Party. On August
26, 1971, the *People's Daily* proclaimed, "Now [that] the new Party committees have been established at all levels, the Party's unified leadership
must be efficiently reinforced. . . . [There must be] absolute submission of
state and army to the Party."

Mao's historic contribution in waging the Cultural Revolution was to
be the first Marxist head of state to recognize and respond effectively to the
fact that after a revolution a privileged class can emerge, one based on
power rather than on private ownership of the means of production. In
contrast to Yugoslavia and the Soviet Union, China has successfully curbed
this "new class." By the end of the Cultural Revolution, the number of
bureaucrats in the central government had shrunk from 60,000 to 10,000,
and there was a corresponding reduction in the managerial ranks in the
factories and communes. This change represents a reversal of the trend
prevailing in most other societies, with their burgeoning political and industrial bureaucracies. We shall now consider how the communes and factories
are functioning after the shakeup of the Cultural Revolution.

China's communes are social and political as well as economic units.
Collectively owned and operated by their inhabitants, they comprise both

factories and fields, and they also take care of the educational, cultural, and medical needs of their members. The communes vary in population from 5000 to 50,000 people. They also vary greatly in wealth. Those located near large cities or in fertile, high-rainfall areas are better off. Despite their differences, all communes have certain features in common. One is their large size, the purpose of which is to make efficient year-round use of hitherto surplus rural manpower. During the slack seasons, when the peasant farmers have time on their hands, they are now able to work communally on projects to combat flood and drought, to reforest the denuded countryside, and to control pests and plagues. The degree to which these cooperative enterprises are transforming the vast territories of the People's Republic is indicated by the fact that within one decade twice as much land has been brought under irrigation as had been brought under irrigation in the preceding 300 years.

Another feature all communes have in common is the emphasis on self-reliance and self-sufficiency. Local labor and raw materials are used to supply local markets with tools, simple machinery, insecticides, fertilizers, and consumer goods. The Red Star Commune, on the outskirts of Peking, has a powdered-milk factory, a flour mill, a soybean-oil mill, and a seed-oil mill—all of which process local products—as well as small workshops to which nearby urban factories farm out the manufacture of parts such as sewing-machine fixtures, small cables and wire, light switches, and lamp holders.

A third uniform characteristic of Chinese communes is the availability of locally controlled educational and medical services. Depending on the size of the commune, its educational facilities will range from a few elementary and secondary schools to an establishment offering all levels of education, including an agricultural school and a research station working to improve seed and livestock strains. Likewise, a small commune may have one clinic with simple equipment and a few doctors and nurses prepared to treat the most common rural ailments—diarrhea, flu, and bronchitis—and to perform relatively simple operations such as appendectomies. A large commune will have several clinics, a well-equipped hospital, and two or three dozen doctors who will undertake all but the most complicated operations, which are referred to the regional hospital. In addition to treating their patients, doctors are also expected to train "barefoot doctors" to provide basic medical care. If the number of patients dwindles, as happens in certain seasons, the doctors will leave their clinics and join the peasants working in the fields.

Finally, all of the communes follow similar general principles in income distribution, with significant variations that are decided locally Roughly five to six percent of a commune's total product is delivered to the state as an agricultural tax in kind. Another five to six percent is set aside for the welfare fund to take care of the sick and aged. Another five to ten percent goes to the development fund to purchase equipment, improve irrigation, erect new buildings, and so forth. The remaining 75 to 85 percent of the commune income is divided on the basis of each member's accumulated work points, which are determined by his work-team members on the basis of the amount of work the person has done and the level of his technical skills, and, since the Cultural Revolution, on the basis of certain political criteria as well. A member who has been particularly active in "serving the people" will be rewarded for his good citizenship by an increase in his work-point assessment, which is determined at meetings of the work team.

Turning from the commune to the urban factory, we again find much more than a mere production unit. The Chinese factory, states an informed observer, Barry Richman of the University of California, Los Angeles,

> is a place where illiterate workers learn how to read and write, and where employees can and do improve their work skills and develop new ones through education and training. It is a place where housing, schools, recreational facilities, roads, shops, and offices are often constructed or remodelled by factory employees. It is also a place from which employees go out into the fields and help the peasants with their harvesting.[32]

Like the peasants in the communes, the workers in the factories are an integral part of the decision-making process. Louis Kraar, associate editor of *Fortune,* toured the Kwangchow Heavy Machine Tool Plant in 1972. He found it, like all factories since the Cultural Revolution, to be run by a Revolutionary Committee elected by the workers. "Before the Cultural Revolution," explained a member of this plant's Revolutionary Committee, "directors and engineers managed production. Now we rely on the broad masses of the people—the workers, who are masters of the country. Politics plays a commanding part in motivating the workers. We use Mao Tse-tung's thoughts to educate the workers and staff members to grasp revolution and to promote production."

"Behind these incessantly repeated stock phrases," observes Kraar, "lies a complex system that does allow a lot of worker participation in management."[33] In addition to the elective Revolutionary Committees, which have replaced the former management, "three-in-one" combinations of workers, technicians, and administrators work together to humanize the workshop operations and to increase output. In the Peking General Knitwear Mill, for example, workers take turns in the hosiery, knitting, dyeing and bleaching, and tailoring shops. This rotation is extended even to the kitchen, where a new group of workers takes over every six months—a system designed to counter the prejudice against kitchen work as menial.

The overall trends since the Cultural Revolution have been a sharp drop in the proportion of administrators to workers and a correspondingly sharp increase in productivity. A *New York Times* correspondent found a reduction from 500 to 200 in the size of the administrative staff of the Peking Heavy Electric Machinery Plant, and he reported that other enterprises visited in a number of Chinese cities had made similar cuts in their administrative personnel.[34]

It is symptomatic that foreign visitors to Chinese factories usually express surprise at being unable to distinguish managerial personnel from workers in dress or comportment during meetings. Official titles and other status symbols are scrupulously avoided. Those in leadership positions are introduced simply as the "responsible persons." And each of these "responsible persons" spends a full day each week performing manual labor on the work floor. "The practice," observes Louis Kraar, "thrusts managers into continuing contact with the realities of the production process."[35]

Pay differentials have also been minimized with the Cultural Revolution. The old incentive bonuses and overtime pay have given way to wage rates determined by workers' committees. The guiding principle in determining wage schedules is the same as that for the communes. Not only technical skill and length of service but also social service to the community are taken into account. The result is that the income differential within a factory rarely exceeds 5 to 1. "As to whom the production is for," concluded John Kenneth Galbraith after a 1972 visit, "there is a quick and easy answer. It is for everyone in about the same amount."[36]

In conclusion, the Maoist economic system, as it is evolving in communes and factories, is as different from Western individualistic capitalism as from Soviet meritocratic socialism. For this reason, both Western and Soviet experts initially predicted that the Yenan type of egalitarianism would prove counterproductive. The Russians warned against tampering with the Soviet-type plans, which had proven themselves in raising productivity in the U.S.S.R. Representing the Western capitalist viewpoint, Barry

Richman concluded a massive study of the Chinese economy with the prediction that "centuries of world history and experience strongly indicate that the Chinese regime will not be able to eliminate self-interest and material gain as major motivating forces for managers, technicians, or workers, and at the same time achieve sustained and impressive industrial progress in the long run."[37]

The significance of the Cultural Revolution in the economic sphere is that it has demonstrated the error of the latter assumption. Dependence on moral incentives is not self-defeating. David Rockefeller, Chairman of the Board of the Chase Manhattan Bank, reached this conclusion following a visit to China in 1973: "Considering the problems to be overcome, economic growth in China over the last 25 years has been quite remarkable, with an average rise in gross national product of 4 to 5 percent. For the 1971–75 period this growth should range between 5.5 and 7.5 percent a year."[38] Equally revealing is this conclusion by an economist after several visits to China:

> It may seem paradoxical in the West, but the acceleration of productivity follows a nationwide attack on material inducements and the elimination during the Cultural Revolution of piece rates and bonus systems. The motivation in Chinese industry today is largely social ("Serve the People") and political ("Produce for the revolution and for international commitments").[39]

Green Shoots in the Workplace

People's attitudes toward work have been ambivalent through the ages. The ancients regarded manual labor as degrading and as incompatible with the superior contemplative life of the philosopher. Religious creeds interpreted labor as a punishment for sin or as a road to salvation. The Reformation bestowed sacred significance on work as an activity through which one might glorify God. With the Industrial Revolution, Adam Smith pointed out that the factory worker condemned to repeat a few simple operations "becomes as stupid and ignorant as it is possible for a human creature to become." Today such dehumanization still prevails and is still accepted as the unavoidable cost of industrial productivity. The political scientist Harry Eckstein asserts that "some social relations simply cannot be conducted in a democratic manner. . . . We have every reason to think that economic organizations cannot be organized in a truly democratic manner, at any rate not without consequences that no one wants."[40] But increasingly this assumption is being challenged, and many theories and strategies for humanizing the workplace are being discussed and tested throughout the world. Some have been analyzed in this chapter, and from these analyses certain conclusions emerge.

First, the decisive factor determining the degree of worker alienation is *not* physical hardship but social organization—the extent to which the worker shares in determining the nature of his tasks. Second, worker self-management is *not* incompatible with worker productivity; both theoretical studies and workshop experience demonstrate the precise opposite. But experience also demonstrates that successful revolution does not necessarily mean successful self-management. The Yugoslav experience shows that external intrusions, institutional failings, and a low educational level among workers can vitiate worker control despite wholehearted government support and enabling legislation. On the other hand, worker control has been relatively successful in China, where the workers' educational background is even more limited than in Yugoslavia. Therefore the prime prerequisite for effective self-management seems to be *political* education and activization, whether it be the built-in type of political education found in the Israeli kibbutzim, the revolution-inspired political activiation that flourished briefly in Chile, or the massive, indoctrination-induced activation that characterizes Maoist China.

Given the high levels of modern technology and organizational knowledge in the West, the manner in which most human beings are still earning their living is as disgraceful as it is crippling. But there is a promising change in attitude abroad today; more than at any time in the past, dehumanization in the workplace is being challenged. What has been unquestioningly accepted as the inescapable fate of humankind is now being increasingly rejected as incompatible with human dignity. Consider this diary entry by a meek English farrier in 1774:

This is the journal of John Smith, farrier to Sir Thomas Troke of Hampshire. My father was farrier before me, and his father afore him, and my son, the firstborn of as good and honest a woman as ever lived, is even now driving nails in the door beam as in the manner born. I serve God, I honour the King, I am the servant of my master, I work from dawn to dark to earn my daily bread, and I rejoice a happy life.[41]

And consider these remarks made by President Johnson in 1964:

> There is the worker who gets to work at 8 and works to 5, and has twenty-seven seconds to put the number of rivets in that car or that plane. . . . If he doesn't get them in the twenty-seven seconds he goes to twenty-eight. That car or that plane moves on down the line—and it doesn't have the rivets in it! And you've wound up with a car that is missing a rivet a time or two yourselves. We all do that. But that poor fellow gets a coffee break twice a day. The rest of the time he has twenty-seven seconds to do that job and handle that machine.
>
> He is the worker, and he hopes someday he can have a little hospital care, he can have a little pension, he can have a little social security, he can have a place to take Molly and the babies when he retires. That is his great love. His boys go to war, they fight to preserve this system. He likes his boss and he respects him. He believes in free enterprise.[42]

Although L. B. J.'s remarks were made in the mid-1960s, many workers reading them today would find them almost as quaint as those of John Smith two centuries ago. Such is the pace and significance of the change taking place in human minds—or, to use Pete Seeger's imagery, such are the green shoots sprouting through the concrete of the workplace.

5

FROM REPRESENTATIVE DEMOCRACY TO PARTICIPATORY DEMOCRACY

I heard citizens attribute the power and prosperity of their country to a multitude of reasons, but they all placed the advantage of local institutions in the foremost rank.

—*Alexis de Tocqueville*

. . . the task is not to construct ever-larger structures but to decompose the organizations that overwhelm us, and to seek less abstract and remote dependencies. After all, this is what the revolt of two hundred years ago, the revolt against a vast, impersonal, and distant imperial structure, was originally about.

—*Sheldon S. Wolin*

Too Much Democracy or Too Little?

A global participatory impulse is astir not only in the realm of economics but also in the realm of politics, where there is a similar striving to shift decision-making power from the few at the top to the many below. The roots of assertiveness in these two realms are comparable. Just as the Industrial Revolution led to the assumption that hierarchical economic organization was necessary, a corresponding political revolution prompted a similar assumption of the need for hierarchical political organization.

This political revolution was the emergence of Big Government in modern times, alongside Big Business and Big Labor. Big Government became a necessity for mediating the periodic confrontations between the other two goliaths. It was also stimulated by the traumatic experiences of the two World Wars and the Great Depression. The "night watchman state" of the early nineteenth century gave way to the vast bureaucratic state that today has assumed responsibility for social welfare and the functioning of the economy. The result has been the bureaucratization of both political and economic life. In American industry, the number of administrators per 100 productive workers has risen from 10 in 1899 to 38 in 1963, but this increase in the administrative apparatus has not been accompanied by a corresponding increase in productivity. The same pattern can be seen in American government. In 1930, when the total U. S. population was 123 million, there were 601,319 federal civilian employees and 2,622,000 state and local employees; by April 1973, when the total U.S. population was 210 million, the number of federal civilian employees had jumped to 2,650,000 and the number of state and local employees to 10,800,000. Thus one person in 38 was a government employee in 1930, and one in 16 was a government employee in 1973.

This bureaucratism in government has its defenders, as it has in business. Just as Harry Eckstein maintains that "economic organizations cannot be organized in a democratic manner," so he and other academicians warn against the dangers of too much democracy in political affairs. They point to totalitarian fascist and communist regimes based on at least a measure of mass participation as examples of participation leading to authoritarianism rather than to democratic self-management. "The electoral mass," states Joseph Schumpeter, "is incapable of action other than a stampede, so that it is leaders who must . . . initiate and decide."[1] Democrary should therefore be limited to free competition among leaders for votes, free participation by citizens in selecting leaders in periodic elections, and free expression of views to the elected leaders between elections. The preservation of this democratic system can best be assured by restricting mass participation to the minimum activity necessary for the functioning of the electoral machinery. The people, states political scientist Giovanni Sartori, should not "act" but should "react" to the initiatives of the competing elites.[2]

This form of representative but nonparticipatory democracy has been the rule in the Western world in modern times. Whatever intellectual rationalizations are marshaled in its defense, the fact remains that it is becoming increasingly nonfunctional throughout the world for two basic reasons. One is that the modern citizen is no longer willing to be the obedient servant of God, King, and master, as was John Smith the farrier in the eighteenth century. The combination of physical and intellectual isolation and the daily struggle for bare survival left the peasant masses relatively passive in past centuries. They have been replaced by self-conscious citizens enjoying a steadily increasing income, much more education, access to a mass of information denied to their ancestors, bargaining power in their workplace, and participation in the electoral process. Under these new circumstances, elitist leaders and practices are no longer acceptable, even within a framework of representative democracy that allows for periodic elections. "It is arguable," states the British cabinet member Anthony Wedgwood Benn, "that what has really happened has amounted to such a breakdown in the social contract, upon which parliamentary democracy by universal suffrage was based, that that contract now needs to be re-negotiated on a basis that shares power much more widely, before it can win general assent again."[3]

The other reason for the current fragility of the bureaucratic state is that modern society is far too complex to be directed and controlled from any one power center, whether it be the White House or Downing Street or the Kremlin. No single person or party can run a large modern society today, even with computers and mass media and all the other resources of modern technology. Consider the difficulty in performing even such basic tasks as maintaining law and order, protecting the physical environment, providing education suited to national needs, and maintaining minimum standards in housing and public health. A September 1973 Harris Poll found that 61 percent of Americans cited "the inability of government to solve problems" as a high-priority complaint, and 71 percent faulted the federal government for failing to improve conditions or for making them worse. Whereas a few decades ago the federal government had been regarded as the protector of the "little man" against vested interests, now it is viewed as being in collusion with those interests.

Equally significant is the prevalence of these same feelings of frustration and powerlessness on the other side of the fence—among government officials in Washington. Thirty congressmen and seven senators—an unprecedented number—retired before the 1974 elections; the main reason they gave was a sense of ineffectiveness in coping with national problems. "There is an erosion of confidence in the government," declared Representative Edith Green of Oregon on retiring after 20 years in Congress. "The federal government has tried to do too much and to be all things to all people. . . We are not doing anything well." The overextension of government, she noted, is reflected in the overload of legislation: 17,528 bills were introduced during the first half of the 1974 Congress, and 726 reached the floor in 1973, or more than double the 351 that reached the floor in 1969.

> If you have several hundred pieces of legislation, how could you possibly know what is in all of them? There is no question but that the federal government has gotten too big and far too remote, and the federal bureaucracy clearly is out of check. There is no way that Congress can check on what it is doing. . . . Congress dishes out hundreds of millions in contracts and grants, but there is such a chaos that the General Accounting Office, the investigative arm of Congress, says it does not know where the money is going.[4]

Ineffective and unmanageable bureaucratism is a problem in Western Europe as well as in the United States. Election returns during the early 1970s show a general drift away from the traditional Right and Left—a common reaction against parties backed by business and labor, respectively, when they follow similar policies in office, with a similar lack of success.

Voters in Western Europe are responding increasingly to appeals against bigness and remoteness in government and showing concern for local interests and local rule. Hence the revival of support for the Liberal Party in Britain and the success of anti-welfare-state parties in Scandinavian countries. Likewise, a survey by the University of Michigan Center for Political studies in early 1974 showed that 41 percent of American voters now classify themselves as independents, 36 percent as Democrats, and 21 percent as Republicans, leaving 2 percent completely nonpolitical.

The functioning of the Western democracies and the reactions of their citizens indicate that the source of political malaise today is not too much democracy but too little. The need is not to restrict mass participation, as some argue, but rather to facilitate it and broaden its scope. In the political world, as in the economic, the current trend is toward more self-management, although the specific manifestations of this trend vary from region to region in accord with local traditions and conditions. The following sections will analyze the present state of self-management and its future prospects in four major regions: the United States, the Soviet Union, the Third World, and the People's Republic of China.

"An Exploring Society"

"The U.S.A. can now be termed an exploring society," asserts the anthropologist Luther P. Gerlach, "exploring its way into its future, generating the future through trial and error experimentation. What appears to be its time of troubles may indeed be its time of discovery and transformation."[5] This estimate is fully justified, for we are now in a period of extraordinary reappraisal and soul-searching in the United States. The root cause is that the two pillars of the "American way of life," universal education and interest-group pluralism, have not proven so effective as commonly assumed in providing meaningful equality of opportunity.

First let us consider the conditions surrounding the goal of universal education. According to the findings of Christopher Jencks and his associates at the Center for Educational Policy Research at the Harvard Graduate School of Education (*Inequality: A Reassessment of the Effect of Family and Schooling in America*, 1972), present inequalities in educational attainment, occupational status, and income are not significantly affected by what goes on in schools, and they probably never will be. The reasons are that children are more influenced by the home environment (including television) than by that of the school, and that, even when the school does exert important influence, this influence is not likely to persist into adulthood. "The character of a school's output," states Jencks, "depends largely on a single input, namely the characteristics of entering children. Everything else—the school budget, its policies, the characteristics of the teachers—is either secondary or completely irrelevant. . . . Equalizing opportunity is almost impossible without greatly reducing the absolute level of inequality." These findings concerning the predominant influence of the home environment have been found to be as valid for social democratic Western Europe and communist Eastern Europe as for the United States.

The second traditional assumption, that interest-group pluralism provides for equality of political opportunity, likewise is now being challenged by studies such as Theodore J. Lowi's *The End of Liberalism* (1969). Conventional wisdom has held that Western pluralistic society is an equitable and genuine meritocracy because its various interest groups are homogeneous and preserve a self-correcting balance. The role of the government, accordingly, can be limited to ratifying agreements reached by the competing interest groups. As Theodore Lowi puts it, this interpretation of the dynamics of American politics constitutes "the Adam Smith 'hidden hand' model applied to groups."

But this "hidden hand" assumption, a useful one as it was applied in the eighteenth and nineteenth centuries, is as irrelevant to present-day politics as it is to present-day economics. The course of events has demonstrated repeatedly and clearly that conflicting interests do not maintain a self-correcting balance. The poor—in Europe as well as in the United States—lack the education, experience, and self-confidence to organize and make themselves heard in the pluralist cacophony. Consequently they are generally excluded from the benefits of society, and their efforts to break in have led not to accommodation but to continued discrimination in schools, trade unions, housing, and other areas, despite official claims.

In early modern times advocates of democracy argued that an aristocrat should not enjoy an enormous head start in life simply because of the hereditary privileges of his family. Modern-day democrats hold that educated, affluent people often are given comparable unearned head starts in life regardless of the availability of public education. Therefore democrats demand not a theoretical equality of opportunity but rather equality of results—to be realized through self-management in schools, in politics, in the workplace, and in other arenas.

This demand is particularly clamorous in the United States, where the traumatic experiences of the 1960s have engendered unprecedented challenging of hitherto sacrosanct American institutions and values. Such challenging is itself in line with American tradition. Over a century ago de Tocqueville observed:

> No sooner do you set foot upon American ground than you are stunned by a kind of tumult, a confused clamour is heard on every side, and a thousand simultaneous voices demand the satisfaction of their social wants. Everything is in motion around you; here the people of one quarter of the town are met to decide upon the building of a church; there the election of a representative is going on; a little farther, the delegates of a district are hastening to the town in order to consult upon some local improvements; in another place, the labourers of a village quit their plows to deliberate upon the project of a road or a public school. . . . The great political agitation of American legislative bodies . . . is a mere episode, or a sort of continuation, of that universal movement which originates in the lowest classes of the people and extends successively to all ranks of society.[6]

This sort of personal involvement, or direct democracy, is beginning to reappear after a long interval of acquiescence to Big Government. "Not since the days of the New Deal," writes James Reston in the *New York Times*, "has there been so much insistent questioning of the institutions and purposes of America as there is now."[7] In fact, today's questioning is more radical and comprehensive than that of the 1930s, when expectations were relatively modest—a man then demanded little more than a job for the support of his family. Now not only capitalism but the work ethic itself is questioned. Also subject to question are traditional laws, customs, and beliefs governing relations between the sexes, relations among generations, the family, and other important institutions and areas of human behavior.

Given the relative freedom of the American political world, Americans' efforts toward self-management have taken many forms. One is the radical caucus, which has appeared in nearly every professional association— those of scientists, teachers, architects, economists, lawyers, physicians, historians, priests, anthropologists, and chartered accountants. The last, for example, organized as Accountants for the Public Interest, have chapters in every large American city. Their role is to dig up crucial financial data on important public issues—low-cost housing, medical care, public-utility rates, school-district financing—and to make it available to public-interest groups so that they will have the accounting data necessary to cope with opponents who can afford the services of professional accountants. Another example of radical caucus is the Medical Committee on Human Rights, organized in 1964 by physicians and medical workers. Among their activities have been providing medical aid during civil-rights campaigns and antiwar demonstrations, giving testimony to legislators, developing alternative approaches to health care, staffing and publicizing free clinics, promoting progressive resolutions at medical conventions, and publishing a newspaper, *Health Rights News,* to foster debate on controversial issues.

Another manifestation of self-management in the political arena are various counterinstitutions that seek to provide an alternative from the outside, rather than to bore from within as do the radical caucuses. In education, for example, "free schools" are designed to avoid the competitiveness and conformity of public schools and to encourage student participation in school governance and curriculum. In religion, "underground" churches often serve as counterinstitutions to the established churches. They combine political involvement with new forms of liturgical celebration ranging from street parades to Eucharistic feasts of pretzels and beer. The best known has perhaps been the Free Church of Berkeley, whose programs included a 24-hour telephone switchboard that offered help on problems ranging from drug abuse to finding a "crash pad" for the night.

More important are the communal groups that have proliferated in recent years throughout the United States and Western Europe. Like their eighteenth- and nineteenth-century forebears, they have assumed many forms. Probably the most numerous are those clustered around colleges and universities. "We're trying to share our lives and ideas in a way never possible in a dormitory or in separate apartments," explains a Harvard graduate student in a Cambridge commune. "It's an attempt to be truly human beings in the way we've always been taught to believe human beings were supposed to live with one another—with love and understanding."[8] Similar to these college-based communes are those oriented toward politics or social service. Their members support causes such as women's liberation or gay liberation, or work in birth-control and abortion clinics or day-care centers. Another type of commune is organized around work situations, including crafts centers, food cooperatives, nonprofit free medical clinics, alternative radio stations, and underground newspapers. Finally, there are communes based on religious principles or the search for a utopian life. Most of these are rural. One large commune near Nashville, Indiana, cultivates its 500 acres exclusively by organic methods; three communal farms in Alabama are operated by Black Muslims; "The Children of God," a sect based on conservative Christian principles, has organized communal farms in California, Texas, and Kentucky. In northern New England a new wave of settlers from urban areas has reclaimed old hill farms, opened craft shops and woodworking mills, rejuvenated abandoned towns, and started new communities, newspapers, and restaurants.

Whereas the communes of China make up Chinese society itself, Western communes are an escape from or an alternative to the established society. Its members are the frontiersmen of late twentieth-century Western society, seeking not new lands but new human relationships. "Why should I work 30 or 40 hours a week," asks an Albuquerque commune member, "for someone or something that doesn't give a shit about me so I can get money to buy things I don't give a shit about owning?"[9]

Between the communes and "straight" society lie a broad assortment of organizations with the general goal of neighborhood self-management. Among these are the Community Development Corporations (CDCs), funded by the Special Impact Program of the Office of Economic Opportunity. Over 40 programs exist in metropolitan ghettos and in sparsely populated rural areas such as the Appalachians, northern New Mexico, Alaska, and northeastern Oklahoma. Their activities range from sophisticated subcontract manufacturing to housing developments and retail outlets. Some are cooperatives, others are nonprofit corporations, and still others are profit-making corporations owned by resident shareholders. Whatever their structure, they are all controlled by the residents, or the representatives of the residents, of the poverty-stricken areas they seek to serve.

An example of these CDC enterprises is one we shall call the Centerville Fund Inc. (CFI), operating in the southern town of Centerville (a fictitious name), which has a population of 100,000, of which 35,000 are black. Funded in September 1968, by September 1972 CFI employed 51 persons full time on a budget of $200,000. Currently operating ventures include a supermarket and a factory for modular housing. Land has been purchased for housing and new industries such as a community cannery and a laundromat. CFI is organized as a profit-making corporation with a board of 24 directors, 16 of whom are elected by stockholders, who must be poor (according to stated criteria) and must reside in the area served by CFI. Thus low-income representatives have control of the corporation. Yet they have had difficulty in exercising their control. The problem is the same one that has plagued worker control in Yugoslavia—lack of education and self-confidence. The shareholders, who had never owned corporation stock, were naturally ignorant of their rights and responsibilities. Although they formed the majority of the Board of Directors, they accepted the proposals of the educated minority. Because this tendency violated the self-management rationale of the CDCs, the Executive Director called a series of meetings for low-income directors alone. The minutes of the first meeting, held on June 18, 1969, recorded the following comments:

> Our president . . . explained that we have a job to do and the only way to get it done is through 100 percent [participation]. We have to help carry the ball, and thus far we have let others carry the ball.
> Mrs. F. [not a board member] stressed the importance of low-income members' participating in the regular meetings. She then asked for some reasons as to why [they] do not participate.
> Mrs. C. [a low-income director] said some of the reasons are because [the other] members talk too fast. And "some of the words they use we do not understand."[10]

The meetings revealed once more that equality of opportunity is meaningless unless the participants have the experience and confidence to take advantage of the opportunity. A recent study of the small Vermont town of Selby elicited the following comments by poor farmers, who shunned the town meeting or, if they did attend, kept quiet:

> I know what I think, but I can't put it across to people. I've got no education, I can't get it across. Sometimes I'm just speechless. Or I get mad. I'd say too much. If I had education, it'd be a difference.
> If you get up and say your piece, they'll call you out of order, whether you are or not. It is all cut and dried before town meeting. They'll pass right over you if you get up to nominate. It's organized their way before the meeting. No, I never speak. I've seen so many called out of order.[11]

Let us return to Centerville. The low-income directors prepared themselves for active participation with formal training programs and in caucus meetings held before the full board meetings. As the poor board members learned to take their part, it was discovered that they were able to make unique contributions in some matters, such as in the design of low-cost housing, precisely because they were poor. CFI is now effectively managed by its low-income constituents, and community involvement is growing. The CDCs are demonstrating their value for decreasing the economic dependence of poor areas and for increasing individual and community power. Perhaps they may assume a broader role than that for which they were originally founded, as one analyst predicts:

> Many existing CDCs are themselves open to membership or stock ownership by *all* residents, even though control at this stage rests with the poor. Moreover, CDC activities, as in Centerville, serve the total community. A good supermarket or well designed modular homes are not patronized merely by the poor. If anything, the reverse tends to be true. CDCs, in short, are not isolated activities, though *controlled* by representatives of the poor, but part and parcel of the economic life of the area. One can therefore expect that, as other people begin to see that these organizations serve their own interests, CDCs will develop broader constituencies, which will, in turn, enable them to acquire needed resources.[12]

Not all neighborhood self-management efforts are dependent on government funding, as are the CDCs. Many are independent in their origins and operations. Let us consider four of the latter: Sto-Rox near Pittsburgh, Pennsylvania; AMO in Washington, D.C.; CAL on the West Coast; and ACORN in the South and Midwest.

Sto-Rox is shorthand for two separate municipalities just outside Pittsburgh—Stowe Township and McKees Rocks Borough. The two communities are contiguous, and each has approximately 10,500 residents. About 96 percent of them are white workers in the $5000–$6000 income bracket; about 1000 of them are on public assistance. Eighty-five percent are Catholic, and two of the first leaders in setting up their self-help organization, Focus on Renewal (FOR), were Father Donald Fisher and Sister Paulette. The Diocese of Pittsburgh and private foundations have contributed to FOR, whose objectives were defined in the first issue (July 25, 1973) of its newspaper, *Focus on Neighborhood:*

> People in Sto-Rox, as in many other communities across the country, have long ago turned over their responsibility for public life to representatives.
>
> The representatives, whether School Board members or Boro Councilmen or Commissioners, have, for the most part, mismanaged their heavy burdens and have selfishly taken power for themselves. The end result in Sto-Rox and in city after city is a wide communication gap between "politicians" and people, mistrust and resentment of those in power, and crippling loss of liberty for the people. This is not a condemnation of any particular person or party; it is a criticism of a system which has made it almost impossible for people to creatively

and directly participate in a process which should be very natural for them as American citizens—*democracy*, or self-government.

Last May [1973], F.O.R. took a step forward in the direction of a cure by creating the Neighborhood Corporation. The Corporation's mainstay is the regular assembly meetings of the 21 natural neighborhoods in the Sto-Rox community. Every resident of or worker in Sto-Rox is invited to participate in a one-person-one-vote status in the monthly assembly in his respective neighborhood and also at the quarterly community assemblies when all Corporation members gather.

Any program, activity, or issue which people are interested in can become the order of the day for the Corporation—the ambulance problem, Shared Revenue, the new school issue, child health, credit union, etc.

The Corporation is really the beginning of a new process of decision making in the public life of the community. It is people assembling, voting, and taking new responsibility for their own turf.

It is difficult work but it is people's work and it can be a glorious task if we pick it up with pride and hope. One thing is certain—the common good will be vitalized and the dignity of each person will be enhanced by such responsible use of freedom. To go this way is to place an act of faith in people—something which is greatly needed in our present time.[13]

Since the 21 neighborhood assemblies of Sto-Rox began working in 1969 to take over "their own turf," they have achieved impressive results, including

- a resident-owned and -operated union
- a mental-health program with a counselor, psychiatrist, social worker, and secretary working full time
- a Senior Citizens' Program with five full-time and six part-time employees, providing door-to-door information referral, minor house repairs, transportation, and financial counseling
- a transportation service—the "Anywhere-in-Town Bus"—a van making four runs around the community each day and open to everybody on a donations-only basis
- a self-sustaining children's health-care center with a pediatrician, serving 1500 to 1800 children
- an ambulance for emergency cases
- a school lunch program

In planning and operating the programs described above, all major decisions—including hiring, spending, and formulating policies—were made by the neighbors gathered in their community assemblies, not by representatives or by hired staff. The Sto-Rox model, like the CDCs, could have an impact extending far beyond the two townships. On April 13, 1972, Governor Shapp of Pennsylvania signed into law a bill providing home-rule rights to local communities. Citizens of these communities may elect government-study commissioners, who then have one year to prepare new charters to replace the existing ones, which for the most part have been drafted by the state legislature. These new charters, if voted in by the electorate, replace the old ones and become the new governing documents of the communities. The commissioners have free rein in designating the structure of government in the charters; the only limitation is that the governing bodies must be elected by the people. Thus the nature of future local government in Pennsylvania will depend on citizen interest and participation.

Equally impressive is the work of the Adams Morgan Organization Inc. (AMO), in northwest Washington, D.C., mentioned earlier on pages 31 and 32. The Adams Morgan area includes about 30,000 people—60 percent black, 35 percent white, and five percent Spanish speaking. About 21 percent earn less than $3200 per year. Apart from a few expensively restored houses, it is a run-down neighborhood. Efforts in the 1950s to secure government funds for urban renewal were turned down by Congress. Independent local action during the 1960s proved more successful in coping with problems such as crime, inadequate schooling, and slum landlords. In 1972 AMO was incorporated as a nonprofit organization, its stated objective "to improve the quality of life substantively for as many people as possible, and to be the voice and action vehicle of the community." Power is vested in the Community Assembly, of which every person who lives or works in the community can be a member. The Assembly passes on all projects and elects a chairman, committees, and an Executive Council. The Council is composed of four members from each of the five neighborhoods of the community. AMO membership now totals about 3000.

The services organized by AMO include a free medical clinic, a "Runaway House" for teenagers in need of help, a video center that produces TV programs and provides training, a weekly newspaper incongruously entitled *The Daily Rag,* an experimental nonaccredited university offering courses on topics proposed by residents, about 20 parent-operated free schools ranging from kindergarten to high school, and a variety of crafts enterprises, including woodwork, leatherwork, pottery, painting, and house and car repairs. AMO has also generated a federation of 20 retail stores that are collectively owned and nonhierarchical and nonprofit in operation. They include three retail food stores, a pharmacy, a community bookstore, a record cooperative, and a printing house. The food stores, which are part of the Washington Food Federation, are currently negotiating with small farmers in the area and with the National Share-croppers group in the South for a long-term contract designed to bring food more directly from the food producer to the consumer.

These community enterprises have hitherto depended on loans from residents or from local Washington foundations for capital, but AMO is now considering a Community Sustaining Fund to be financed by a sales tax on the community businesses and service organizations. This plan is seen as the first step toward opting out of the municipal taxation system, under which the community is taxed to support what it views as a bloated city bureaucracy and administration of services over which the residents have no control. "Eventually we hope," states an AMO representative, "that the neighborhood, through AMO, will be able to make the following proposition to the D. C. bureaucracy—don't take our money and don't give us any services. We ask nothing of you and want you to take nothing from us. Since Adams Morgan is a poor neighborhood (though not the poorest in D.C.) such a proposal might well pass, since to refuse would be to have to say, 'We can't let you do this or the bureaucrats cannot make their paychecks.'"[14]

The Citizens Action League (CAL) and the Association of Community Organizations for Reform Now (ACORN) are similar in that they, along with a considerable number of other groups scattered throughout the country, follow the strategy advocated by community organizer Saul Alinsky for helping people to help themselves. Their basic objective is to show people how to win the power needed to influence the events affecting their lives. Whereas social workers act as intermediaries between the powerful and the powerless, CAL and ACORN seek to prepare the powerless to do their own "jolting" whenever and however they see fit. Action is directed against what they view as the major adversaries of the public interest: corporate wealth and power, and bureaucratic ossification and insensitivity to popular needs.

Within this common framework, the different citizens' action groups vary according to local conditions and traditions and according to the personalities and backgrounds of their leaders. CAL is the creation of Mike Miller, who, after experience in the student and civil-rights movements, now teaches urban studies courses at Stanford University and San Francisco State University and serves as chairman of CAL. CAL comprises a canvassing division, which raises funds to supplement the ten-dollar yearly membership dues; a training division, which makes organizers out of recruits; and an organizing division, which builds up the local units, the county chapters, and the overall state apparatus.

CAL follows three general strategies in its activities. One is organizing peoples' financial power toward specific objectives, such as support for the Farm Workers' boycotts and the withdrawal of private, institutional, and state funds from banks and savings and loan institutions that do not practice affirmative-action hiring or that discriminate in granting loans. The second strategy is direct mass action to compel corporate or public officials to negotiate and make concessions on specific issues. For example, in April 1975, 20 busloads of CAL members descended on Sacramento and proceeded to buttonhole over 100 legislators in behalf of the so-called lifeline legislation providing that a minimum amount of gas and electricity be provided to individual citizens at a low set rate. This highly significant reversal of the traditional practice of high rates for low consumers and low rates for high consumers was passed by the Assembly and signed by the Governor on September 23, 1975. Other successes resulting from direct mass action include improvement of water quality in the East Bay, exposure of massive underassessment of some downtown business property in San Francisco, and allocation of more San Francisco Unified School District funds for direct classroom needs and less for bureaucratic expenditures.

These activities merge into the third general strategy now being developed by CAL: building a statewide organization for exerting decisive influence on California politics. The legal institutions of initiative, referendum, and recall, which date from earlier reform eras in California politics, provide valuable tools for such grass-roots political action. In line with this objective, CAL is now extending its base from the San Francisco region, where it started, to the Los Angeles and San Diego regions. More long-range plans include expansion into neighboring states—Arizona, Nevada, Oregon, and Washington.

ACORN is the creation of Wade Rathke, who, after experience with the National Welfare Rights Organization in Massachusetts, went to work in Arkansas, where 70 percent of the people live on incomes of less than $7000 per year. He focused on low- to moderate-income families, organizing them to cope with specific problems existing in their communities. ACORN began in 1970; by 1975 it had grown to include over 5000 dues-paying families (dues are one dollar per month or ten dollars per year). It has nine regional offices in the state, 70 neighborhood groups, and three non-geographical membership groups. The membership is roughly 60 percent white and 40 percent black.

ACORN's emphasis on learning how to help yourself has yielded outstanding results. Hitherto frustrated Arkansas citizens have improved school conditions for their children, gained recreational facilities and parks in neglected areas, quickened service at food-stamp centers, improved treatment for returning Vietnam veterans, organized food-buying clubs, rerouted the Wilbur Mills Expressway that threatened to disrupt three neighborhoods, stopped rate increases by Arkansas Power and Light, stopped block-busting by real estate interests, and won control of the influential Pulaski County quorum court, which approves the county budget. These successes have made ACORN a model for similar organizations throughout the country and have encouraged Rathke to expand his operations into South Dakota and Texas in 1975 and plan for later expansion into other states.

In addition to these community and neighborhood organizations, all striving for local self-management, several national organizations have this same goal. One is Ralph Nader's Public Citizen, Inc. Nader is usually considered a "consumer advocate," but he is much more than that. His avowed objective is to close the "citizen gap" that exists because citizens remain passive in the face of business and government abuses. His organization strives to persuade people to learn the skills of citizenship and to become citizen activists. A Public Citizen's Action Manual, distributed to the over 100,000 members of his organization, describes how to cope with local problems—from checking the honesty of a TV repairman to investigating a government agency, and from projects requiring nothing more than writing a letter to those requiring lawsuits and public hearings. It discusses hospital and health projects, tax reform, deceptive advertising, and employment discrimination. In short, the essence of the Nader movement is self-management, as summarized in its watchword: "Activate, don't delegate."

Very similar is Common Cause, organized in September 1970 by the former Secretary of Health, Education and Welfare John W. Gardner, and numbering by 1974 over 300,000 dues-paying members. On the basis of his experience in Washington, Gardner decided that national problems could not be solved by the White House or Congress or the state legislatures. "Even if the ideal man were elected President, or the Congress was vastly improved, it would have very limited effect. . . . We are up to something much bigger. There has got to be an outside force to bring pressure, to open up the doors and windows and give this country back to the people." Common Cause has lobbied effectively on a variety of issues, including the Vietnam War, congressional reform, the Equal Rights Amendment, political-campaign spending, tax reform, and welfare legislation. At the outset it operated primarily in Washington as a national citizens' lobby; but now it is working on the state level as well, on issues such as campaign-spending controls, political contributions by lobbyists, and the disclosure of financial interests by public officials. The basic objective of Common Cause is to introduce "a vital new ingredient into the American political and governmental system—a means of insuring continuous accountability to the citizen—a means of 'voting' between elections."

Finally, some members of Congress are talking about returning government to the people and are doing something about it. One of these is the Republican Senator Mark Hatfield of Oregon, who introduced a bill entitled "The Neighborhood Government Act of 1973," by which the federal government will allow citizens to contribute as much as 80 percent of their income tax to neighborhood corporations that are taking over local services now provided by Washington. The bill also offers financial grants to such corporations organized under state law. Senator Hatfield views this bill as the first of a series designed to decentralize the handling of such services as local welfare, justice, and child care. The rationale behind such bills, explains the Senator, is to make American government "democratic, effective, close to the people."

> If people have the power to deal with their own resources in their own ways, I can see America begin to be revitalized. . . . If, for example, every church and synagogue were to take over the responsibility of caring for ten people over the age of 65 who are presently living below the poverty level, there would be no present welfare programs focused on the aged. If each church and synagogue took over the responsibility of eighteen families who are eligible for welfare today, there would not be any need for federal or state welfare programs to families. . . . We must learn to rely on the spirit of our people, and create new structures, rather than adhering to the sterile institutions of the past.

Senator Hatfield spoke these words before the founding convention of the Alliance for Neighborhood Government, held in Washington, D.C., in May 1975. This body seeks to play the same role in the area of neighborhood government that People for Self-Management plays in workplace organization. The first meeting was attended by 100 delegates representing

40 neighborhood groups from six eastern cities. Resolutions passed asserted the right of neighborhoods to review in advance and decisively influence all actions by governmental and private institutions that affect them; the right of neighborhoods to determine their own goals and initiate and execute their own programs; the obligation of neighborhoods to concern themselves with the problems and rights of the poor, the disadvantaged, and the minorities; and, conversely, the obligation of neighborhoods to avoid oppressive or irresponsible decisions, even those reached in democratic process by neighborhood residents. The convention also agreed to hold further meetings in other regions in order to broaden the organization, and to start a monthly newsletter to exchange ideas and experiences.

Similar to the convention of the Alliance for Neighborhood Government was the National Conference on Alternative State and Local Public Policies, held in Madison, Wisconsin, in June 1975. This conference was attended not by representatives of private organizations but by leftward-leaning public officials seeking to move local politics in a populist direction. Among the participants were Tom Hayden, one of the defendants of the Chicago Seven trial, then running as a candidate for the United States Senate from California; John Froines, another Chicago Seven defendant, who held state office in Vermont; Sam Brown, who ran the 1969 Moratorium against the Vietnam War, also an office-holder in Vermont; Paul Soglin, Mayor of Madison; Jeff Fried, Mayor of Austin, Texas; Justin (Chuck) Ravitz, a Marxist judge from Detroit; a judge from Zavala County, Texas, where the Chicano organization La Raza Unida has won political power; two city councilors and an elected city auditor from Berkeley; a state senator and a clerk of courts from Lincoln, Nebraska; representatives from the legislatures of Michigan, Vermont, and Florida; and city councilors from Chicago, Cleveland, Washington, Madison, Urbana (Illinois), and Montpelier (Vermont).

The discussions at the conference centered on how to cope with local problems without waiting for federal intervention and funds. One common theme was that states and cities should play much larger roles in their local economies through state-owned banks and insurance companies, publicly owned power companies, and a state agency to oversee and control all energy transactions. Another theme was the need for new or better governmental services in transportation, health care, and control of land use. Corollary themes were tax reform to finance the new services and strategies for distributing revenues directly to those in need rather than financing an expanding bureaucracy. Jim Lorenz, then director of California's Employment Development Department, proposed that unemployment funds be spent not on leaf-raking and paper-pushing jobs but on enabling unemployed auto workers to set up a car-repair cooperative, for example, or on enabling construction-workers' unions to hire unemployed workers to insulate the homes of the elderly.

Some authors and organizers supporting political self-management are Milton Kotler, Director of the Institute for Neighborhood Studies and author of *Neighborhood Government* (Bobbs-Merrill, 1960), David Morris, codirector of the Institute for Local Self-Reliance and coauthor of *Neighborhood Power* (Beacon Press, 1975), Karl Hess, community organizer in Washington, former editor of *Newsweek,* speechwriter for Senator Goldwater, and author of *Dear America* (Morrow, 1975), and Marcus Raskin, codirector of the Institute for Policy Studies and author of *Notes on the Old System* (David McKay, 1975). The extraordinary range and creativity of the ideas set forth in these books attest to the significance of the neighborhood movement for the future of the United States.

The New American Revolution

Radical caucuses, communes, CDCs, ACORN, CAL, Sto-Rox, AMO, Public Citizen, Inc., Common Cause, and Senator Hatfield's bills all represent Pete Seeger's grass sprouting on the American political landscape. This greening has prompted foreign observers like Jean Francois Revel to write of the "Second American Revolution."[15] But the fact is that this second revolution is stalled at an incipient stage. The grass is not firmly rooted and the concrete is far from crumbling. In the Adams Morgan Organization, for example, is the recognized danger that the alternative nonprofit retail stores may become camouflaged Ma and Pa stores and that the member workers may vote themselves generous medical benefits and paid vacations that would be the equivalent of cash profits. AMO also faces the problem that the community is mostly black but the alternative businesses are almost all white, and that the blacks want community control whereas the whites want worker ownership.

Aside from the fragility of alternative institutions, another obstacle is the generally hostile social environment. The combination of the 1968 and 1972 election results and the Watergate revelations has generated widespread defeatism and alienation. Bill Moyers has warned of "the nothing-can-be-done" disease and the "danger that we will suffer permanent loss of faith and begin to doubt our capacity for self-government."[16] We must also recognize that the United States lacks the mass radical parties that could provide a base for countering the political and economic power of the major corporations and their allies in Washington. Under the circumstances, the final beneficiary of the frustrations engendered by Watergate, inflation, and unemployment may be a leader like the Governor of Alabama, George Wallace, who for years has been demagogically representing himself as the champion of ordinary working people and as the adversary of the educated elite of the North and the politicians and bureaucrats in Washington. Public-opinion analyst Patrick Caddell found, in surveys conducted in 1974, that 65 percent of Americans agreed with the statement "Things are too complicated for the average person to understand." He also found that agreement with that statement correlated closely with support for George Wallace.[17]

And yet an entirely different scenario could emerge in the American future. The Consitution and the Bill of Rights remain a precious reality and the handling of the Watergate revelations reflects the significance of a free press and a free judiciary. Whereas Soviet dissidents are an isolated and beleaguered "one percent" (see the next section), their American counterparts, although by no means free from attacks ranging from ridicule to physical force (and including such "dirty tricks" as spying, intimidation, and character assassination), nevertheless enjoy freedoms for which a Sakharov petitions in vain. It is revealing that, although Jean Francois Revel favored Senator George McGovern in the 1972 election and presumably was disappointed by its outcome, he nevertheless wrote two years later:

> The French know down deep, though they don't admit it frequently, that 20 Watergates could take place at home—and apparently have taken place—without those responsible being taken to task or without even public opinion being informed. . . . Among democracies then, and not even speaking of the other political systems, with Watergate American democracy has supplied proof that it is perhaps the one in which the mechanisms of control over the abuse of power function with the greatest and most irresistible efficiency.[18]

Neither should the educational impact on the American public of the current upsurge of inflation, unemployment, and corruption be underestimated. The "silent majority" may have accepted with equanimity Nixon's policies regarding civil rights or intervention in Southeast Asia, but the same people kick over the traces when they realize that *they* are the victims each time a factory shuts down or supermarket prices go up.

Finally, citizen activism in a wide variety of cooperative enterprises is an important American tradition. Whereas Americans tend to be suspicious of political activism and to take a negative view of politics as a "dirty game," they still participate more than most other nationalities in community undertakings—a bond issue for a new hospital or a new swimming pool, PTA affairs, neighborhood health centers, and the like. If such projects really allow citizens to participate and to make substantive decisions, experience shows that there is no lack of volunteers who give generously of their time and energy. The Harvard psychiatrist Dr. Robert Coles, in testimony before the Senate Committee on Labor and Public Welfare, reported the reactions of a worker to bona fide versus sham participation:

> Who asks us anything? Do they really go out to us, try to let us know in advance what they're thinking of doing in the schools or about a road they're building or about the kind of television our kids are going to be looking at? You hear all the time that people don't care, they're apathetic. But it takes two: the companies and the government—do they really want to get a lot of people down their backs, speaking up with their ideas? I doubt it. It's easier just to go ahead and start something, then take on the few people who complain! Sure I'm tired, and how many hours do I have left each day when I come home? But if there was something really important going on—some meeting or program that affected my wife and kids, that really meant something to us, I'd try to find the time.[19]

This man's statement poses squarely the overriding question of the future: is it better to perpetuate representative democracy, with its one-way communication through the mass media, by which candidates can manipulate support with images and slogans and sell themselves to a market of consumers, or to develop participatory politics, which will activate and mobilize a community and enable its members to take part in "something really important going on"?

The first course has resulted in the gutted American countryside, the expanding but increasingly uninhabitable American megalopolis, and the unprecedented lack of public confidence in traditional institutions and leaders. Therefore the problem boils down to how to get started on the second course toward decentralization and local self-management, both rural and urban. This problem requires reappraisal of hitherto unchallenged liberal political strategy. The 1973 Harris Poll found not only citizen disillusionment but also a large although largely untapped potential for citizen action. Asked what actions they would take to change an unjust law or oust a corrupt politician, 94 percent were ready to go to the polls, 91 percent to talk with friends, 84 percent to write to congressmen, and 79 percent to join one of the new citizen-action groups; and 49 percent agreed that such citizens' groups "are having more effect in getting government to get things done than they did five years ago."[20]

What might be the dividends today if a small percentage of the human and material resources expended in the confusion of the 1968 and 1972 presidential campaigns had been invested instead in grass-roots community mobilization, so that citizens had gained experience and confidence in managing their local affairs? Might there now be less feeling of frustration and powerlessness, and correspondingly less vulnerability to the demagogues waiting to exploit such feeling?

It might be argued that the failure of George McGovern's 1972 presidential campaign proves that participatory politics is not the answer for America. McGovern himself dubbed his venture the "little guy" campaign and opened his drive for the Democratic nomination an unprecedented 18 months before the convention. His aim was to air the issues and mobilize grass-roots support for his reform platform based on withdrawal from Indochina, substantial tax reform, and sharp reduction of arms expenditures. The day before the Democratic National Convention opened in Miami Beach, McGovern described his following in unmistakably populist terms:

> The new constituency first of all embraces a much stronger voice for the women of this country. They are apparent in this convention as they have never been before. It embraces a stronger voice for young people than they have had before, and they are here in much greater numbers than ever before. It embraces the whole spectrum of people that are anti-war, that are opposed to our involvement in Vietnam. It embraces the alienated blue collar worker, not the labor leader at the top, but the rank and file blue collar worker who voted for me in one state after another. It embraces the small farmer, as against the corporate farmer. It embraces the little independent businessman, as against ITT. . . .
>
> What is forming in this country in my opinion is a new mainstream, a new coalition of people who are dissatisfied with the status quo.

This statement was not mere rhetoric for McGovern. He was unquestionably sincere, and for this reason he went down to overwhelming defeat.

Anyone basing his campaign on "a new coalition of people who are dissatisfied with the status quo" must expect the bitter-end opposition of all those satisfied with the status quo. And those included, in McGovern's case, not only the business community but also city bosses like Mayor Daley of Chicago, labor leaders like George Meany of the AFL-CIO, rival Democratic leaders like Senators Hubert Humphrey and Henry Jackson, and wealthy Democratic supporters like W. Averell Harriman. When it became apparent that McGovern would win the nomination, an ABM ("Anybody But McGovern") coalition was organized, including representatives of AFL-CIO's COPE (Committee on Political Education) and supporters of Senators Humphrey and Jackson. In meetings held while the convention was still in session, the strategy agreed upon was to ignore McGovern during the campaign and then "pick up the pieces" after the election.

In line with this strategy, Democratic chieftains such as Robert Strauss either whispered their endorsement of McGovern or, like George Meany, turned benevolently neutral toward Nixon. After the election, the AFL-CIO political director, Alexander Barkan, announced that "Gravel Gertie [party chairman Jean Westwood] and the crazies have got to go."[21] Robert Strauss had the backing necessary to replace "Gravel Gertie," and the Democratic Party found itself again under traditional leadership. In the words of I. W. Abel, President of the United Steelworkers, "I'd like to see democracy exercised to the fullest in our union or any other union, but democracy in the labor movement, as in various segments of life, can be carried to an extreme."[22]

McGovern has been accused of many tactical mistakes—of having "insulted Daley's political manhood," of having ignored old party leaders and favored the minorities, and so forth. But the fact is that, even if endowed with the charm and astuteness of a Roosevelt or a Kennedy, McGovern would still have had to face an implacable ABM coalition as long as he was serious about a mass-based "coalition of change" against the status quo. The fact that he was serious is what Meany and Daley and the Democratic Party's leadership found unforgivable. The gut issue was whether or not in American democracy decision making should be the prerogative of the few at the top or should include the many at the bottom as well.

The lesson is clear for any future McGovern who opts for the many at the bottom. He stands a chance only if the many are actively organized behind him, aware of the issues, and knowledgeable about the political process. Thus his campaign demands that he gain preliminary grass-roots experience to secure a strong base at the local level before making a bid for power in Washington. What goes on at the Capitol and at the grass roots obviously act and react upon each other. But the fatal mistake of American liberalism in the past has been to ignore the grass roots, thus permitting easy victory for the well-organized few and the preservation of the status quo.

The Soviet "One Percent"

Future world events will be influenced not only by the course of the Second American Revolution but also by the fate of the self-styled "one percent" of the Soviet population, its beleaguered group of dissidents. This one percent apparently faces a dismal future, because there is no counterpart in the Soviet Union to the "exploring society" of the United States. Although the Soviet revolutionary tradition goes back only to 1917 rather than to 1776, Soviet society, to use Pete Seeger's image, is already covered by a double layer of concrete. One layer is socioeconomic, composed of a self-perpetuating elite (analyzed in Chapter 6, pages 146 to 154), which derives its power and privileges from control of public office rather than of private property. The second layer is political, composed of the authoritarianism of the Communist Party Secretary, in the case of Stalin, and later of the ruling Party oligarchy, under Khrushchev and Brezhnev.

Soviet authoritarianism is paradoxical, in view of the traditional Marxist-Leninist emphasis on mass involvement and "proletarian democracy." In the *Communist Manifesto* Marx stressed that revolution was impossible unless the majority of workers was imbued with communist consciousness. Likewise, Lenin in his *April Theses* of 1917 called for "All power to the Soviets," but he stressed that this did not mean a coup or a Party revolt but rather an upheaval involving a whole class aroused by revolutionary consciousness. With such an ideological background, why did the Soviet state, from the beginning, develop along authoritarian lines?

One reason is that, despite Lenin's theoretical insistence on mass support for any uprising, his own revolution resembled a coup in certain respects. Certainly it was a coup in comparison with the later Chinese, Yugoslav, and Vietnamese revolutions. In February 1917 the Bolsheviks numbered about 23,000, and by October they barely exceeded 100,000. The actual seizure of power in October involved merely the overthrow of Kerensky's moribund authority in the cities of Moscow and Petrograd. There was none of the protracted guerrilla warfare and the gradual evolution, by trial and error, of peasant-based administration of liberated provinces that occurred under the leadership of Mao, Tito, and Ho. It was in keeping with their historical origins, then, that the Russian Bolsheviks proved from the beginning to be much more authoritarian in thought and action than their rural-based successors.

Soviet repressiveness also has roots in the ambiguity of Marxist-Leninist ideology, which views the Party as both servant and master of the people—as both their tool and their lash. In his essay *What Is to Be Done?* Lenin wrote that the Party must be firmly based on the masses but at the same time must preserve its identity and integrity as "an organ of revolutionaries capable of maintaining the energy, stability, and continuity of political struggle." The Party must follow the exceedingly thin line between "tailism," or the passive following of mass desires, and "commandism," or elitist exercise of dictatorial power over the masses.

This is precisely what Mao preaches today in his "mass line" doctrine; and, unlike Lenin, Mao has survived his revolution and has been able to use his "mass line" to build a society that is socialist in fact as well as in name. What Lenin might have achieved had he not died in January 1924 is one of the great "ifs" of history. Instead we have the history of his successors, who lacked the patience, or capacity, to evoke the same measure of mass support that Lenin had enjoyed. Faced with desperate domestic problems and foreign threats, they imposed their will by naked force both on Party members and on the population as a whole. By a process of substitution, as Trotsky put it, the Party substituted itself for the working class, the Central Committee substituted itself for the Party, and its General Secretary ultimately substituted himself for everyone else.

Stalin's purges of 1936 through 1938 decimated the Bolshevik Old Guard as well as the leadership of the army, the economy, the trade unions, and the police. Stalin ignored even his own Party advisors in reaching decisions. Thirteen years elapsed between the Eighteenth and Nineteenth Party Congresses, held in 1939 and 1952 respectively, and during those years Stalin consulted the Central Committee and even the Politburo ever less frequently. Even victory in World War II did not bring significant relaxation of the dictatorship. Indeed, new purge trials appeared to be imminent when Stalin died in 1953.

By this time the Soviet Union had become a great industrial power. This very success made an undiluted continuation of Stalinist despotism impossible. Russia had been transformed from a land of peasants (*muzhiks*) into a country with a literate population, a complex economy, rapidly expanding urban centers, and a large corps of technicians and scientists.

Khrushchev responded with his "thaw," a policy that, in the realm of politics, involved a shift away from purges, secret police, and slave-labor camps. At the Twentieth Party Congress of 1956, he delivered his sensational attack on Stalin, attributing Stalin's transgressions and terror not to the Soviet political system but to Stalin's personal perversions of Marxist principles. The need, he concluded, was to "return to and actually practice in our ideological work the very important Marxist-Leninist theses about the people as the maker of history and the creator of all mankind's material and spiritual benefits." Five years later, at the Twenty-Second Party Congress in October 1961, he stressed the need for a "steady flow of new, promising people" into leadership positions. Accordingly, the Congress adopted new rules limiting members of the Presidium to three consecutive terms in office, and requiring that no fewer than one quarter of the members of this body and of the Central Committee be replaced at every Congress. Similar provisions on a more drastic scale were stipulated for lower Party units and also for non-Party governmental bodies such as the soviets.

Krushchev's great contribution, in retrospect, was his de-Stalinization of the Soviet Union. But he was far from his stated goal of "the people as the maker of history" when he was overthrown in October 1964. The fact that he was the victim of a coup by a handful of top leaders is itself significant, highlighting the chronic Soviet problem of the lack of machinery enabling orderly political succession. It also highlights the more basic problem of the relationship between bureaucracy and people. During Stalin's early years, the illiterate *muzhiks* could be ordered around with impunity. But a half century of industrialization, urbanization, and education now confronts the Soviet leadership with new problems and new tasks. There are the needs for meeting the rising expectations of an educated populace and for realizing the potentialities of a new industrial-scientific order that requires mass participation rather than mass regimentation.

Khrushchev appeased popular discontent by ending the Stalinist terror. He relieved the people from oppression but denied them freedom. Today, any new concessions must cut into the bureaucratic structure itself, and the new leadership cannot countenance this undermining of its power and privileges. Under Stalin the bureaucracy was only a subservient body with no independent power or identity. Now it has become the ruling clique that delegates but does not abdicate power to its leaders. It wants enough rule of law to protect it from another Stalin terror but not enough to jeopardize its privileged status. In short, the Soviet ruling elite now enjoys an internal democracy that it refuses to extend to the intellectuals and lesser bureaucracy, let alone to the workers and peasants.

Opposition to this repressiveness is limited because the success of the Five Year Plans has significantly improved the lot of the average citizen. The Soviet share of total global industrial output rose from 1.5 percent in 1921 to 10 percent in 1939 to 20 percent in 1966. This economic leap forward has made possible a corresponding social leap forward. Literacy rose from 28.4 percent in 1897 to 56.6 percent in 1926 and to 98.5 percent in 1959. The number of physicians rose from 23,200 in 1913 to 425,700 in 1961, and during the same period life expectancy rose from 32 to 70 and infant mortality fell from 273 per thousand to 32 per thousand. Soviet citizens now also enjoy free medical care, old-age pensions, sickness and disability benefits, maternity leaves, and paid vacations. The Soviet system is paying off in a material sense, and this fact, along with unrelenting repression of any organized opposition, has left Soviet dissidents a tiny and isolated minority.

A large potentially dissident element are the minority nationalities of Central Asia, the Ukraine, and the Baltic republics, but they do not appear sufficiently organized to be considered an active dissident force. The same may be said of an amorphous group of philosophical dissidents that looks primarily to religion for support and believes that Soviet society should be based on Christian moral principles. Alexander Solzhenitsyn falls into this category, with his Slavophile-type opposition to Western ideas and Western industrialization. "All that 'endless progress,' " he wrote in his *Letter to the Soviet Leaders,* "turned out to be an insane, ill-considered, furious dash into a blind alley."[23] Solzhenitsyn, however, is unique among the religiously inclined dissidents because he has been able to win a worldwide audience through his literary achievements. Russian Jews are both organized and vocal, but they cannot be considered a serious threat to the Soviet Establishment because the goal of those who are dissatisfied is more often to escape abroad than to force reform at home.

The Soviet dissidents who are best known in the West may be described as liberals who wish to combine the social achievements of the Soviet system with the personal freedoms of the West. They consist primarily of physical scientists, who are allowed more latitude than artists or writers because their cooperation is considered more important for Soviet economic and military strength. Some distinguished scientists have taken advantage of this privileged position to speak out on critical issues. The leader in this movement has been Andrei Sakharov, the brilliant theoretical physicist who was made the youngest member of the Academy of Sciences for his leading role in the development of the Soviet H-bomb in 1950. Since then Sakharov has acquired a different kind of fame for writings and public statements in which he has expressed unorthodox views on both Soviet and global problems.

In 1968 he issued the pamphlet *Progress, Peaceful Coexistence, and Academic Freedom,*[24] in which he set forth the following propositions: that the scientific revolution has made old ideological divisions obsolete and extremely dangerous for mankind; that modern technology enables capitalism as well as Communism to provide economic security for all; that the advantages of a socialist society must be demonstrated in its moral values rather than in alleged economic superiority and consequent historical inevitability; and that the future of the human race depends on American-Soviet cooperation to avert nuclear disaster and to promote global economic development. Since this publication, Sakharov has been inspired by the increasing repressiveness of Khrushchev's successors to address himself to domestic Soviet problems. In March 1970, along with a fellow physicist and a historian, he addressed an *Appeal of Soviet Scientists to the Party-Government Leaders of the USSR;* and in November 1970, along with two fellow scientists, Sakharov founded the Committee for Human Rights to ensure personal freedom in the Soviet Union.

The 1970 *Appeal* merits extensive quotation because it offers a penetrating analysis of Soviet ailments and a forthright program for reform.

In the 'twenties and 'thirties the capitalist world underwent a period of crisis and depression. At that time we, by exploiting the upsurge of national energy which had been unleashed by the Revolution, were creating industry at an unheard-of tempo. That was the time when the slogan "Overtake and Surpass America" was coined. And we really were overtaking it in the course of the next few decades. Then the situation changed. The second industrial revolution came along and now, at the onset of the 'seventies we can see that, far from having overtaken America, we are dropping further and further behind. . . .

Why is this? Why have we not only failed to become the pioneers of the second industrial revolution but, as it transpires, are we even incapable of keeping abreast of the developed capitalist countries in this revolution? Can it be that the socialist system does not present the same opportunities as the capitalist system for the development of productive forces and that in the economic competition between capitalism and socialism capitalism will emerge victorious?

Of course not. The source of our difficulties does not lie in the socialist system at all, but, on the contrary, in those features and circumstances in our life which run counter to socialism and are alien to it. This source lies in the anti-democratic traditions and norms of public conduct which were laid down during the Stalinist period and which have not been eradicated even to this day. . . .

Our economy can be compared to traffic at an intersection. As long as there were only a few cars the man on point duty could cope and the traffic flowed freely. But the volume of traffic is growing unceasingly and so a traffic jam builds up. What can be done about it? The drivers can be punished and the man on point duty changed, but this will not save the situation. The only solution is to widen the crossing. The obstacles blocking the development of our economy lie beyond it, in the socio-political sphere, and all measures which fail to remove these obstacles are doomed to inefficacy. . . .

From our friends abroad we sometimes hear the U.S.S.R. compared to a huge truck, whose driver presses one foot hard down on the accelerator and the other on the brake. The time has come to make more intelligent use of the brake! . . .

What has our country to expect if a course leading towards democratization is not taken? It can expect to lag behind the capitalist countries in the second industrial revolution and to gradually revert to the status of a second-rate provincial power (there have been such instances in history); economic difficulties will grow; relations between the Party-Government apparatus and the intelligentsia will be exacerbated; there will be a danger of outbursts to right and left; national problems will be exacerbated, for in the national republics the movement towards democratization, coming from below, inevitably assumes a national character.

At the time of the 1975 Helsinki summit meeting, Sakharov made public an essay entitled *My Country and the World* in which he depicts the Soviet Union as a bureaucratically controlled society with its government behind closed doors, social inequality between the ruling elite and the nation at large, and a disproportionate use of resources for military purposes. "Despite inflation, fuel crisis, and problems of unemployment," he wrote, "the Western economies are on a much healthier foundation than the chronically strained, militarized, and chaotically managed economy of the USSR." Giving qualified praise to Khrushchev, Sakharov stated that the late Soviet leader's attempts to reduce the privileges of the elite and to cut the defense budget were the chief causes of his downfall in 1964. In his critique of Soviet society, Sakharov referred to lack of initiative, inferior working conditions, and poor medical care for the majority of citizens. He offered a 12-point reform program that included establishment of a multi-party system and amnesty for political and religious prisoners, whose numbers he estimated at 10,000 out of a total prison population of 1,500,000.

The response of the Soviet government to Sakharov's campaign has been unequivocally negative. It is following precisely the course against which he warned, slamming on the brake rather than making "more intelligent use" of it. Because of economic setbacks and the resulting need for foreign technological aid, the government has adopted a policy of diplomatic détente and closer economic ties with the West. But to counter any possible ideological contamination from these ties the Kremlin is tightening its control over the movement of ideas and people. *Pravda* has charged that only "hawks" favor more exchange across East-West borders. "They are linking such movement with the infamous strategy of 'building bridges,' which could be used for subversive activities against the socialist countries of Europe."[25]

Certain tactical concessions have been made by Soviet authorities, such as allowing the emigration of Jews and of a number of internationally known dissenters—the scientists Zhores Medvedev and Valery Chalidze, the cellist Mstislav Rostropovich, the poets Iosif Brodsky and Naum Korzhavin, the scholars Yefim Etkind and Pavel Litvinov, and the writers Andrei Sinyavsky, Volodya Maksimov, Victor Nekrasov, and Alexander Solzhenitsyn himself, who was forcibly deported. Western observers had long assumed that new dissidents would emerge to take the places of the émigrés, but this does not seem to be happening. The government is appeasing the more prosperous and articulate segments of the population with private cars, better apartments, and other symbols of bourgeois life. "We live better now than our parents did," asserts a middle-aged man, "or better than we ourselves did 10 years ago, and we hope for better yet."[26] Young people also generally go along with the present system, especially since they do not perceive an appealing alternative model beyond their frontiers. The American correspondent Georgie Anne Geyer, after extensive first-hand study of Soviet youth in 1971, concluded:

> In my experience, more young Soviets feel that their system, despite its brutalities—which they hope and believe are now a thing of the past—has "delivered" for the average person while the U.S. system has not. . . . It is clear that many of these young people, while highly critical of their own society, also have been deeply disillusioned

by the United States—which they once looked upon as an attractive alternative—because of Vietnam, economic failures, racism, violence, and social inequalities. "We hate the totalitarianism in our society," one young Soviet man said, "but then we ask ourselves, what good is your freedom if you can't solve your problems?"[27]

The net result is an absence of anything that could be described as an organized movement of dissidents. There appears to be little more than intermittent debate on the nature of detente and the future of Soviet society among a handful of personalities protected by their prestige and by world opinion—the scientist Andrei Sakharov, the historian Roy A. Medvedev, the mathematician Igor R. Shafarevich. "We are living on a moonscape," observes a literary critic who has remained behind. "There is no one left. We are all alone on the moon."[28]

Doubtless the critic is as alone as he feels he is, but the question is whether he is alone because the mass of the population is contented and apathetic, or because relatively well-to-do intellectuals are isolated from the masses, who are not so favored and who conceivably might not be so satisfied and passive as the critic assumes. Are the increasing income and status differentiations among workers negating the positive effect of the rise in absolute living standards? The answer to this fundamental question will decide the course of future events within the Soviet Union. But the answer is extraordinarily difficult to determine because of the impossibility of testing mass public opinion in Russia.

A few reports of working-class discontent have reached the outside world. When the scientist Pavel Litvinov, grandson of Stalin's Foreign Minister Maxim Litvinov, left the Soviet Union in March 1974, he reported that during the four years he spent in Siberia for protesting the invasion of Czechoslovakia he had close contact with workers and found strong discontent with the Soviet system "on all levels of the working class."[29] Andrei Sakharov likewise attested to widespread discontent among Soviet workers, during a telephone interview on the occasion of the Danish Parliament's announcement that it would form a tribunal in Copenhagen to investigate the condition of human rights in the Soviet Union. Sakharov testified to

the sorry—even tragic—state of Soviet workers. Their wages are insufficient to support a family of four. Therefore, the wife is forced to become a wage earner, and destructive results are felt in child-raising and in the creation of other insoluble social problems.

The working hours of the Soviet laborer are much longer than those in any Western European country, and his medical and public health care are inadequate. Improvements in that area have been negligible.

If the Copenhagen tribunal can deal with the condition of Soviet workers—and my facts are correct—I would consider it the most important issue. This is particularly true since the rest of the world is completely misinformed on the situation of workers in the Soviet Union.[30]

Finally, we should bear in mind that the positive effect of generally rising living standards may be neutralized not only by an increase in income disparity but also by the possibility that less attention is being paid to projects that can be enjoyed by large numbers of people, and more paid to the production of luxury goods for the affluent minority. The recent shift of Soviet industry toward greater reliance on the "profit index" may explain consumer complaints that stores are stocking primarily expensive items, on which there is a greater profit margin, and it may also explain worker complaints of excessive speedup, or demand for more output per employee, and of unemployment for the resulting surplus employees.

So the crucial question remains: are the literary critic and his friends in fact alone on the Soviet moonscape, or are they alone in their private and relatively comfortable ivory towers?

"Dirty Phnom Penh"

The expulsion of the United States from Southeast Asia in the latter half of the twentieth century was a major turning point in modern history, ranking with the Russian Revolution in the beginning of the century and the Chinese Revolution in mid-century. The spectacle of United States Ambassador Graham Martin fleeing Saigon, the American flag under his arm, symbolized a sudden shift in the balance of power. But another dramatic event that occurred at the same time symbolized something much more basic than a mere power realignment. This was the forced evacuation of what the Cambodian Communists called "dirty Phnom Penh," "the great prostitute on the banks of the Mekong River," "the Western cesspool of hooliganism, graft, embezzlement, gambling, prostitution, alcoholism." The Western superstructure that had evolved during the past century was rooted out in a matter of hours, leaving the capital "an echo chamber of silent streets." This uprooting represented a more drastic break with the past than had the winning of political independence by several dozen former colonies in Southeast Asia following World War II. It signified a qualitative change within the Third World itself as well as in relations between the Third World and the Western powers.

The underdeveloped societies of the Third World are by definition sick societies. Their traditional institutions—political, economic, and social—have been exploited and distorted in the process of these countries' integration into the global market economy. Their sickness can be cured only by restructuring their now obsolete institutions and practices. But it is precisely this restructuring that has been adamantly opposed by those who profit from the obsolescence—the native elite and their foreign patrons, who have blocked modernization and thereby maintained the underdevelopedness and poverty that are the hallmarks of the Third World.

From the beginning of the West's expansion in early modern times, there have been native reformers who realized that the adoption of certain Western techniques and institutions was essential in order to be able to resist the West. But such development was resisted by local Establishments, which were usually backed by Western powers that had a substantial investment in the status quo. This investment, both private and governmental, developed naturally through the years and took such forms as loans to the established government, favorable trade treaties, industrial and mining concessions, and ongoing military and financial missions. Hence the paradox that has persisted since the beginning of Western expansion overseas—the fact that the Western powers are the implacable opponents of Third World westernization. In China the Western powers supported the moribund Manchu dynasty against the Taiping rebels, and later, after the collapse of the dynasty in 1911, backed the conservative Yuan Shih-kai against the republican Sun Yat-sen. Likewise, in India the British systematically supported the native landlords and princes against the nationalist Congress Party. In the various states of Indochina the French propped up the indigenous royal houses as convenient puppets to be manipulated against the local nationalists. In the Philippines, under the guise of liberating the islands from Spanish oppression, President McKinley turned on the indigenous nationalist movement and crushed it with 60,000 soldiers in a bloody two-year struggle suggestive of the later American intervention in Vietnam. In Persia, both Russia and Britain backed the Kajar dynasty in order to keep the constitutionalists out of power. Throughout Africa, the various European powers in their respective fashions supported tribal chieftains against the Western-educated nationalists. Even in czarist Russia, which was economically a semicolony of the West although a great power in its own right, the Western powers intervened decisively to prop up the Romanov dynasty during the 1905 revolution with large loans.

Because the strategy of counterrevolution prevailed, a small peninsula on the western tip of Eurasia ruled the entire world until the early twentieth century. Then came the two World Wars, which damaged irreparably both the prestige and the power of the hitherto invincible white colonialists. Most of the Asian colonies won their independence during the first decade after World War II, and most of the African colonies during the second decade. But formal political independence did not dissolve the traditional marriages of convenience between local elites and foreign patrons. Common interests and mutual support persisted, although in forms that were changed to suit the new constitutional structures of these countries.

To begin with, independence was granted only when local leaders' interests were judged to be in harmony with imperialist interests, and these leaders were therefore not likely to adopt policies damaging to their former ruler. This selective granting of independence meant that nationalist leaders were acceptable only if they were not social revolutionaries. Hence the willingness of the French to free so many of their colonies in equatorial Africa while at the same time fighting to the bitter end in Indochina, where the leader was the Communist Ho Chi Minh. Likewise, the British were willing to relinquish India, their prize imperial jewel, but refused independence to Guiana until the Marxist Dr. Cheddi Jagan had been ousted from leadership by various clandestine measures.

After the selective granting of independence came the equally selective granting of preferential treatment to "friendly" regimes. Aid was lavished on Emperor Haile Selassie of Ethiopia but not on Julius Nyerere of Tanzania, on King Hussein of Jordan but not on Abdel Nasser of Egypt, on the generals ruling Brazil but not on Dr. Salvador Allende of Chile. The network of aid operations and operatives also provided political leverage that could be, and was, exerted at all levels of the recipient government. This aid proved effective not only in economic matters but also in the security and military fields, where officers of Third World forces have usually been trained abroad and are dependent on foreign arms. And, if all else failed, there remained the options of covert political intervention, as in Greece, Iran, and Chile, or overt armed intervention, as in Cuba, the Dominican Republic, and Vietnam.

Since these counterrevolutionary strategies have proved generally successful, the Third World has been ruled primarily by a succession of elites. The colonial administrators of the preindependence period were followed by those nationalist leaders favored by the departing colonialists, and later by the military bureaucrats who seized power when the politicos proved incapable of satisfying basic needs and curbing the ensuing popular unrest. Such military coups have been so numerous that when President Francois Tombalbaye of Chad was deposed and killed by rebellious troops in April 1975, he was the victim of the thirty-fourth coup to take place in Africa since the end of World War II.

The significance of the Southeast Asian events of 1975 is that they have put an end to this succession of elites in a strategic part of the Third World. The revolutionaries of Vietnam, Cambodia, and Laos were able to organize a mass revolutionary movement mobilizing the great bulk of the population to such a degree that victory by the Western interventionists was simply unattainable by any means short of extermination using nuclear weapons. Washington did try everything else—genocidal inventions such as antipersonnel devices and B-52 carpet bombing, depopulation measures such as relocation camps and free-fire zones, and ecocidal techniques such as crop destruction and massive defoliation with chemical herbicides, which, according to the United States National Academy of Sciences, caused ecological wounds that may take at least a century to heal. Over the years of American involvement in Southeast Asia, every strategy was followed in the pursuit of victory, beginning with money, arms, and advisers to the local oligarchies, escalating to counterinsurgency teams, and culminating in an invasion army of half a million men.

In addition, an attempt was made to supplement this massive physical force with land reform that was intended to remove the socioeconomic roots of revolution by promoting (1) a more equitable distribution of agricultural output and (2) higher living standards, thereby lessening the appeal of the Communist-led revolutionaries. In actual practice, however, *effective* land reform is not viable as a counterrevolutionary tool, for it disrupts the traditional patterns of land tenure and exploitation, undermines the economic and political power of the landlords, and unleashes radical and unpredictable opposition movements.

This discrepancy between theory and practice explains why, despite liberal rhetoric and initial reform measures, American policy in the Third World generally, as well as in Vietnam, has ended up supporting landlords in the countryside and conservative anti-Communist political parties in the cities. Hence the postponement of land reform in mainland China until the Nationalist government was virtually defeated. In the Philippines, reform was sustained until the revolutionary wave subsided and then was abruptly dropped, to be resumed again in 1973 with the renewal of insurrection. And in South Vietnam, American soldiers and officers repeatedly expressed disillusionment in observing South Vietnamese landlords following them into newly occupied regions and resuming the collection of exorbitant rents from peasants who had been freed from such imposts by the National Liberation Front (NLF).

The American failure to effect structural reform meant a corresponding failure to win people over, and, therefore, the inevitable failure of modern military technology to win the Vietnam War. The failure was inevitable because the Communist-led revolutionaries regarded land reform and the struggle for national independence as interdependent and mutually reinforcing. Landlords never showed up in guerrilla-held territories to reclaim their estates. Equally important were the contrasting types of leadership on the two sides, as is evident in the following comparison by the North Vietnamese leader Nguyen Khac Vien:

> The first directive issued by the Communist Party in Vietnam shortly after its founding ordered its political activists to work in the mines, become rickshaw pullers and to live and work among the peasants—to build a solid base of support among the people. Bourgeois politicians, on the other hand, spent their time primarily in contacting other politicians, journalists, and foreign governments. Being city people by birth and education, they were unfamiliar with their own country, never having shared the life of the nine-tenths of the Vietnamese population who are poor peasants.[31]

This difference explains why the printouts of Pentagon computers indicating inevitable victory over a few million rice farmers were consistently proven wrong over the years. Despite the relentless U.S. bombing, the revolutionary forces were steadily replenished and supplied. This constant reinforcement was possible because of the mobilization and involvement of the entire countryside, which transformed the war into a struggle between foreign machines and local inhabitants. A group of captured United States Air Force officers who were allowed to travel south of Hanoi with visiting American correspondents were astounded by the human and very visible supply chain. In South Vietnam, night travel on roads was always perilous because of the numerous guerrilla bands. In North Vietnam, since the only danger was from American planes overhead, traffic at night was heavy and unhindered. During the day the convoys parked under the rows of trees lining the roads. "I used to fly over this place," remarked a lieutenant, "and it seemed uninhabited. But look, it is teeming with life. . . . We could never see those things from the air. And the moment someone comes down to get a better look at them—blam, man!" "It is technology against ideology," observed a major. "I just wonder how far technology can go, because the Vietnamese habitually beat it."[32]

The significance of recent events in Southeast Asia is that they demonstrate that what Mao has achieved with a quarter of the human race and the resources of a subcontinent behind him can also be achieved by a small country if its people are fully activated and mobilized. This proposition has already been proven in Africa by the successful revolution in the Republic of Guinea-Bissau, the small former Portuguese colony of 800,000 people on the coast of West Africa. This little-known but outstanding success story is highly implausible, for the country is only half the size of Maine. Its population is divided into five main groups and over a dozen smaller ones, each with its own language, cultural traditions, and sense of separate identity. Their social systems vary from the primitive democracy of the village to a form of semifeudalism, with no genuinely urban element among the 100,000 Africans living in the towns. Under Portuguese colonial rule the infant-mortality toll was about 600 babies in every 1000; a grand total of eight doctors and one hospital were available for the entire rural population; not more than one percent of the population could claim elementary literacy; only one secondary school existed in the whole colony; and there were no higher educational institutions of any kind.

Such were the conditions when in September 1956 Amilcar Cabral and five companions organized the African Independence Party of Guinea and the Cape Verde Islands (PAIGC). By January 1963 the recruiting and organizing had reached the point where armed resistance could begin. A decade later, in April 1972, a United Nations team visiting the area reported that the guerrillas controlled at least two-thirds of the territory. On November 2, 1973, the U.N. General Assembly declared Guinea-Bissau an independent sovereign state, and on August 26, 1974, the Portuguese government itself recognized that independence. The Portuguese government that did so was itself of revolutionary origin—ironically, a product of the African resistance, for the protracted colonial wars in Guinea-Bissau, Angola, and Mozambique had contributed decisively to the 1974 overthrow of the Portuguese dictatorship that dated back to 1933.

The reason for Cabral's remarkable success is that he recognized from the beginning the necessity of organizing mass support at the grass-roots level. He set out systematically to "reafricanize" himself, since he had become one of the *assimilés* while training in Portugal as an agricultural engineer. His duties in the colonial administration, which involved the preparation of an agricultural census, gave him the opportunity to travel throughout the colony. From this experience he realized that Cubans and Vietnamese were far more culturally advanced than the indigenous inhabitants of Portuguese Guinea, and that only a revolutionary strategy that recognized this could have any chance of success under such circumstances. To evolve such a strategy it was essential to live with the people and, in Cabral's words, "practice revolutionary democracy, hold frequent meetings, hide nothing from the masses of people, tell no lies, claim no easy victories."[33]

Another basic principle was self-reliance. Military equipment was gladly accepted from the outside, as well as diplomatic backing and training for nonmilitary personnel. But foreign volunteers or military advisers were not accepted: "They would rob my people of their one chance of achieving a historical meaning for themselves: of reasserting their own history, of recapturing their own identity."[34] Finally, Cabral sensed from the beginning that the aim of insurrection must be social revolution and not merely the substitution of an African elite for the departing Europeans. Only basic structural reshaping of all aspects of life could justify the bloodshed and suffering that the people endure in the course of an armed uprising.

These principles were consistently followed during the years of revolutionary struggle. No operation was undertaken without long discussion, continued until consensus was reached, on why the operation was necessary, how it should be conducted, and what each member should do. This process of education along with military action enabled the guerrilla fighters to overcome their fear of operations at night or in dark forests where spirits were believed to reside. It is revealing that precisely the same educational process was conducted among the NLF in Vietnam, and for the same reasons. In both countries the guerrillas eventually were launching most of their attacks at night, when they were less vulnerable to air strikes. A popular song among the Guinea fighters went:

> The guerrilla walks proudly on the land
> While the little Portuguese commands the clouds.[35]

In accordance with the principle of creating a new revolutionary society during the course of the armed struggle, the PAIGC built hundreds of schools in the liberated areas, established health services staffed by doctors and nurses trained abroad, and conducted a ceaseless educational campaign to politicize and inspire the populace.

> Frequent meetings must be held to explain to the population what is happening with the struggle.
>
> Oppose tendencies to militarism and make each fighter an exemplary militant of our Party.
>
> Educate ourselves, educate other people, the population in general, to fight fear and ignorance, to eliminate little by little the subjection to nature and natural forces which our economy has not yet mastered. . . .
>
> Learn from life, learn from our people, learn from books, learn from the experience of others. Never stop learning. . . .
>
> Nothing of this is incompatible with the joy of life, or with love for life and its amusements, or with confidence in the future and in our work.[36]

Although it has attracted much less attention than Vietnam, Guinea-Bissau, along with another ex-Portuguese colony—Mozambique, is likely to have an impact on the rest of Africa comparable to that of Vietnam on Southeast Asia. Both struggles demonstrate that the prerequisite for winning full independence is a participatory mass liberation movement that stimulates the people to cast off not only the physical yoke of colonial rule but also the mental yoke of superstition, illiteracy, and fatalism.

Consider, as a striking example, the contrasting careers of Amilcar Cabral and Ché Guevara. Whereas Cabral spent years "reafricanizing" himself so that he could comprehend and be comprehended by the Guinean villagers, Guevara cherished the illusion that Bolivian Indian peasants would flock to the sound of guns in the hands of liberators whose language many of them did not understand and who had made no effort to learn their language. Significant in this connection is Cabral's exchange with another Latin American revolutionary leader. "When I was in Cuba I met a revolutionary from Central America. I said to him: 'What about the Indians in your country—after all, they're a big part, aren't they, of your rural population?' And he said to me: 'Oh, the Indians: yes, you see, the Indians are a sort of reserve. . . .'"[37] The inevitable sequel to such revolutionary elitism was Guevara's isolation and death among an apathetic, and even hostile, peasantry. "The peasant mass," he wrote toward the end of his diary, "aids us in nothing and is turning into informers."[38]

The harnessing of intelligence, the firing of imagination, and the offering of a new vision of the future are essential for postrevolutionary reconstruction as well as for the revolutionary struggle itself. Nguyen Khac Vien emphasizes that "underdeveloped countries need *first and foremost an ideology of progress* which is able to mobilize, organize and educate their people."[39] It is easy enough, he warns, for technicians to prepare blueprints, for economists to formulate plans, and for politicians to legislate. But the real problem is to transform all this into reality, and this task can be done only by the peasants. To galvanize the peasants for this undertaking, the North Vietnamese leaders are waging a two-pronged campaign of "rectification" and "emulation."

"Rectification" means simply the holding of mass discussion meetings where everyone can discuss his or her daily problems—how to modify the old method of planting rice, how to change the blade on a plow, how to make a small wheelbarrow instead of carrying everything on the back, why the manure and human waste in the villages should be collected and used as fertilizer, why cooperatives are desirable, why polygamy and child marriage are forbidden. Each person is to feel free to criticize the ideas of others and to be ready in turn to have his ideas criticized, so that correct information is transmitted and errors corrected.

When the rectification process is completed, the "emulation" campaign begins to implement the agreed-upon consensus. This is the "doing" stage, when obscure peasants suddenly become famous because they have collected so many tons of fertilizer, or found a better way to breed water buffalo, or broken records in the yield of their rice paddies. Their names and achievements fill the newspapers and magazines. All media resources are directed to help concrete personal experiences to become the standards guiding everyone's efforts. Vivid slogans are popularized to drive home the principles of the emulation campaigns: "Free your shoulders" to persuade peasants to build wheelbarrows; "Clean villages mean well-manured rice land" to induce villagers to collect garbage and manure; "Break the chains of the one-tenth hectare" to stimulate peasants to clear more land for cultivation.

In this way, explains Nguyen Khac Vien, rectification and emulation prepare the Third World peasants for their leap into modernity. It is easy to distinguish those who have been so prepared from those who have not.

> In the first case, the peasants are a new people, ready to seize the initiative; in the second, they have remained as they have been for

centuries, resigned and slaves to the habits of the past. . . . Dare to think about progress, dare to take initiative, dare to transform your ideas into reality. . . . An underdeveloped society is essentially a feudal and pre-capitalist society which totally excludes any ideas about progress. . . . Ideological liberation of the great majority of the people is the *sine qua non* of development. There is no question that for developing countries, liberty is the most precious of all blessings—not the negative liberty which demands "leave me alone," but a true liberation of spirit and energy.[40]

Unprecedented social experimentation and innovation is under way in many parts of the Third World today. Examples are Tanzania, where President Nyerere has a monthly salary of $570 and no car of his own, where politicians do not get rich, and where an "African democratic social-ism" stresses rural development in the Ujamaa villages, which are producers' cooperatives; Cuba, where, according to Herbert L. Matthews, "Fidel Castro is not giving Cubans the consumer goods and prosperity they would like, but is giving them a great deal else they never had, such as honesty in government, excellent educational, medical, and social services for every citizen, and almost full employment,"[41] and Peru, where a military regime is dividing estates, nationalizing banks and public utilities, issuing industrial- and mining-reform laws, and advancing its *Sin Amos* ("without masters") program with the express purpose of creating a fully participatory social democracy. "We have laid the juridical basis for our revolution," states one of the Peruvian generals, "but now the most difficult part of the battle lies ahead: to convince the people of the need for change."[42]

This task is indeed the "most difficult" and also the most essential. For the decisive factor that will decide the long-run success or failure of any regime or undertaking, in the developed world as well as in the underdevel-oped, is whether the bulk of the citizenry is actively involved. Degree of mass participation is today, as always in the past, the most meaningful test of modernity. Attainment of such mass participation does not demand that a revolutionary society emulate the policies of Mao or Ho or Cabral, as any of these three would be the first to insist. Indeed, their triumphs stem precisely from the fact that all were independent revolutionaries, receptive to principles and precedents but eschewing dogmas and blueprints.

All this is not to suggest that a simple shift to participatory politics will solve the problems of the Third World. In the first place, such a shift has rarely been seriously and purposefully tried, and when it has it has failed far more often than not. For the traditional alliance of local elites and foreign patrons remains a formidable combination that is still operative throughout the world. Washington policymakers have not been moved by the Southeast Asian debacle to reappraise their global counterrevolutionary strategy of supporting rightist regimes, regardless of the unpopularity of these regimes with those they govern. The much-publicized "reassessment" of American foreign policy after Vietnam was a reassessment not of basic strategy but merely of the tactics for implementing that strategy. Any doubts on that score were soon dispelled by President Ford's visits to Seoul and Madrid and by Secretary of State Kissinger's repeated assurances that existing commitments would be honored.

Washington obviously is also counting on certain subimperialist powers to serve as junior partners in preserving the global status quo. Thus Brazil is provided with generous economic and technical aid in support of her role as watchdog of Latin America, as are Iran and Saudi Arabia for their similar role in the Middle East.

This counterinsurgency strategy has been generally successful, thereby dashing romantic illusions of new winds of change sweeping through the Third World. The successes of Mao, Ho, and Castro raised hopes that Marxist revolution, having petered out in the West, would be reborn among the peasant masses in the backlands. Now the pendulum is swinging to the other extreme, and the American-Soviet détente is viewed as a new Holy Alliance that will buttress for decades the status quo of the entire globe. This forecast of a new political Ice Age is as unrealistic as the earlier expectation of instant world revolution.

Relevant to this connection is the appraisal by the conservative British Member of Parliament J. Enoch Powell of the January 1973 Vietnam agreement. "The United States has just succeeded in terminating the most humiliating war not merely in its own history but in that of most Western nations in modern times. It is comparable with the defeat of Russia by Japan in 1905."[43] The implications of Powell's analysis may be deduced from the following considerations: that Japan's defeat of Russia inspired a series of explosions in the colonial world between 1905 and 1914—in Persia, India, China, and the Ottoman Empire; that the Third World today is much more combustible than was the colonial world at the beginning of the twentieth century; that there is little evidence to indicate that the Shah of Iran or the generals of Brazil will be able to escape the fate of the Hashimite dynasty of Iraq or to extinguish the revolutionary fires growing in their respective regions; and that the existence today of the Soviet bloc and of independent Communist societies provides Third World peoples with sources of support and alternative models that were not available to colonial peoples before the First World War.

The Mass Line in China

Maoist China, probably more than any other society, is purposefully striving to demystify "boss, bureaucrat, and expert." The Norwegian sociologist John Galtung concludes that China's Cultural Revolution is *"perhaps the first antimeritocratic revolution in human history* to downgrade the professionals, to put them firmly together with the people, with the masses, by means of rotational schemes, completely new definitions of jobs. . . ."[44]

One reason for this participatory egalitarianism of contemporary China is Mao's deep-rooted populist faith in the people, particularly the peasants. As early as 1927 he wrote in his *Hunan Report:* "All revolutionary parties and all revolutionary comrades will stand before [the peasants] to be tested, and to be accepted or rejected as they decide."[45] To the present day the slogans most commonly encountered in China reflect this populist tone: "The people, and only the people, are the motive force in world history." "Merge with the masses." "Learn from the masses." "Become students of the masses."

Maoism unalterably opposes meritocratic elitism, considering it to be the antithesis of socialism and an insuperable obstacle to its realization. Whereas hereditary meritocracy is regarded in the Soviet Union as necessary for building an industrialized socialist society, in China it is rejected as the "revisionist" road to capitalism. Mao has gone further and warned that the issue between capitalism and socialism in China remains unresolved because the danger of regression to capitalism is ever-present. He recognizes that the development of a modern society requires the services of political experts (Party and state cadres) and of economic experts (managers, technicians, and scientists). For fear of following the Russian path toward a hereditary elite, the Chinese warn against "the private ownership of knowledge," which they consider to be a threat as great, if not greater, than the private ownership of the means of production and distribution. Hence the objective of the Cultural Revolution to make the expert also "red"—that is, a comrade who does manual work as well as physical, and who is devoted to serving the people rather than himself.

The basic operational strategy for realizing this populist objective is the "mass line," which was evolved during the 1940s in Yenan. In his essay *On Methods of Leadership* (1943), Mao summarized the meaning of the mass line:

> In all the practical work of our Party, all correct leadership is necessarily "from the masses, to the masses." This means: take the ideas of the masses (scattered and unsystematic ideas) and concentrate them (through study turn them into concentrated and systematic ideas), then go to the masses and propagate and explain these ideas until the masses embrace them as their own, hold fast to them, and translate them into action, and test the correctness of these ideas in such action. . . . And so on, over and over again in an endless spiral.

The mass line, then, is essentially a technique for narrowing the traditional gap between rulers and ruled. It seeks to maximize the input from below—from the masses—and to secure genuine response to that input from above—from the cadres, or trained personnel. This interaction between the masses and the cadres is a continuous process. No policy decision remains fixed once it is made. There is constant testing of its reception and effectiveness among the people, reformulation, retesting, reappraisal, reworking, and so on—the "endless spiral," as Mao put it.

With Mao's triumphant entry into Peking in 1949, the basic issue was whether the "Yenan Way" could be applied on a national scale as well as on a local scale, and in a society in the process of rapid industrialization as well as in a primitive frontier community. At times the answer appeared to be negative, particularly with the launching of Soviet-type Five Year Plans based on material incentives, marked discrepancies in income distribution, and a rising new mandarinate comprising technical experts, party officials, and state bureaucrats. During the 1950s Mao made repeated efforts to reverse this trend; the outstanding attempt was the Great Leap Forward in 1958, whose rallying cry was for everyone to be "red" as well as expert, in order to narrow the gap between the masses and the political-technical elites and to attain "organization without bureaucracy." Although successful in some of its undertakings, the Great Leap Forward generally failed to change the prevailing developmental pattern substantively. The resulting stress was aggravated by the "three bitter years" of natural disasters (1960–1962) and by the withdrawal of Soviet support in 1960.

At this point, as described in Chapter 4 (pages 74 to 80), Mao instituted the Cultural Revolution to reverse the prevailing trend and restore the principles and practices of the Yenan Way. Consequently, the China of today is altogether different from the China of the mid-1960s. The authoritarian and bureaucratic predispositions of the earlier period have been castigated in countless mass meetings as the abhorrent "revisionism" of the "capitalist roaders" striving to steer China onto the road of Soviet "state capitalism."

This Cultural Revolution was not an isolated, one-shot affair. Mao warned repeatedly that every revolution results in the emergence of a new technical-bureaucratic elite. The ever-present danger of revisionism should be guarded against in two ways: by introducing "counterinstitutions" to counter or restrain this inherent tendency toward regression, and by launching periodic Cultural Revolutions to eliminate whatever backsliding does occur. Both policies have been followed during the years since the first Cultural Revolution.

The counterinstitutions are ubiquitous and unique. In one way or another they mold the lives and thoughts of China's millions, and the one goal of this molding is to avoid the bureaucratic elitism that Max Weber and other Western intellectuals have assumed to be the unavoidable concomitant of modern technology. Let us look at some examples of these counterinstitutions.

One is economic egalitarianism, which allows only minimal, and essentially meaningless, income differential. Payment is not according to need, as the Communist principle dictates; income differential within a plant may be as much as five to one. But this differential signifies little, because basic needs—food, housing, medical care, and education—are available to all free of charge or very cheaply. The more highly paid workers who have a surplus after taking care of their basic expenses can buy very few extra commodities—a bicycle, wristwatch, sewing machine, radio, camera, and TV set. Once these are acquired, the limit has been reached in personal possessions. Surplus funds are deposited in the state bank, where they draw modest interest. Since basic necessities are in effect guaranteed, the chief satisfaction gained from having a bank account, and one that is often articulated, is that the money is available for national development. Conspicuous consumption is literally impossible, as well as socially unacceptable. "Keeping up with the Joneses" does exist in China, but the competition is in social service rather than in material wealth.

Another counterinstitution is an educational system (analyzed in Chapter 6, pages 155 to 161) that combats the "private ownership of knowledge." The "May 7 cadre schools" are farms established and run by cadres such as teachers, state administrators, and party functionaries. They work periodically on these farms for three- to six-month periods and sometimes longer. The basic objective, again, is to forestall the emergence of an intellectual aristocracy. The cadre members must do the hard labor necessary to maintain the farms, do supplementary work with peasants on neighboring communes (for the mutual education of peasants and cadre members), and engage in concentrated study of Marxism-Leninism-Maoism and of domestic and international developments in the light of this ideology.

Another example is the *Hsia fang* ("going down") principle, providing that those at the top must spend part of their time working at the bottom. This principle means that factory managers work on production lines, university professors clean dormitory rooms, hotel managers wait on tables, and surgeons clean operating rooms. As a specific example, the Huihsien County Committee of the Communist Party of China reports that, between 1969 and 1975, the first secretary of the Committee averaged 110 days of work per year in collective production, members of the standing committee of the County Party Committee 96 days, members of commune cadres 175 days, and members of brigade cadres 265 days.

Finally, two more counterinstitutional measures are the autonomy of the communes and the mass participation in internal commune affairs. One illustration of this autonomy was the decision to vest control of tractors and other machines in the communes rather than to follow the original Soviet model of giving this responsibility to government-operated Machine Tractor Stations. Likewise, the communes are now responsible for the financing and administration of elementary and secondary schools, ensuring that children will receive schooling geared to local production and research needs rather than that a handful are groomed for higher education. As for mass participation in the running of the commune, the Cultural Revolution has had a decisive influence, as reflected in the following statements. The first is by the chairman of a commune Revolutionary Committee; the second is by a commune teacher.

> Formerly, before the cultural revolution, I thought that the masses at Liu Ling were stupid. After all, I knew best what needed to be done. And I told them. . . . It was for their own good, I thought. After all, they didn't understand as much as we, their leaders, did. . . . During the Cultural Revolution I was much criticized for this. After the masses' criticism of me and others and after the great criticism against Liu Shao-ch'i I began to realize I'd been wrong in setting myself up above the masses. I became self-critical. . . . Now I don't try to

teach the masses lessons and tell them what they're to do. Now we take up problems at study meetings. And solve them there. This is a big change.

When all the pupils had learned to speak up and criticize in the right way, our discussions clarified what was right and what was wrong, and I explained why such or such a piece of criticism against me had been wrong. I showed them that it didn't agree with the facts. But I had not used my authority as a teacher and an adult to fight back at my pupils. And that was important. Only in that way could they develop. As a teacher I enjoy a sort of authority now different from that which I had before the Cultural Revolution. For now we are working toward other goals. We aren't chasing high marks or driving ourselves to trying to educate so-called "educated people." Now we learn from each other.[46]

In addition to the counterinstitutions, the Cultural Revolution of the 1960s has been followed, as Chairman Mao forecast, by a second Cultural Revolution that got under way in early 1974. Some observers have interpreted this new campaign as the by-product of a domestic struggle over the succession to Mao. Whatever the reason for this campaign, the nature of the charges leveled is revealing. On February 20, 1974, the official Communist Party paper, *Jenmin Jih Pao,* called on the people to struggle against "the restoration of certain new tendencies that the Cultural Revolution of 1966–69 sought to wipe out, such as an overly bureaucratic Party and narrow academic education." Other Chinese newspapers published numerous charges against army officers who got their sons into college "by the back door" and against Party officials who used their influence to save their children from being sent to remote rural communes for their labor service, where at least 8 million educated youths from the cities have had to go. Wall posters in Chinese factories once again denounced the "evil tendency" to offer overtime payments and other material incentives to workers rather than to depend on their sense of service to the community. Posters also appeared in Peking and other large cities urging public support for the fight against "hooliganism" ranging from petty theft to murder. According to Western reporters, these crimes are perpetrated by deserters from the ranks of the millions sent to work on the communes. Some of these youngsters refuse to accept the physical hardships of the countryside and resent what they consider to be the waste of their education on primitive agricultural tasks. So they flee to Hong Kong or to any other accessible large city. But there, because they lack the money and coupons necessary to purchase fuel, cooking oil, meat, and other necessities, they resort to the crimes now being reported in the press.

"Both Centralism and Democracy"

The Constitution of the Communist Party of China, adopted by the Tenth National Congress on August 28, 1973, states unequivocally that "The organizational principle of the Party is democratic centralism. . . . It is essential to create a political situation in which there are both centralism and democracy, both discipline and freedom, both unity of will and personal ease of mind and liveliness" (Chapter III, Article 5). This statement brings to mind the Soviet Union, where "democratic centralism" has been the proclaimed watchword from the beginning, but where the "democratic" component has long since been forsaken, in practice if not in rhetoric. The question is therefore what democratic centralism means in China in practice.

On paper, Mao spelled out in a January 1962 speech on democratic centralism why the word "democratic" is as essential as the word "centralism."

> When opinions do not originate from the masses, it is impossible to formulate good lines and guiding principles, and policies and methods. In terms of formulating lines, guiding principles, policies and methods, our leading organs are merely a processing plant. As everybody knows, a plant cannot process anything without raw materials. . . . When democracy is absent there is a lack of comprehension of the situation and objective conditions; there is an insufficient collection of opinions from all parties; upper and lower levels do not communicate; and higher level leading organs make decisions on problems based on unilateral or false information.[47]

Likewise, Wang Hung-wen, who emerged at the Tenth Congress as the third-ranking party official after Chairman Mao and Premier Chou En-lai, stated flatly at the Congress that the remnants of "commandism" in the party must be eliminated.

> There are still a small number of cadres, especially some leading cadres, who will not tolerate differing views of the masses inside or outside the Party. They even suppress criticism and retaliate, and it is quite serious in some individual cases. In handling problems among

the people, Party discipline absolutely forbids such wrong practices as resorting to suppression if unable to persuade, and arrest if unable to suppress. . . . We must have faith in the masses, rely on them, constantly use the weapons of arousing the masses to air their views freely, write big-character posters and hold great debates.[48]

Turning from theory to reality, the issues are less simple and clear-cut. On the one hand, there is ample evidence of the "faith in the masses" demanded by Wang. Self-management is operative in the day-to-day affairs of the communes, where the great majority of the people live. Workers' participation is encouraged in the factories through a variety of institutions and practices. The main thrust in education is to give control of the schools to the local communities so that teachers and curricula will be responsive to local needs. At the grass-roots level, the Communist Party follows Wang's injunction by giving veto power to non-Party mass meetings regarding applications for Party membership and by facilitating popular criticism of Party and state officials. And the new constitution adopted in January 1975 by the Fourth National People's Congress confers the right to petition for redress of grievances (Article 27) and to enjoy freedom of speech, press, and assembly and the right to strike (Article 28). Article 13 provides for the application of these rights in the conduct of public affaris: "Speaking out freely, . . . holding great debates, and writing big-character posters are now forms of carrying on Socialist revolution created by the masses of the people. The state shall insure to the masses the right to use these forms to create a political situation in which there are both centralism and democracy. . . ." "So far as we could tell," concludes Professor Thomas I. Emerson of the Yale Law School, following a visit to China, "these rights of free expression were meant to be observed and are in fact exercised."[49]

On the other hand, there is also ample evidence of stringent controls, both internal and external, on the Chinese people. The internal controls are the result of the unprecedented amount of "political education" being administered. It certainly has not produced robots, for its purpose is the exact opposite, yet popular reactions in China today do suggest "the merciless masochism of community-minded and self-regulating men and women."[50] Although a few of these men and women kick over the traces and flee from the communes, the great majority internalize the values and goals propounded in their political education. For example, a mother may yearn for more free time to spend with her growing children. She is likely to express this natural feeling to her fellow workers, and together, in a self-criticism session, and after many references to Mao, they will analyze the feeling in its social context. They will probably agree that it is understandable for the mother to want to spend more time with her family. But by remaining on her job, and thereby contributing to the community, she is "serving the people," including her own children.

Obviously, the mother is paying a price for this internalization of Maoist values and goals. These goals, and their effects on people's lives, are somewhat akin to the Protestant ethic. Chairman Mao, not unlike Benjamin Franklin, calls for hard work, frugality, responsibility, and self-reliance. But the crucial difference is in the end objective—community welfare in the one case and personal advancement in the other.

In addition, the dictatorship of the proletariat, proclaimed in the 1975 Constitution, "suppresses and punishes all treasonable and counterrevolutionary activities" (Article 14). The terms "treasonable" and "counterrevolutionary" are interpreted broadly to include differences over basic policies. The functioning of this dictatorship of the proletariat is manifest throughout Chinese society. When a Liu Shao-chi or a Lin Piao falls from grace, he promptly becomes a nonperson. History is rewritten, photographs withdrawn, and slogans reordered. Phrases such as "renegade," "scab," "capitulatist," and "hidden traitor," used to refer to those who once were second only to Mao, are grating to Western ears—as much for their orchestrated uniformity as for their stridency. Wang's "faith in the masses" and toleration of "differing views of the masses" is applicable only within the parameters of the current Party line. Differing views are definitely not allowable should they be those of a nonperson. Then they become dissent, and those who persist in holding such views are castigated as "revisionists" and subjected to "reeducation" until they have seen the error of their ways. Should they be so obstinate as to resist reeducation or attempt to propagate their revisionism, they are sent off to jail.

The Chinese do rely more on reeducation than on the exiling and incarceration (in mental asylums as well as prisons) that the Russians favor, but in the final analysis all of these coercive methods arise from the same insistence on the dictatorship of the proletariat. Dictatorship of the proletariat is evident in matters intellectual as well as political, and the functioning of Peking University after the Cultural Revolution is a good example. Like every institution in China—whether hospital, factory, commune, or hotel—Peking University is run by an elected Revolutionary Committee. In 1972 the committee comprised 39 members: six from neighboring factories, six "cadres" or university administrators, nine "staff" or faculty, seven students, three "university workers" or maintenance personnel, seven

People's Liberation Army soldiers, and one faculty housewife. The Revolutionary Committee had a Standing Committee of 13, and in addition the Communists associated with the university elected their Communist Party Committee of 15. In general, the Revolutionary Committee and its Standing Committee are responsible for administrative matters, whereas the Party Committee is responsible for political indoctrination and for the application of the Party line. It is the Party Committee that determines the guidelines or slogans for each university department. In the spring of 1972 the History Department had been assigned the task of combating "the hero theory of history," the Political Science Department was to "repudiate the three appeasements" (revisionism, imperialism, and reactionism), and the Philosophy Department was to "reject idealism."

The question arises of what these academicians and other intellectuals would be doing now if Mao had not prevailed against his opposition. Recall that after the failure of the Great Leap Forward Mao had few supporters in the top levels of his own revolutionary government. "At that time most people disagreed with me," he observed later. "Sometimes I was alone. They said my views were out of date. . . . It appeared quite probable that revisionism would triumph, and that we would lose."[51]

Because Mao did not lose, the Peking University historians now are fighting the hero theory and the philosophers are repudiating idealism. But if Mao had lost, as he thought he might, the Party directives being handed down to them would be altogether different. How could they challenge those directives? How could they defy those who now are castigated as "revisionists" and "capitalist roaders"? Would not China then—and might not China sometime in the future—be vulnerable to unchallengeable dogmas such as those of Lysenko, which did so much harm to Soviet science and agriculture?

For this reason, Western intellectuals tend to have more reservations about Maoist China than do Western financiers, such as David Rockefeller, who note the economic progress, or Western journalists, such as James Reston and Joseph Alsop, who report the national cohesion and buoyancy. Western intellectuals question the nature and meaning of the mass line, especially because of the travesty of "democratic centralism" in the Soviet Union.

Accordingly, one of their reactions is to dismiss the mass line as something really nonexistent—that is, merely a rationalization designed to mask Communist Party manipulation from above with feigned attention to opinions and initiatives from below. This assumption of deliberate deception is difficult to accept, given the circumstances of the mass line's origins and evolution during the Yenan years, as well as the *raison d'être* of the Cultural Revolution, which was essentially the restoration and further development of the mass line.

A second Western reaction is to accept the sincerity of Maoist rhetoric concerning the objective and practice of the mass line but to insist that in the final analysis manipulation, rather than participation, is decisive. The mass line, after all, explicitly requires leaders to be leaders rather than simply carry out the expressed wishes of the people. "It sometimes happens," writes Mao, "that the masses objectively need some reform but are not yet subjectively awakened to it and willing or determined to bring it into effect."[52] The duty of the party leaders is to "awaken" the masses to the need for the "reform" of which they are not yet aware. "Our comrades who are engaged in practical work," states Mao, "must realize that their knowledge is mostly perceptual and partial and that they lack rational and comprehensive knowledge." Since the leaders do possess such knowledge, they must assume the task of "synthesizing the experience of the masses into better articulated principles and methods."[53]

These formulations can be taken to prove that Mao's mass line is, at bottom, mass manipulation—regardless of the sincerity of his populist insistence that leaders must be the pupils of the masses in order to lead effectively. An alternative conclusion is that these formulations reveal how thin the line is between manipulation and participation. The Soviet experience demonstrates that democratic centralism can indeed be simply manipulation from the center or, if necessary, outright coercion. But the Chinese experience demonstrates equally that the mass line can be a creative synthesis of the "mass" component from below and of the "line" directive from above.

Mass line is being implemented in practice as well as in theory if there is constant and purposefully lubricated interaction from top to bottom and bottom to top, if the mass line is based on what is learned from this interaction, if feedback concerning the application and results of the mass line is uninhibited, and if there is adjustment or even reversal of the line on the basis of the feedback. It can be reasonably deduced that these conditions do prevail in China and explain the successes to date. "Is it conceivable," concludes Richard M. Pfeffer, "that the Chinese Communists won because they really did 'serve the people' in different ways, during different periods, and at different places? . . . [Because] they had developed to maturity certain institutions, styles, concerns and commitments that encouraged the leadership to learn from the rural masses of the concrete problems they faced and stimulated the movement to serve the needs of the rural masses and gain their support."[54]

A third Western reaction to the mass line is to concede that it is viable now but to question its continued viability in the future. What will happen if Mao's successors are not committed to the principles of the Cultural Revolution? And will the Chinese people be able "to maintain an unremitting Revival atmosphere . . . to view life as permanent, unremitting struggle?"[55] The possibility of regression after Mao dies is, of course, fully recognized and continually warned against. Hence the elaborate precautions noted above—the variety of counterinstitutions and the unceasing ideological indoctrination designed to forestall moral backsliding. As for the strain of the "unremitting Revival atmosphere," it is noteworthy that Western critics rarely consider the possibility of a gradual internalization of moral values oriented toward community welfare rather than personal gain. Western scientists agree that human nature is a "vast potentiality" and that nothing in our genetic makeup compels us to strive for personal power or riches regardless of the consequences for the community. It follows that, if social values, institutions, status systems, and material rewards are all oriented toward realizing human potentiality for social service rather than personal aggrandizement, in time it will be the former rather than the latter that will come to be considered natural and in accord with human nature. In this case life would not need to be a "permanent, unremitting struggle"—at least not a struggle between personal and social interests and values.

In any case, China today is set on a course dramatically different from that of most of the world. The crucial question, which cannot be answered now, is whether Maoism will survive Mao. If the answer proves negative, revisionism will emerge and China will follow in the wake of Russia. But if Maoism prevails, China will profoundly influence future global trends, not as a blueprint for others to copy but as a precedent indicating what is possible for human society.

6

FROM SELF-SUBORDINATION TO SELF-ACTUALIZATION

We shall once more value ends above means and prefer the good to the useful. We shall honour those who teach us how to pluck the hour and the day virtuously and well, the delightful people who are capable of taking direct enjoyment in things.

—John Maynard Keynes

Beyond the Age of Pericles

The spirit of self-management is manifest not only in the workplace and in the political arena but also in people's minds—in their perceptions of themselves and of their relations with others. They are groping away from self-subordination to authority and toward self-actualization. This trend is not unexpected, for the current Second Industrial Revolution is enabling man to cast off his age-old shackles of poverty and to gain security and self-confidence. The casting off of economic shackles facilitates the casting off of psychological shackles as well—the shackles of age-old acceptance of poverty and exploitation as the divinely ordained and unavoidable fate of man.

The significance of this liberation can be explained most clearly in terms of the hierarchy of human needs defined by the psychologist Abraham H. Maslow. These needs begin with the basic physiological needs (food, water, sex) and work up to the need for "self-actualization," or the realization of one's full potential. In the past the great majority of mankind could think only of satisfying primary needs, and only a privileged few had the opportunity for self-actualization. Today this opportunity is being extended from the few to the many, thanks to the liberating potential of technology and of the accompanying participatory impulse. "I am just as convinced as can be," states the geochemist Harrison Brown, "that man today has much more power than he realizes. I am convinced that man has it within his power today to create a world in which people the world over can lead free and abundant and even creative lives. . . . I am convinced that we can create a world which will pale the Golden Age of Pericles into nothingness."[1]

The Golden Age that Harrison Brown foresees remains, of course, only a hope for the future. The brutal fact is that in the real world of today more people are sick and starving than at any time in the past. Yet is is also a fact today that for the first time the people of the world know that misery is not their inescapable fate. They know from radios blaring in village squares and in city streets that modern science does offer a way out, and that in some societies the traditional scourges of mankind no longer afflict the great majority of ordinary citizens. Once these revolutionary facts have been grasped, old allegiances and constraints are undermined, and sooner or later, by one means or another, the climb upward begins—from satisfying basic needs to fulfilling individual potential.

On the other hand, the experience of affluent societies suggests that, even when the benefits of the Second Industrial Revolution are evenly distributed and made generally available, escalation up Maslow's ladder need not be automatic. Potential does not mean realization—in psychological matters any more than in material matters. The rampant consumerism in the United States, which has spread to Western Europe and Japan since World War II, suggests that in consumer-oriented societies the satisfaction of basic material needs stimulates more material desires rather than a striving for self-actualization. Thus Erich Fromm sees man reduced to "an appendage of the machine" and transformed "into *Homo consumens,* the total consumer, whose only aim is to have more and to use more."[2]

Self-gratification undeniably is the prevailing trend in the affluent countries, but it does not follow that this trend is irreversible. Unbridled consumerism is by its very nature a transitory, self-destructive phenomenon. It is self-destructive because an ever-growing GNP means accelerating depletion of natural resources and deterioration of the physical environment. "The goal of a happy, high-consumption world," states the scientist Peter Medawar, "cannot be fulfilled even for the 3.5 billion people now alive, much less the 6 billion expected by the year 2000. At the American standard of living, the Earth could support only 500 million."[3]

A consumer-oriented society is self-destructive psychologically as well as ecologically. The comforts and gadgets of technology are intriguing and satisfying, but only in the short run. Eventually the satiated consumer becomes bored and frustrated, and yearns for something more creative than mere satisfaction of artificially stimulated material desires. This phenomenon is seen among all classes. The auto workers at General Motors' Lordstown Vega plant struck against their dehumanizing assembly-line jobs despite the relatively high pay; the idle rich who have everything money can buy are often nevertheless desperately unhappy. An example of the latter can be seen in the following news item concerning life in the wealthy Florida city of Boca Raton, "a splendid community, a real garden spot." Dr. Elizabeth Faulk, a clinical psychologist with an office across the street from a string of expensive condominiums, testifies of the human misery amid purposeless affluence: "The trouble is that so many of the wealthy fail to get involved with anything more than rich food, alcohol, and golf. Most of the patients I see here are depressed, psychosomatic and impotent. . . . They are flocking to doctors to escape from their loneliness. They are bored with themselves."[4]

It may be argued that a consumer society could be preserved indefinitely through vigilant indoctrination and by taking adequate precautions against outright ecological disaster. Certainly, past civilizations along the banks of the Nile, Indus, and Tigris-Euphrates rivers dragged on for millenia past their prime despite their manifest decadence. But they were able to do so because their isolation allowed them to stagnate with little danger of outside intervention. Today no civilization can do so, for an unprecedented range of diverse social systems are competing within a rapidly shrinking world. Under these circumstances, any innovation in one country that copes successfully with any of the problems plaguing modern man exerts an irresistible influence on all other societies, whether open or closed. Likewise, it is impossible for injustice to exist within one nation without international effect: "I can say with conviction," declared Alexander Solzhenitsyn, "that a return to [a Stalinist] regime is impossible in our country. The most important reason for this lies in the flow of international information, the infiltration and influence, in spite of everything, of ideas, facts, and human protest."[5]

These are the reasons why the current worldwide ferment is not confined to the desire for the satisfaction of material needs. It also involves new images of society and of man. In the West, Lewis Mumford foresees the "new person," while in Russia and China the resources of society are mobilized for the realization of the "new Soviet man" and the "new Maoist man."

The New Western Man

The pluralistic Western societies do not enjoy the disciplined unanimity of the Communist societies regarding goals and methods. This is especially true in the United States, where violent dissension has prevailed in recent years regarding almost every question concerning national values and policies. But the roots of this dissension go back to the origins of the republic. The origins were indubitably revolutionary and egalitarian, as is evident in the history of the American Revolution itself and in the stirring rhetoric of the Declaration of Independence: "All men are created equal"; the "unalienable rights" of man are "Life, Liberty, and the Pursuit of Happiness"; "Whenever any form of government becomes destructive to these ends, it is the right of the people to alter it or abolish it. . . . " Yet at the same time, one of the great leaders of the American Revolution, Alexander Hamilton, openly expressed his scorn for "the people" exalted in the Declaration of Independence. "Your people," he declared, "is a great beast." And so Hamilton devoted his formidable talents to promoting the interests of the landed families, shipowners, manufacturers, and financiers of America.

Hamilton was by no means alone in his support of property and its owners. What he stood for has remained a major force in American society to this day. The perceptive Alexis de Tocqueville noted in 1835 in his *Democracy in America,* "I know of no country, indeed, where the love of money has taken stronger hold on the affections of men, and where a profounder contempt is expressed for the theory of permanent equality of property." A few decades later Mark Twain similarly observed that money was the established religion of America: "What is the chief end of man?—to get rich. In what way?—dishonestly if we can; honestly if we must. Who is God, the only one and true? Money is God." America's humorists today see their country in the same light. Witness Lennie Bruce's quip: "It's time to grow up and sell out."

And yet the revolutionary and egalitarian spirit of 1776, although usually overshadowed and unfavored, remained a constant countervailing force in the country of its birth. It found expression in the works of Ralph Waldo Emerson and Henry David Thoreau, who personified the moral insurrection of mid-nineteenth-century America and prefigured the moral insurrection of the present. Emerson warned against American civilization's becoming "essentially one of property, of fences, of exclusiveness," while Thoreau advocated civil disobedience against such a civilization. "How does it become a man to behave toward this American government today? I answer that he cannot without disgrace be associated with it. . . . If the injustice . . . is of such a nature that it requires you to be the agent of injustice to another, then, I say, break the law. Let your life be a counter friction to stop the machine. . . . "

This spirit of resistance against institutionalized injustice is still very much alive in America today, as was demonstrated during the 1960s and 1970s by the civil-rights movement, the anti-Vietnam War movement, the McCarthy and McGovern presidential campaigns, and some of the undertakings of the New Left. The common thread running through these efforts was the basic demand for self-actualization, as articulated in the contemporary student slogan "We don't want to have more; we want to be more." Although the demand for self-actualization is expressed most vocally and explicitly by students, it is at least implicit in the current aspirations of minorities, women, workers, and other elements of American society.

Minorities, for example, constitute over one-third of America's total population; they comprise roughly 40 million "ethnics" (foreign-born and first-, second-, and third-generation Americans of European ancestry), 23 million blacks, 9 million Spanish speakers, 1 million Indians, and others. These groups are discovering increasing pride in themselves and in their heritages, and they increasingly reject assimilation into the traditional melting pot. They seek more opportunity for self-actualization as members of their race or ethnic group in order to be able to make their individual contributions. Not only is black beautiful in contemporary America, but so are brown and red.

This new emphasis on color in turn has stimulated another minority group, the white ethnic Americans, who see themselves as "the most ignored group in America." They feel trapped in a crossfire between (1) working class blacks and Spanish speakers, who demand a share of political and economic power, and (2) upper class white Anglo-Saxon Protestants, who refuse to yield their privileges. This predicament has driven the ethnics to the outbursts against busing and neighborhood desegregation that have attracted nationwide publicity. But there is also a small minority among the ethnics who see the solution to their predicament in cooperation rather than confrontation with the blacks and Spanish speakers. "When we get the Polish Women's Alliance, its Greek equivalent, its black equivalent, and every other ethnic minority all together," declares the Baltimore community organizer Barbara Mikulski, "think what kind of a march on Washington that would be. It's going to shake Congress so they won't know what hit them. That's what's going to reorder national priorities."[6]

Women are a "minority" group, actually 52 percent of the population, who are increasingly rejecting the traditional life pattern by which they have served first as somebody's daughter, then as somebody's wife, and finally as somebody's mother. Many are challenging this self-sacrificial,

Madonna-like role, especially in the Western world, where women now enjoy in varying degrees more opportunities for higher education, more legal protection against sex discrimination, and the personal freedom afforded by new birth-control methods. These opportunities are encouraging women to make demands for equal rights, child-care centers, and unrestricted abortion. The radicals in the women's liberation movement go much further, seeking through "consciousness-raising" sessions to arouse women to fight against self-deprecation, to view themselves as human beings rather than sex objects or advertising targets, and to struggle for basic changes in society's institutions. Educated middle-class women have traditionally been the most active in the liberation movement, but since the 1960s they have been joined by increasing numbers of working-class women. Whereas working-class women formerly tended to report that they found security and emotional satisfaction in husband, children, and home, a 1973 study showed that increasing numbers hold jobs or are active in PTA, volunteer work, and recreational groups. Almost a third of those surveyed said that they would not choose homemaking as a career if they could go back to being 15 years old. "From their own personal experience, the women know life can be improved and upgraded, and they don't want to stop."[7]

Some American fathers, as well, are striving for their own liberation. Many have decided that a man has as much responsibility as a woman for raising children; that nurturing is as natural for a man as for a woman; that paternal deprivation, as well as maternal, can be injurious to children; consequently, some believe that fathers as well as mothers should accept only part-time jobs so that both may function as homemakers. In 1974 some 200 of New York City's 28,500 male teachers secured unpaid paternity leave to devote more time to the care of their children.

Some workers are finding the absence of self-management in the workplace just as intolerable as its absence in the political arena, and therefore are concerned with more than how many hours they work and for how much per hour. One such worker is Nora Watson, a writer for an institution that publishes health-care literature, who told interviewer Studs Terkel: "This is what all of us are looking for: a calling, not just a job. Most of us, like the assembly line worker, have jobs that are too small for our spirit. Jobs are not big enough for people."[8]

Some clergymen, such as the Jesuit priest Philip Berrigan, hold that "to be either human or Christian or both, man *must* be a revolutionary." Berrigan accordingly invited arrest by destroying draft cards and served a prison sentence. Other members of the clergy—nuns, ministers, priests, rabbis—are questioning hierarchical dictation on issues such as divorce, birth control, celibacy, and political involvement; they have either dropped out or remained within the fold to challenge established policies or to concentrate on community work.

Finally, the outcasts of American society—those who depend on public aid and for that reason are looked down upon as lazy, shiftless, and undeserving—are also asserting themselves and demanding certain rights as citizens and as human beings. Their National Welfare Rights Organization seeks to build a coalition with other low-income groups—low-salaried workers, women, senior citizens—around the "common cause of need in the world's richest nation." Likewise, disabled Americans have organized groups to demand transportation and physical access to public places, as well as equal opportunity for employment.

This all-pervasive ferment is impelled in the final analysis by the self-actualization ethic, with its primary emphasis on the development of the individual. Social scientists at the Stanford Research Institute[9] interpret this trend as the opening of a new American frontier. Whereas the first frontier was open land, and the second industry and technology, this new third frontier is one of individual and social change—the realization of personal and collective human potential. To hasten this realization is the objective of Assemblyman John Vasconcellos of California in launching in 1975 what he terms "Self-Determination: A Personal-Political Network."

> We're at once committed to our own evolution as persons *and* to working for political change to humanize our society and institutions. We believe humanistic politics is the best way to live our commitment. . . . Humanistic politics explicitly challenges that self-denying, self-defeating traditional culture which is no longer enough for many of us, nor for life itself. It offers instead a self-actualizing, self-realizing vision. . . . Already in California many persons are into personal growth, and many are into political change. We want to converge/fuse those two—by a humanistic politics that makes explicit the connection that inherently exists between these two processes—so that the persons involved in each may share the persons and resources of the other. . . . We intend our network to operate especially at the grassroots/community level, but also statewide. Its purpose and effort will be to legitimate and intrude into the political dialogue—at every level and place and person where politics is done in California—a platform of the fundamental questions about being human, about the human condition, about self-determination.

More is being written and said about self-actualization in the United States than in any other Western country, but the people of some of the smaller and more homogeneous nations of Western Europe may be closer to its actual realization. Holland, for example, is a country whose citizens enjoy economic well-being, stable and democratic political institutions, and a highly developed social-welfare system. Consequently, they have reached a new level of discontent and questioning and are consciously groping toward the self-actualization now within their reach. "No one goes hungry," says W. A. Wamsteeker, secretary of the executive board of the largest trade-union federation. "When you reach that state, the interest in non-material things grows." In the same vein, Housing Minister Hans Gruyters observes "We have always proclaimed high ideals. Now one has the feeling that the ideals can be realized." Among these ideals, as verbalized in the early 1970s by numerous political-action groups, were environmental protection, more equal distribution of wealth, opposition to American intervention in Indochina and to the Portuguese colonial wars in Africa, better housing, and a more participatory and less centralized political democracy at home. The participatory impulse is manifest throughout Dutch society. Wamsteeker describes its impact on the labor unions:

> Until the last few years contracts were decided by three people—a representative from the union federation, a management man, and someone from the Ministry of Social Affairs. After that there were membership meetings, but the issue was decided. In theory the members had a say, in effect not. Now the union officials like myself are mere advisers of the membership, not leaders. This is more difficult, but much better.
>
> Consistent with the new mood, labor's concerns go far beyond wages, hours and working conditions. It demands of both government and the employers the right to share in industrial decisions and insists that the decisions be made for the benefit of society.[10]

Sweden is another country where Lewis Mumford's "new person" is more than a rhetorical phrase. This nation, the wealthiest on earth (figured in per capita gross national product), supports a cradle-to-grave welfare system. About 90 percent of the population votes in elections in which three major parties compete. Recent legislation provides that two employee representatives be named to all corporate boards of directors and empowers local safety ombudsmen (ordinary workers specially trained in safety) to order the shutting down of unsafe or unhealthy operations. Also in the wind is legislation for a six-hour working day that would give working mothers and fathers more time with their children.

Citizen groups, unions, and government bodies have been involved for some time in a sex-role debate. The purpose is to decrease women's vulnerability to exploitation by their families and employers. Schools and teachers are seeking to minimize the traditional distinction between "man's work" and "woman's work." All children, regardless of sex, are taught manual work and given household training. Between the ages of 7 and 10, boys and girls learn together how to sew and do woodworking; between 10 and 12, to cook and to keep a family budget; between 15 and 16, to care for young children. As a result, adolescent boys in Sweden do not feel their self-esteem threatened by learning how to change diapers. A recent survey disclosed that 92 percent do not consider it "unmanly" to take training in housework and child care.

Prime Minister Olaf Palme's views concerning Sweden's values and policies reflect the serious thought his society gives to gross social product as well as gross national product—quality of life as well as quantity of goods. The following statements were made by Palme during an interview with an American correspondent:

> We are past the stage of waste-makers. We've reached a point where people can question the value of gadgets, where people can see that consumption is not a goal in itself. We are at a point where a change in life styles is essential.
>
> It's all a question of how you organize society. If society decides that human needs should be given priority—to improve care for elderly or handicapped or sick or children—then these needs can be fulfilled by expanding public services. By doing this you create new jobs, and you don't need great amounts of energy or natural resources. You create growth by providing human services rather than by building plastic gadgets. . . . I'll give you an example. In our recent budget proposal there was an increase of some 100 million kroner ($22 million) for creating some 7,000 new *hemsamarit* jobs. These are "home samaritans"—women (or men) trained to help elderly or ill or shut-ins with household tasks. These home samaritans would be able to help some 30,000 to 40,000 people. This is a very valuable service; it creates contact among people. . . .
>
> All the time you have a number of choices. If the aggregate benefits to society clearly show that you should invest in social benefits, such as home samaritans, rather than in plastic gadgets, then you take that choice.

I'd say [Sweden] will be the first country to try to cure the hangover of industrial society. We've made tremendous advances in production and in raising the standard of living.

But slowly people are learning the price they pay for progress: there are gaps between groups of people, there is dissatisfaction with industrial life as it is. A lot of crackpot theories are offered as solutions: conservatism, or back to nature, or revolution. This leads nowhere; it only aggravates a clash. What we must do is see what we can do about renewing production to make work meaningful, to increase equality, improve environment, and to try to create a new, gentle society . . . we need a gentle society when it comes to relations between people. Don't ask what you can do for yourself, but ask what you can do for your fellow man.[11]

The New Soviet Man

The original dream of Marx and Lenin of creating a new socialist man along with a new socialist society has had a sad outcome. Below are two complaints that could have been made in any American city. The first was made by a Moscow cab driver to his Western passenger:

The cheating's wrong, I know that. I hate it and I'd gladly stop it. I want to stop. But it would make no sense now. I cheat because everyone else does. The . . . high-ups live like kings—on the people's money. Factory directors take a share of their plant's profits. Foremen take wage "kick-backs," workers smuggle out what raw materials they can under their coats, shop assistants water the wine. And we drivers fiddle the meter. That's the way it is. You know the proverb . . . When in Rome, do as the Romans do. . . . Cheating's the thing to do. The boss of my taxi park has made a fortune selling gasoline and spare parts, and all the shift supervisors take their cuts too. Spare tires on the black market, batteries and things. Why should I be a martyr? I would if it would help, but it wouldn't change a single thing.[12]

The second is from a report by the Secretary of the Central Committee of the Lithuanian Communist Party:

It is no secret that, with the higher material standard of living, many families seek to protect their children from any kind of work. Then we are surprised when families of good and industrious people rear softies, people with no sense of responsibility. It is gratifying that

today children do not have to undergo the poverty and misfortune
that many people of our generation experienced. But it is bad that the
content of their lives becomes idleness and the search for casual ad-
ventures and friends. . . . It is necessary to take a more decisive
stand against the frame of mind in which young people demand only
rights and privileges of various kinds for themselves but have no sense
of duty and refuse to give anything to society. . . . Long-haired
sloppy individuals who no longer look like human beings. . . .[13]

As far back as 1850, Karl Marx exhorted workers to struggle "not
only in order to transform the social system, but in order also to transform
yourselves."[14] Likewise, a 1919 Bolshevik publication, *The ABC of Communism,* asserted: "Within a few decades there will be quite a new world,
with new people and new customs."[15] But Lenin himself, before his death
in 1924, reflected ruefully that his Soviet society was socialist more in appearance than in substance—"a bourgeois, tsarist mechanism with only a
Soviet veneer." If a resurrected Lenin were to look about in the Soviet
Union today, he would see little to lead him to a different conclusion. A
Soviet journalist pinpointed the key issue when he commented to his Western colleagues that Russia's basic problem was not the shortage of consumer
goods, which the Westerners were stressing in their reports, but rather the
meshchanstvo of Soviet society.[16] By this he meant the growth of middle-
class values, the cultivation of self-serving private concerns, and the con-
notation of the word "they," used by the Russian man-in-the-street to refer
to Party and state leaders as though they were strangers from another
planet. Such a society is, of course, the complete antithesis of the new society envisaged by Marx in the mid-nineteenth century and by the Bolsheviks
in 1917.

This regression is particularly ironic in view of the fact that, as noted
in the preceding chapter, Soviet economic and military achievements have
been outstanding. The underdeveloped czarist Russia of the nineteenth
century has been transformed into a superpower of the twentieth, and the
living standards and cultural attainments of the Russian people have risen
correspondingly. Yet despite these impressive advances, the USSR is no
longer regarded by citizens of either the West or the Third World as a
beacon for the future. Today the Russian Revolution is played out.

A basic reason is the shift from egalitarianism to meritocracy that
occurred early in the evolution of Soviet society. It began with the 1921
New Economic Policy (NEP), which legalized private enterprise and
profit in small-scale production and exchange, as well as in agriculture.

Lenin was quite aware that this new policy represented a retreat, and he always referred to the NEP as such. The ensuing Five Year Plans did improve the lot of the peasants by wiping out the "nepmen" (petty capitalists) and the *kulaks* (rich peasants who exploitèd other peasants), but they did not establish the egalitarianism envisaged in Marxist theory. On the contrary, the Five Year Plans made necessary the purposeful adoption of a system of wage differentials in order to attract scarce technical experts and to provide material incentives for workers. With the influx of droves of peasant boys and girls into industry during the early Plan years, veteran factory workers came to resent receiving the same flat weekly wage that the much less productive newcomers received. Hence the introduction of a piece-work system of remuneration providing for progressively higher pay for output above an established norm. Similar considerations led to the abandonment of the "Party Maximum" rule, by which Communist Party members, regardless of their rank or responsibility, could not receive higher pay than workers. As the Plans progressed and thousands of workers received technical training, those who joined the Party, with all the extra duties that this involved, found that they were receiving one-half to one-quarter of the pay of their fellows who had not joined. The ensuing protests resulted in the rejection of the "Party Maximum" rule along with the flat-rate wage.

Meanwhile, this switch to wage differentials was spreading from the shop floor to management, white-collar, and professional work. Since workers were paid according to piece work, managers were often receiving less than their subordinates, and able men were consequently refusing promotion to management. Bonuses were therefore introduced, to be awarded either to individual managers or to collectives on the basis of performance.

By 1931 Stalin was denouncing *uravnilovka*, or "equality-mongering," as a "petty bourgeois" deviation, and the wage differential of highly skilled to unskilled workers had reached 3.7 to 1. Furthermore, income taxes were drastically reduced and the inheritance tax virtually eliminated. Khrushchev followed this course in strongly repudiating proposals for wage leveling during the Twenty-Second Party Congress in 1961. "Such proposals are profoundly erroneous. Embarking upon such a road would be tantamount to undermining the material stimulus to raise labor productivity and put a brake upon the construction of communism."

Along with income differentiation came special privileges for the bureaucracy. Party officials were provided with their own hospitals, free rest homes, *dachas* (country houses), and special stores that supplied them (and still do) with low-priced luxuries not available elsewhere. From possession of such privileges it was only a short step to outright corruption. The dissident Soviet historian Roy Medvedev describes the process of degeneration.

> The small circle of high officials was protected by the creation of a system of special stores, distributing centers, and dining rooms, where goods could be obtained at fixed prices. Gradually they acquired other privileges too. . . . In the same period [1930s] a peculiar habit began to appear: the Party *aktiv* were given expensive gifts for holidays, congresses, and conferences. . . . Many officials increased their salaries even more through a system of pluralism; that is, one man held several offices, receiving full pay for each. . . . During the war [World War II] and the first postwar years . . . the disgraceful system of "packets" (*pakety*) was introduced in the higher state and Party institutions. Each month almost every high official would receive an envelope or packet containing a large sum, often much higher than the salary formally designated for his post. These payments passed through special financial channels, were not subject to taxes, and were kept secret from the rank-and-file officials of the institution. Some Communists found the courage to refuse these packets. E. P. Frolov tells how M. D. Kammari, an editor of the journal *Kommunist*, never went to get his packets from the bookkeeper's office, which put the head bookkeeper in a difficult position. "I don't need so much money," Kammari used to say. "My salary is enough for me." But he had few imitators among his colleagues. On the contrary, many of them began to look at him suspiciously, regarding his behavior as a challenge and a protest.[17]

Does this mean that the U.S.S.R. is becoming a class society? Not at all, insist Soviet spokesmen—because class division is rooted in the ownership of productive property, and since such ownership does not exist in the Soviet Union there can be no classes. Many Western scholars assert that, on the contrary, classes have emerged—simply as a product of the dynamics of modern industrialism, which requires certain reward structures regardless of the political ideology of the industrialized society. The same conclusion is reached by dissident Marxists, although their reasoning is that a new exploitative class has risen that does not own property but that does control the allocation of goods and services, with end results similar to those under capitalism.

Whatever term is used to describe Soviet social relationships, certain facts seem reasonably clear. One is that a hierarchy of both reward and status does exist in the Soviet Union. At the top of the pyramid are the leading Party and state officials. Their salaries are unknown but are irrelevant in any case, since their life-style depends not on income but on the privileges of office. They lead cushioned lives, attended by servants and chauffeurs, housed in grand style in city and country homes, consuming the finest native and imported foods and liquors—all on a level that matches the life-style of their counterparts in Western governments and corporations.

Below them a pecking order exists; the most prestigious workers are the white-collar intelligentsia filling the professional, managerial, and administrative positions, and then following in descending order come the skilled manual workers, unskilled white-collar workers, and unskilled laborers. This hierarchical structure has engendered in the U.S.S.R. an elitist status-consciousness and a contemptuous attitude toward physical labor that is much more pronounced than in a capitalist society such as the United States. The coveted status symbol of Russian bureaucrats is the chauffeur-driven limousine; more of them are to be seen in Moscow than in any Western capital. When Yevgeny Trubitsyn, Minister of Automotive Transport, attempted to phase out some of these limousines, he admitted that the officials who used them presented him with "a whole tangle of psychological problems." He has given these officials three years to learn to drive their own cars, and to soften this demeaning prospect he explains that in Europe and the United States he "personally saw company managers, company directors and even government ministers driving their own personal cars." [18]

This privileged minority of state and Party officials is rapidly becoming self-perpetuating, because its children enjoy educational advantages from their favorable home environment and their parents' political influence. Thus the attainment of higher education promotes and entrenches class differentiation and a form of "hereditary aristocracy" even without private ownership of productive property or the passing on of political or managerial offices from generation to generation. Soviet sociologists have conducted considerable research on this subject and published their findings. For example, here are some results of a study of hereditary privilege in higher education:

> Given the number of applicants, which is now several times greater than the number of vacancies in first year courses at higher schools, society is interested in selecting those who in a few years are capable of becoming the best specialists. . . . It is quite obvious that, given equal abilities of youngsters, those families in which the parents have

higher educational attainments provide greater opportunities for preparing young people for the competitive examinations. . . . In ignoring the conditions under which applicants are trained, and in making judgments based only on the applicants' knowledge, admissions committees in effect sanction inequality of opportunity.[19]

And from a study on elitist disdain for manual labor:

Sociologists have noted a highly critical attitude toward physical labor, bordering on squeamishness, exists among some upper-grade secondary school students in Leningrad. It was this, actually, that the Resolution of the Central Committee of the Party on the School Reform (1959) dealt with: "Some of those who graduate from school regard it as demeaning for them to engage in physical labor." . . .

In our country (and this is by no means limited to the ranks of the salaried professionals) people are prepared to condemn a juvenile—and, even more, the parents of one—who will work *for pay*. . . . Abroad, children from diverse strata of society (except the elite, of course) regularly earn money by working as baggage-handlers, salesmen, dish-washers, maintenance workers, and so forth. Should one be surprised that having been trained from childhood only for mental work, for study, the Leningrad secondary students . . . had decided that they were born only for the professions and not for any other kind of work? When life compels them to "become a worker," this is taken as demeaning and even as a catastrophe. . . .

It is dinned into the ears of the young person that he has free access to all occupations which enjoy standing in his eyes, and that he can advance to the highest status in our society. . . . In effect, this aphorism strips all but the thoroughly intellectual occupations of all attractiveness, and thus misleads young people by picturing as excessively easy the difficult choice of a "place in life."[20]

On hereditary domination of the professions, another sociologist found that the more prestigious the school, the higher-class the background of those who gained admittance.

This is a completely understandable phenomenon. Such higher educational institutions as the Medical Institute and the University are attended by larger numbers of children of doctors, teachers, and the like, for among the intelligentsia these occupations are often "hereditary."[21]

This crystallizing social differentiation, combined with the political authoritarianism noted in the preceding chapter, is responsible for the proliferating deviance in the behavior of Soviet citizens. The three major concerns of law-enforcement officers are theft of state property, alcoholism, and juvenile delinquency. Alcoholism for long was viewed as a hangover from czarist times, but since alcoholism is now especially serious among young people and women this explanation is no longer acceptable. In June 1973 a highly publicized measure prohibited the sale of alcohol between 11:00 A.M. and 7:00 P.M. on weekdays and reduced the number of sales outlets. But this measure has been circumvented, according to *Literaturnaya Rossiya,* by an "army" of speculators, who buy vodka during the legal hours for about five dollars a pint and sell it after hours for seven dollars. As for juvenile delinquency, it assumes forms quite familiar in the United States: street fighting, petty larceny, and vandalism such as smashing of telephone booths and store windows. Newspapers also complain of the indolence and materialism of the pampered younger generation. "They are all bored if there are no outside stimulants such as record players, television sets, tape recorders, telephone calls from friends."[22] The "in" thing among many of the young is to acquire *modny,* (from the word "mode"), and indulgent parents are blamed for "spoiling" their children—for providing them with the money to buy the latest fads.

As serious as illegal deviancy is the all-pervasive ethic of self-advancement and self-gratification regardless of the social consequences. On the fiftieth anniversary of the founding of the U.S.S.R., the Communist Party leader Leonid Brezhnev complained of "social sores . . . such as [an] unconscientious attitude toward work, indiscipline, grubbing, and various violations of the norms of the socialist way of life."[23] The Soviet press provides rich details on these "social sores." It documents the indifference of waiters, sales clerks, and repairmen in state-run shops unless they are galvanized by tips, which formerly had been denounced as a demeaning bourgeois vice. It describes the "Uncle Vasyas" and the *levaks*—literally, "lefties," or illegal operators—who for a price will repair broken windows and leaking faucets, install doorbells and curtain rods, lay floors, sell flowers or apples, deliver natural-gas cylinders to outlying homes, and perform countless other chores and services that state agencies administer incompetently or not at all.

So serious is the problem that the Writers' Union weekly, *Literaturnaya Gazeta,* has suggested that private enterprise be allowed in the operation of small shops and retail trades—cafes, dressmaking, hairdressing, repair shops, and hotel restaurants. "Obviously we could use the experience of East Germany, Hungary and Poland, where the individual under certain conditions and under state economic control is given certain freedom of action in the sphere of services." These measures would ensure that, instead of having to wait endlessly in line or do without services, consumers would find "servicemen knocking at the door, because they will be looking for profit."[24]

The implications of this suggestion for a socialist society are self-evident and are fully recognized by Soviet leaders. In 1963 L. F. Ilichev, then Secretary of the Central Committee of the Communist Party, stated: "Unless we eradicate the moral principles of the bourgeois world, unless we rear people in the spirit of Communist morality, unless we spiritually regenerate man, it is impossible to build a Communist society. The very nature of Communist social production and distribution requires a new man . . . a new morality."[25]

All evidence indicates that the essential "new man" and "new morality" are not being realized. Soviet officialdom, by its very nature, cannot treat the causes of the profound national malaise. It treats the symptoms instead, by stratagems such as adopting a 12-point New Moral Code and disseminating it assiduously through schools, collectives, factories, and mass media. The code calls for "devotion to the communist cause . . . conscientious labor for the good of society . . . unpretentiousness in social and private life . . . an uncompromising attitude to injustice, parasitism, dishonesty, careerism and money grubbing."[26] The code had no discernible effect on national morality, of course, because of the excessive gap between such official preachiness and social reality. Thus the end result of corruption and elitism at the top is corruption and self-serving at the bottom. Special stores and *pakety* lead inevitably to "social sores" and Uncle Vasyas.

Discrepancy between official creed and social reality is not peculiar to the Soviet Union. In 1972 President Nixon launched a ten-million-dollar advertising campaign to persuade the American public that "America didn't get rich by goofing off" and that "productivity is not a twelve-letter dirty word representing certain people getting exploited by others."[27] The Nixon campaign had no more impact than did the Soviet New Moral Code, and for the same basic reason. Both sought to treat symptoms rather than causes.

Yet there remains a fundamental difference between the two cases. In the United States the discrepancy between creed and reality can be publicly noted, castigated, and acted upon, as it indeed is by scores of individuals, organizations, movements, and sects. In the Soviet Union such opposition is forbidden, except for complaints in the form of letters to the press, which are used by officialdom as a guide in correcting specific abuses.

Yet when Ivan Yakhimovich, an outstanding collective-farm chairman in Latvia, sent letters protesting political trials in Russia and the invasion of Czechoslovakia, he was examined by psychiatrists, who discovered certain "peculiarities" in his behavior. He "puts the public interest higher than his own," noted the psychiatrists, "wears a beard . . . believes that he has to dedicate his own life to the ideals of communism. . . ." For these offenses Yakhimovich was incarcerated in an insane asylum and sentenced to compulsory "treatment until recovery."[28]

Such occurrences explain why the number of hours spent by the average Soviet worker in public and cultural activities dwindled from 107 in 1924 to 17 in 1959. The number of hours has probably continued to decrease, and with it the dream of a new Soviet man. The fate of this dream can be seen in the experiences in 1975 of Gennady Bogomolov, a particularly zealous and productive Leningrad machinist who was turning out up to ten times the norm for his milling machine. In the 1930s, a coal miner, Aleksei Stakhanov, performed similar feats of overproduction and promptly became a national hero; "Stakhanovite methods" were hailed as a model for all Soviet workers. Today, by contrast, *Izvestia* admits that Bogomolov "is not the pride and joy of his plant's managers or Party officials." Bogomolov's fellow workers are also less than enthusiastic over his production feats, viewing them as threats to their prevailing comfortable work pace. Wages are low, consumer goods are scarce, and it is almost impossible to be fired, so why should a worker exert himself? Given the loss of the original socialist dream, the inevitable conclusion of the average Russian worker is, in the words of one worker, "They pretend they are paying us, so we pretend we are working."[29] After more than half a century under the Soviet system, Russian workers today are repeating the nineteenth-century syndicalist slogan, "Poor work for poor pay."

The New Maoist Man

An American professor of management and international business, Barry M. Richman, has compiled lists of terms commonly used to describe the characteristics of the Chinese people before the revolution and today. Typical words and phrases used before 1949 were "suspicion, nepotism, despotism, favoritism, corruption, the dominance of conservative ruling elites, avoidance of responsibility, venality, face-saving at any cost, sloth, a lust for money, emphasis on family loyalty. . . ." Current visitors to China, on the other hand, describe their impressions with such terms as "hard-working, dedicated, self-sacrificing, nationalistic, proud, pragmatic, flexible, well-disciplined, clear, resourceful, energetic, entrepreneurial, inventive, productive, well-motivated, honest, puritanical, sincere, cooperative with each other, thrifty, frugal, respectful of the virtues and dignity of labor. . . ."[30]

The contrast between the two lists is particularly striking in view of the traditional Chinese passivity and reluctance to challenge the status quo, out of fear of state authority and respect for the Confucian virtues of interpersonal harmony and social tranquillity. The end result of this tradition has been a pervasive anxiety about interpersonal conflict and a sense of individual political isolation and impotence. The ideal new Maoist man is the precise opposite—a self-reliant activist, a "red and expert" jack-of-all-trades, a comrade with a deep sense of mission to "serve the people," and an antitraditionalist who believes that personal and national salvation can be achieved only by casting off the fetters of tradition.

Considerable progress has been made toward realizing this ideal man, as suggested by Richman's contrasting word lists and by the reports of foreign visitors, who are as much impressed by the presence of the new Maoist man in China as visitors to Russia are impressed by the absence of the new Soviet man. The reason for the Chinese success is Mao's fundamental conviction that, unless man himself is changed along with his society, the new society will regress until it resembles the old.

It follows that Mao's egalitarianism involves not only economic but also psychological leveling, not only income redistribution but also demolition of the barrier separating "mental aristocrats" who work with their minds from the masses who work with their hands. Thus the Chinese continually stress their basic proposition that the new man is not the end result of their new society but its prerequisite. And in stating this guiding principle they assert that they have "learned by negative example"—referring not too subtly to the fate of the new Soviet man.

To mold or remold 800 million adults and children, the Chinese Communists have established a number of institutions and practices. As noted in the preceding chapter, these include the May 7 schools, the *hsia fang* or "going down" principle, the pervasive political indoctrination of all citizens, the mass representation and participation in the Revolutionary Committees, and the massive educational system designed specifically to combat the "private ownership of knowledge." This phrase summarizes the Maoist contention that education represents a community investment in an individual person, since all schooling, from kindergarten through graduate school, is virtually free. Schools therefore should turn out students who have sought education as a means of serving the people rather than for personal gain. Students should be models for the rest of the population in living up to the two ubiquitous slogans: "Serve the people" and "Fight self."

For this reason every student, from kindergarten onward, is required to combine physical labor with mental. Toddlers are encouraged to sweep the floor, set the table, wash lunch bowls, and fold their quilts. Elementary and middle schools have adjacent fields where the pupils regularly work and workshops where they produce parts for nearby factories. The graduates of the lower middle schools (corresponding to the American junior high schools), boys and girls alike, are assigned to a two- or three-year labor stint in a commune, factory, railway, mine, hospital, hotel, or dockyard. Their preferences are considered but not necessarily accepted. Whether they continue with their studies after this labor service depends on the recommendations they receive from their fellow workers and from their workplace leaders. These recommendations are based on intelligence (does the applicant have the ability to benefit from higher education?), on reliability (is the applicant a conscientious and dependable worker?), and on citizenship (will the applicant use further training to serve the people or to serve self?).

Those not recommended can, and often do, attend some of the numerous night schools or technical schools. Those who receive favorable recommendations and also are accepted by the institution to which they apply leave their workplace and begin the second phase of their formal education. Some 300 institutions of higher learning are available, including technological institutes, specialized schools for the arts, and regular universities. Many of the regular universities were founded by Westerners and, before the Communist Revolution, were patterned after Western models in their organization and curriculum.

All this changed drastically with the Cultural Revolution, during which all universities were shut down for four years and their faculties required to go to work in factories, mines, and communes in order to be "reeducated by the workers and peasants." In 1970 the universities reopened, and since then they have been cautiously feeling their way by trial and error into their assigned role in the new society. The general nature of this role is set forth in the guidelines laid down by Chairman Mao. All educational institutions are to be "schools without walls," "schools with doors open." Universities must function primarily as agents for modernizing the backward rural areas, where 80 percent of all Chinese still live. "Workers and peasants must be intellectualized," exhorts Chairman Mao, "and intellectuals must be transformed into workers and peasants."

These injunctions have led the schools to practice what might be described as a Chinese version of an "open enrollment" program. Here, this term does not mean that anyone who wishes to attend a university is granted admittance. In fact, enrollment figures still have not reached pre-Cultural Revolution levels. In the fall of 1974 only 167,000 new university students were enrolled, compared with 200,000 before the Cultural Revolution. Rather, "open enrollment" in China means admitting students with a view to preventing the emergence of a hereditary elite such as existed in prerevolutionary China and is developing again in the Soviet Union. Hence the emphasis on citizenship and social responsibility in considering applicants' credentials. In the early 1970s a quota system of admittance was followed: 40 percent workers, 40 percent peasants, 10 percent Peoples Liberation Army, and 10 percent cadre, or administrators. If grade scores alone were the criterion for admittance, those groups now allotted 10 percent would probably end up constituting 90 percent of the student body, as in the past.

This policy has engendered a debate in Chinese educational circles very similar to that which open enrollment has stimulated in the United States. The issue is whether academic standards have been so compromised by the quota system that China will not be able to train the scientists, technicians, and professional men needed in order for the country to reach the proclaimed goal of becoming a "powerful modern socialist state" by the end of the century. In April 1975, students at the Shenyang College of Mechanical and Electrical Engineering debated this question with wall posters. One group of students put up a poster declaring that the graduates of the "new-type socialist universities" should not be treated like "ordinary workers," because they have greater contributions to make. Another group found this "shocking" and slapped up a poster that replied "No matter what you are, you should be an ordinary worker if you want to take a proletarian stand and serve the people. Otherwise you will be an overlord sitting on the backs of the people or an intellectual aristocrat."

The local newspaper, the *Liaoning Daily*, reprinted the wall posters, recommending them for careful study. A Canton broadcast followed up with an analysis concluding that the issue remained unresolved. "The struggle between two classes and two lines is still acute and complex on the higher education front."[31] Education in China today obviously is in transition. The means, not the goal, is in question. How can elitism and hierarchy be avoided without sacrificing the needed expertise? The Soviet Union is held up as an example of what happens when means are subordinated to a goal. The dilemma is not confined to education; inevitably, it permeates an entire society groping its way toward socialism.

The Communist Chinese leadership typically does not seek a solution through decision making at the top. Rather, the problem is defined and discussed on a mass scale, and then grass-roots experimentation is conducted throughout the country. Results are reported, lessons are exchanged, and the nationwide cross-fertilization process continues until a generally recognized satisfactory solution is reached in some locality. This solution is then proclaimed as the model for the entire country, and all the resources of Party and state are used to build it up and to ensure maximum impact.

In agriculture, for example, the village of Tachai in northern Shansi Province was selected as the national model; since 1964 the entire country has been covered with signs urging: "In agriculture, learn from Tachai." Thus a decade later the obscure Chaoyang Agricultural College, in a remote and arid section of Liaoning Province, was selected as the model for education, and a nationwide campaign followed with the slogan: "In education, learn from Chaoyang." Officials and students from all over the country are making pilgrimages to the college and returning home to spread the "Chaoyang Way."

The precise nature of this Chaoyang Way is significant. It is based on what is termed the "going-up and going-down training system"—going up to the college and going down to the village. This two-way process conforms exactly to Chairman Mao's injunction that the university be an open and active agent for modernizing the countryside. The Chaoyang system amounts to a never-ceasing flow of students going back and forth from college to village, carrying home new seeds, new techniques, new ideas. The interaction between school and village is carried to the point at which the two virtually become one. No longer is the village an isolated and exploited backwater, deserted by enterprising youth for the attractions and opportunities of the city.

Precisely what this means for the 80 percent of China's population that lives in rural communes has been revealingly analyzed on the basis of first-hand observation by Silas H. L. Wu, professor of history at Boston College. In 1946, at the age of 16, he left his native village of Chen-t'ou, some 230 miles south of Peking. Like other villages in the area, it had numerous temples that fulfilled various functions in the traditional routine of village life. Old Mother Temple was responsible for human fertility; barren women sought help by placing an offering in one of her open hands. Dragon King was responsible for rain; in time of drought the villagers carried him around under the blazing sun in the hope that the scorching heat would force him to order rain. The Insect King was in charge of the problem of locusts and other pests, and the Drug King was responsible for the villagers' health.

When Professor Wu revisited Chen-t'ou in 1973 after an absence of 27 years, he found the old gods ousted from their temples by new ideas in the heads of the peasants. Like most observers from the West, writes Professor Wu, "I had shared a common notion about 'Mao Tse-tung's thought.' I had taken it as essentially a political ideology. Through the trip [to the village] I realized that Mao's thought was more than political; it was scientific as well. Here *scientific* refers to both methodology and problem-solving."[32]

As an example, old peasant Feng explained how he solved problems in cotton growing when he discovered a certain critical period in cotton's growth cycle. During this period he had to pay careful attention to the three "key points" of water, fertilizer, and management. By prolonged "practical observations," he and his fellow villagers "grasped the law" governing the growing of cotton. In doing so, explained Mr. Feng, they were merely following the problem-solving methodology set forth by Chairman Mao in his two writings *On Practice* and *On Contradiction*.

Another peasant, Li Ming-shan, related how he had followed Chairman Mao's *On Practice* to understand the "rationality" of interplanting wheat and cotton. He had noted that when these two crops were interplanted the number of aphids attacking them decreased drastically, even when little insecticide was used. Since he could find no rational explanation for this phenomenon, he spent seven days and nights in the fields while the cotton shoots were in the budding stage. Finally he discovered the "law" governing the new phenomenon: most of the aphids were eaten by the ladybirds in the wheat planted next to the cotton.

Not surprisingly, productivity in Professor Wu's village rose from a pre-revolutionary average of 150 catties (1 catty = 1.1 pounds) per mou (1 mou = $\frac{1}{6}$ acre) to an average of 600 catties per mou by 1973. In addition, the large number of deep wells that were sunk enabled the village to survive two consecutive years of the worst droughts in half a century. In fact, Professor Wu learned from a family letter that wheat production in 1974 had risen to 700 catties per mou despite the drought.

Improved productivity has made possible a correspondingly improved diet. Whereas wheat flour was formerly enjoyed only by a privileged few, it is now available to all villagers for eight months of the year; cheaper grains are used during the remaining four months. Old Mother Temple has been replaced by a medical clinic concerned more with promoting family planning than with procuring male heirs for ancestor-conscious families. "Today, Mao Tse-tung's thought," concludes Professor Wu, "is more than a political ideology. It is becoming a part of the peasant mentality as an effective tool to solve problems in farming as well as in other areas of rural life."

All this does not mean that China has become a country of 800 million dedicated Maoists. The impact of the educational system and of the assorted counterinstitutions designed to forestall regression is undeniable and impressive. Yet it must be remembered also that China is a country "where two virulent bureaucratic traditions . . . , that of the Chinese mandarin and the Communist *apparatchik,* make their influence felt simultaneously. . . ."[33] In addition to these bureaucratic traditions, there is a corresponding tradition of submission to authority—the precise opposite of the citizen activism and independence that has characterized America from the beginning. A Maoist official once explained to Edgar Snow the problem of weaning the people away from their age-old habit of subservience. His account is obviously significant for any forecasts of China's future.

> During the early years of the revolution there was a strange thing. When the peasants came to the October anniversary and went past the reviewing stand, many did the *k'ou-t'ou* before Chairman Mao. We had to keep guards posted there to prevent them from prostrating themselves. It takes time to make people understand that Chairman Mao is not an emperor or a god but a man who wants peasants to stand up like men.[34]

The plight of dissident intellectuals in Maoist China should also be kept in mind. Those who are committed to the fundamentals of Maoism— and they appear to be the great majority—are enthusiastic participants, feeling that they are no longer locked up in their ivory towers but are now relevant, giving now as well as taking. But those intellectuals who cannot subscribe to Maoist tenets and practices have no place whatsoever in a self-proclaimed dictatorship of the proletariat. Their choice is between discreet silence and incarceration accompanied by unceasing indoctrination to convince them of the error of their ways.

Granting all this, it seems clear that the new Maoist man is much more a reality than is his Soviet counterpart and, for that reason, is likely to have considerable influence beyond the frontiers of China. Here it should be noted that certain specific manifestations of Maoist zeal seem excessive to Western taste and therefore are likely to prove counterproductive to the influence of Maoism abroad. One example is the case of a young soldier, Lei Feng, who for some years was held up as the personification of the Maoist hero. During his short life before he was killed in an accident, this Chinese Frank Merriwell performed an interminable list of good deeds. He kept his army truck in perfect condition, contributed his meager pay to the aid of flood victims, worked in his spare time on public projects, carried a peasant's child for miles in a heavy downpour, and always avoided acclaim or reward. "Learn from Lei Feng," urged Mao. The press emblazoned his good deeds and a film was made of his life.

The social objectives of this didactic moralizing and relentless indoctrination are obvious and laudable, yet to Western tastes they are cloying and disturbing. One foreign correspondent saw the Lei Feng film and noted that the audience left the theater wet-eyed. When he ventured to suggest that the sermonizing was overdone, he met with utter incomprehension.

> Several times, when we thought we could do so without offending those who asked [our opinion of the film], we gave them to understand that the kind of cult dedicated to this Communist saint who reeked of virtue seemed foolish to us. No one fully understood us. "But," said one, "we haven't invented anything. Lei Feng really existed and everything told about him is true. Besides, there are hundreds of thousands of Lei Fengs in China, and we congratulate ourselves on this; it is only with such men that we can advance toward the collectivist society.[35]

Yet social commitment cannot be dismissed as boring banality or ideological servitude because it seems so to the outside observer. Indeed, it is this commitment that makes China today as different from the Soviet world as from the Western. To a much greater degree than dams or factories or full bellies, it is the "hundreds of thousands of Lei Fengs" that have so impressed foreign observers of all political persuasions. The following statement by Jesuit Father William Van Etten Casey in the 1975 issue of *The Holy Cross Quarterly* serves as an example:

> Throughout the tour, I was most impressed with the richness and depth of the virtues of the new Chinese people. I found these people,

variously, warm, friendly, courteous, cordial, cheerful, happy, content, gracious, helpful, sincere, patient, serene, relaxed, confident, diligent, industrious, intelligent, thrifty, clean, sober, naive, unsophisticated, abstemious, curious, ascetical, stoical, puritanical, just, kind, purposeful, intent, dedicated, disciplined, self-sufficient, self-possessed, honest, reliable, trustworthy. . . .

On our way back to the United States, some of us, discussing our reactions to China, tried to recall any awkward or unpleasant situation involving the Chinese people that we might have witnessed. The only such incident that finally came back to memory was the sight of a peasant beating his donkey a bit too enthusiastically. . . .

Since religion is of no consequence in China today, it is obvious that it has had nothing to do with the development of the virtues in the new Chinese people. This fact presents the theologian with a baffling problem: how to account for so numerous a people engaging in such a widespread practice of virtues which in the West have been traditionally associated with religious belief and religious motivation. The prophet Jonah had something of the same problem with the Ninevites.

Whatever the explanation, there is no doubt that the Chinese, if they ever could know, would be appalled at the level of public morality in those Western countries whose birth and development owe so much to the role of religion and who still pay lip service to the importance of religion in their lives. These nations, with religion, are sick from overdoses of violence, greed, injustice, selfishness, prejudice, pornography, crime, drugs and weapons, but China, without religion, is producing a healthy and virtuous people.[36]

The Chinese type of socially dedicated new man also has an obvious appeal for underdeveloped Third World societies that lack a motivated citizenry as well as technology and capital. Thus the revolutionary Frelimo (Mozambique Liberation Front) government of Mozambique announced, when it assumed power on June 25, 1975, that top priority would be given not to administrative or economic measures but to "transforming individual thinking." President Samora Machel explained that this measure was necessary to change "the feudal, traditional mentality which is predominant in the rural areas" and "the colonial, capitalist mentality which is deeply rooted in the urban areas." Leading roles in the molding of the "new man" in Mozambique have been assigned to the Army, of over 10,000 men, and to "dynamic groups," or party units, that exist in almost every institution—factories, shops, schools—slums, and rural areas. The specific objectives are to combat elitism and tribalism, to exalt manual labor as "a link between practice and knowledge," and to "decolonize" all institutions. The judicial system, for example, is to be completely restructured so that justice may be understood by common citizens. "Our aim is to rebuild our Mozambique personality and our culture," stated Machel, "and to create a new mentality and a new society. . . . Leaders should be humble and guard against bureaucratic rigidity. . . . The people should be consulted and involved in decision-making."[37] The Maoist overtones are clear and acknowledged.

7

THE PROMISE
OF THE COMING
DARK AGE

*Man's destiny is to make possible maximum fulfillment for
the greatest number of human beings.*

  Sir Julian Huxley

*I think the Dark Age is already here, only we don't know
it. . . . The small community is going to come back into
its own. . . . Under the surface a new life may be knitting
together, struggling still to find its way. . . . Today is
the seedbed of the future.*

  Lewis Mumford

"The Worst Form of Tragedy"

This is an age of worldwide ferment and innovation. Pete Seeger's green grass is growing everywhere in its manifold varieties. Bosses, bureaucrats, and experts are going the way of kings, priests, and landlords. Why, then, are so many Western spokesmen in the depths of despair? Why do they foresee doom, or urge the acceptance of a technocratic elite as the only way out of our mounting difficulties, or advise the laying in of dried foods in individual foxholes?

Robert Heilbroner gave the answer in his book *The Future as History* (1959), which was revealingly different in tone and outlook from his later study *The Human Prospect* (1975). The historic forces of our day, he wrote in 1959, "can still be said to point in the direction of optimism and progress." But the trouble is that the West is now the target rather than the spearhead of these forces. Consequently, the West is no longer in tune with the forces that are preparing the environment of the future. "It is a crushing spiritual blow," concluded Heilbroner, "to lose one's sense of participation in mankind's journey."[1]

This loss is clearly manifest in the following two statements by Secretary of State Henry Kissinger:

[1] To Americans usually tragedy is wanting something very badly and not getting it. Many people have had to learn in their private lives, and nations have had to learn in their historical experience, that perhaps the worst form of tragedy is wanting something badly, getting it, and finding it empty. And to get this sense of historical humility and of limitation, which is the experience through which we are now going as a people, is extremely painful.[2]

165

[2] I don't see why we need to stand by and watch a country go Communist due to the irresponsibility of its own people.[3]

The feelings expressed in these two statements are causally related. Kissinger is pessimistic because he seeks to apply the American equivalent of the Brezhnev Doctrine (which justified Soviet intervention in the internal afffairs of Eastern European countries) to the entire globe. Such an undertaking is as demoralizing as it is utopian. When the Portuguese dictatorship was overthrown, Kissinger felt constrained to send two missions to investigate the danger of a Communist takeover. When Franco's position in Spain was weakening, Kissinger, along with President Ford, visited the aging dictator to bolster his crumbling power. Because of Italy's political instability, the American embassy in Rome has worked feverishly behind the scenes to block the inclusion of the Communist Party in the Italian government. When the military junta collapsed in Greece, Kissinger branded independent political leaders such as Andreas Papandreou and Archbishop Makarios as "the Castros of the Mediterranean."

Thus events that would have been hailed ecstatically by nineteenth century America as the freeing of the oppressed peoples of the Mediterranean from their bloody tyrants are viewed by twentieth-century official America with foreboding and as a peril that must be crushed by any means. Back in the days when a Greek revolutionary leader could have the city of Ypsilanti named in his honor, it is understandable that Jeffersonian democrats looked forward to the future with confident expectation. Jefferson himself had said, "Old Europe will have to lean on our shoulders, and to hobble along by our side, under the monkish trammels of priests and kings. . . . What a colossus shall we be . . . as a ralliance for the reason and freedom of the globe! I like the dreams of the future better than the history of the past."[4] But in today's world, where wartime quislings and torturers were propped up in Athens for years by American dollars and agents, it is not surprising that Kissinger philosophizes pessimistically about a nation's "wanting something badly" and then "finding it empty." But what is empty and chimerical is not the national future but Kissinger's self-assumed role of mankind's Big Daddy, who decides when an entire nation of people are "irresponsible" and threatens to punish them for it.

In Somalia, for example, a Marxist-oriented group of army officers seized power in 1969. The United States thereupon ended its economic assistance. The officers turned to the Soviet Union for help in building their armed forces and their economy. In response to American charges that the

Russians were constructing a missile-handling installation at Berbera on the strategic Gulf of Aden, a Somali colonel states: "I am a Marxist but we are not taking orders from either Moscow or Peking. What we want to get across is that we are not just a facility—a tiny plus or minus in the balance of power between East and West—but a country, a nation of humans that are poor and want to live."[5] Such aspirations and statements are by no means confined to Somalia. Any Big Daddy, whether in the White House or in the Kremlin, who sets out to punish all such declarations of independence is likely to be afflicted with something more serious than Kissinger's melancholia.

The fact remains that we are witnessing today not the darkening future of mankind, as Kissinger and other establishmentarians assert, but rather the darkening future of the obsolete policies and institutions of the United States as presently constituted. This point has been made specifically by a Vietnamese spokesman who spent some time in America.

> To many Vietnamese, it is understandable that Americans would feel depressed over the state of affairs in their own country given all the things Nixon has done. I have yet to meet an American in the peace movement who doesn't feel the same, and who would not try to transpose his gloom onto the Vietnamese for some obscure reason. Perhaps this is a remnant of America's messianic zeal of the past when "what was best for America must also be best for everybody else." . . .
>
> As a Vietnamese, it is sad for me to see that Americans continue to refuse what is theirs—the current depression due to crises and Nixon himself—and to visualize their problems being with the Vietnamese. As far as we are concerned, this unrequested attention is often more than we can bear. This is in a way a lesson to be drawn from the Viet Nam war.[6]

"The Most Creative International Institution"

If one's vision is directed toward the future rather than the past, one will perceive Pete Seeger's green grass thrusting upward through the layered concrete. This grass, as noted in the preceding four chapters, represents the efforts being made everywhere to alter the global landscape that has evolved since the West began the overseas expansion that created the modern world. More specifically, the basic thrust of world affairs in the late twentieth and early twenty-first centuries will be the fundamental restructuring of the global arrangements and relationships that have evolved since the voyages of Christopher Columbus and Vasco da Gama. This restructuring will occur both within Third World nations and between the Third World nations and the developed world.

Considering first the restructuring of the Third World, we will see a political decentralization reminiscent of the disintegration of the Roman Empire. In the Third World today, as in the Roman Empire nearly two millenia ago, there will be an assertion of local autonomy and traditions against the increasingly restrictive and exploitative domination by metropolitan centers. Rome's imperial structure gave way to feudal fragmentation; today the great nineteenth-century empires have disintegrated likewise. The trend in global reorganization appears to be toward regional autonomy—as suggested by the reemergence of China, by Hanoi's current slogan "Southeast Asia for the Southeast Asians," by the increasing assertiveness of Latin American states against the "Yankee colossus," by the political awakening and growing economic power of the Arab world, and by the successful liberation struggles in the Portuguese African colonies and the ensuing intensification of black Africa's struggle against the racist white regimes south of the Zambezi.

In the economic realm the decline of Rome led, likewise, to the disintegration of the imperial economy and the emergence of manorialism, with its attendant shrinkage of trade and cities and deterioration of roads and harbors. The overall economic trend today is also toward decentralization; the movement is from global to national and even to a local scale of economic operations. The objective of Third World countries is to literally do away with the Third World—by definition, those countries subservient to, and dependent upon, the metropolitan centers of the First and Second Worlds.

This unequal economic relationship was the outcome of the expansion, beginning in the fifteenth century, of dynamic Western capitalism throughout the world, creating for the first time a truly global economy based on a global division of labor. Karl Marx himself paid tribute to this historic achievement of capitalism: "The bourgeoisie, during its rule of scarce one hundred years, has created more massive and more colossal productive forces than have all preceding generations together." World industrial production multiplied six times, and the value of world trade over ten times, between 1860 and 1913.

But there was a dark side to this burgeoning human productivity. The global economic cake was getting larger, but the slices were becoming more unequal. It is estimated that the differential in per capita income between developed and underdeveloped countries was roughly three to one in 1800, was about seven to one in 1914, and is 12 to one today. The cause of the widening gap was the subordination of colonial economies to the needs of the metropolitan centers, which engendered vertical economic linkages in the colonies (that is, links to the economies of the colonialist countries) rather than horizontal economic linkages (those between the various domestic sectors of the colonial economies). Such vertical economic relationships resulted in monoculture economies that produced only mineral resources and agricultural goods for export, that were inherently incapable of overall integrated economic development, and that doomed the Third World countries, therefore, to the dependency and appallingly high unemployment characterizing them today.

This global economic system was justified in the West by the theory of comparative advantages (which holds that certain regions are suited to producing certain goods) and of international specialization of production. Although this theory might be valid for some hypothetical world, such a world of course has never existed, and in actual practice this theory was responsible for the appearance in early modern times of the Third World, comprising countries whose underdevelopment was the by-product of the emergence of the developed world.

The unequal relationship began when early colonies were exploited by mercantilist regulations, which were designed to ship treasure and raw materials to the "mother country." It continued through the nineteenth century, when the practice of "free-trade imperialism" incorporated into the global market economy politically independent lands such as Latin America and the Czarist Empire, semidependent lands such as the Ottoman and Chinese Empires, and outright colonies such as India and the African continent. By this time the West had become so strong economically, due to the Industrial Revolution, that it had no need for formal colonial bonds. Free access to markets sufficed and, indeed, was preferred to the old colonial ties, which imposed the obligations of maintaining expensive bureaucratic and military apparatus in the colonized territories.

This situation remains today, for, although the colonial empires have disappeared, these dominant-subordinate economic relationships persist as strongly as ever. The principal instrument for economic control is the multinational corporation, which is now playing the role formerly played by the Hudson Bay and East India Companies. In earlier times, Hudson Bay Company traders would exchange a long-barreled musket for a number of furs that, piled up on the ground, reached as high as the tip of the musket. East India Company representatives conquered Indian provinces, where they collected taxes, controlled trade, and extorted "gifts" with a gold lust reminiscent of that of the *conquistadores* of the Aztec and Inca Empires.

Today some obervers maintain that the multinational corporations play a role entirely different from that of their predecessors—that the enrichment of the multinationals automatically also enriches the Third World host countries in which they operate. Thus Daniel Moynihan, United States representative to the United Nations, asserted in *Commentary* (March 1975) that "the multinational corporation, combining modern management with liberal trade policies, is arguably the most creative international institution of the 20th century." Moynihan's pronouncement is akin to that of the nineteenth-century spokesmen of the Manchester school of economics, who, extolling the virtues of global free trade, insisted that it benefited Europeans and colonials alike, the benefits accruing from the international division of labor. All the while, nevertheless, India's textile industry was being ruined, the peasants of Java and India were being compelled to grow jute and cotton and indigo rather than the foodstuffs they needed to avert recurring famines, and China was punished by force of arms for daring, in defiance of the sacred principle of freedom of trade, to prohibit the importation of British opium from India.

So it is today. What is good for the multinationals is considered good for their host countries, even though the exact opposite is glaringly evident in almost every Third World economic indicator—rising unemployment, growing indebtedness, declining standards of nutrition and health, and declining per capita real income—a decline both absolute and relative to those of the developed countries.

Even with the escape hatch that Moynihan providentially left himself by inserting the word "arguably," he finds himself hard pressed to defend his statement in the face of data presented in recent studies of the global economy, such as *Global Reach* by Richard Barnet and Ronald Müller (Simon and Schuster, 1974) and *Persistent Poverty* by George Beckford (Oxford University Press, 1975).

It has been argued that multinationals provide the capital necessary for the economic development of backward areas, but in fact the precise opposite is the case: it is the underdeveloped areas that furnish capital for the developed areas. A 1970 United Nations study revealed that, between 1957 and 1965, American-based multinationals financed 83 percent of their Latin American investments locally, either from reinvested earnings or from Latin American savings. Only 17 percent of the total American investment represented an actual transfer of capital from the United States to Latin America. In addition, the global reach of the multinationals enables them to buy and sell to their own subsidiaries, and hence to export Third World commodities at bargain rates and to price their imports at inflated levels. The end result is a net flow of capital each year from the poor to the rich countries, a trend accelerated by the mounting debt load of the poor countries. Between 1960 and 1970 the external public debt of Third World countries rose from 19 to 66 billion dollars, and in the process of paying these debts these countries pay each year to the developed countries an amount larger than they receive in the form of aid.

It has also been argued that the multinationals provide jobs in countries where they are desperately needed, but the nature of these jobs is not usually examined. Fairchild Camera and Texas Instruments are among the numerous American corporations that have set up plants in Hong Kong, where 60 percent of the adult labor force works seven days a week. There is also a child labor force in Hong Kong that includes 34,000 children of age 14 or younger, half of whom work ten hours or more per day. Rollei Camera Company of Germany has moved its camera plant to Singapore, where the wage level is one-sixth the German level and the government guarantees freedom from union trouble. Gelmart Industries makes bras (Maidenform, Sears, Montgomery Ward, Kresge, and so forth) in the Philippines, where the minimum wage is $1.20 a day and where workers with 15 years of service can earn $1.40 a day. The largest number of American plants abroad are in Mexico; in 1974 a total of 586 plants employing 68,000 workers were located near the border. The attraction is the minimum hourly wage, which was 58 cents for adult males in 1973. But when union pressure raised the wage to $1.13, the companies began looking toward Haiti, where the minimum wage is $1.30 for a full day's work.

Such low pay perhaps could be justified if these jobs provided a means for the transmission of technological skills needed for local development. But not much skill is required to assemble electronic equipment, toys, clothes, or sports goods. And the skills that workers may acquire are for the most part irrelevant to local needs; thus, if a foreign plant shuts down, its employees are left stranded without applicable skills. More serious is the fact that, when a multinational company signs a contract with a Third World government for the transfer of technology, the fees are usually exorbitant; in addition, 80 percent of the contracts, according to a U.N. study, prohibit the use of the technology for producing exports. The multinationals' wish to restrict competition is understandable, but the effect, nevertheless, is to prevent Third World countries from earning foreign exchange through exports. Furthermore, the transferred technology is usually of the capital-intensive, labor-saving variety, which is quite counterproductive for the underdeveloped world, suffering from capital shortage and 30-percent unemployment.

The inappropriateness of much of the technology transferred to the Third World is especially evident in agriculture. Agricultural research, whether conducted by multinationals or by metropolitan governments or their universities, is designed to meet the needs of monoculture plantations producing for export. Hardly any research, subsidies, or infrastructure facilities have been aimed to benefit the subsistence farming of the peasants. The results of this situation can be seen, for example, in Africa's Sahel, where agribusiness corporations use scarce water and land resources for growing cotton and vegetables and raising cattle for foreign markets. The resulting neglect of agricultural production for domestic needs exacerbated the shortages and suffering during recent droughts. In India and Latin America, the imported Green Revolution (as noted in Chapter 3, pages 42 to 44) has primarily benefited the landowners who can afford the necessary expensive fertilizers, pesticides, and irrigation, and who, despite staggering unemployment rates, import machinery to enhance their profits and eliminate labor problems.

As detrimental as the economic impact of multinationals on the Third World is their cultural impact. American television programs are geared to entertain and hold audiences long enough to get across commercials designed to create consumer wants. But the uneducated citizens of underdeveloped countries need instruction more than entertainment, and depression of consumption aspirations rather than their stimulation. Nevertheless, shows like "I Love Lucy," "Batman," and "Hawaii Five-O" are dubbed in six languages and sold in about 50 countries. American corporations offer these old shows at a fraction of what it would cost local producers to create new programs. So these shows are seen all over the world, carrying added local advertisements and making America's consumption culture a global model.

This high-consumption model is also responsible for what Derrick Jelliffe, professor of public health at the University of California, Los Angeles, labels "commerciogenic malnutrition." Unsuspecting peasants are brainwashed into hankering for relatively expensive white bread and soft drinks, while they and their families suffer malnutrition from protein shortage. In countries such as Nigeria, baby-food companies employ female "milk nurses" to push their products more directly and effectively. These women visit doctors, clinics, and individual mothers under the guise of dispensing nutritional advice; in reality, they are promoting the use of processed baby food over homemade and bottle-feeding over breast-feeding. The Nairobi City Council has banned "milk nurses" from its clinics; the British aid agency War on Want has issued a report, *The Baby Killers,* which charges that the very survival of infants in underdeveloped countries is in direct conflict with the profit aims of the baby-food corporations.

In view of the facts cited above, it is scarcely surprising that multinational corporations show generally higher earnings than single-nation corporations, that the multinationals gain higher profits from their overseas operations than from their domestic operations, and that the gap in per capita income between developed and underdeveloped countries has widened rapidly during the decades since World War II, when the multinationals have grown the fastest.

Third World Responses

One response of the Third World to this subordination and exploitation is symbolized by the statement of President Houari Boumedienne of Algeria at the "preparatory meeting" of raw-materials producers and consumers held in Paris in April 1975. The objective of the meeting, declared Boumedienne, was to achieve "the economic emancipation of the underdeveloped countries" by promoting "the destruction of the unfair economic structure which governs the world today." A few years ago such a statement would have been dismissed as rhetorical bluff, but the dramatic successes of the Organization of Petroleum Exporting Countries (OPEC) suggest that the balance of economic power between developed and underdeveloped countries is no longer tipped hopelessly to one side. Boumedienne and others of like mind seek to expand OPEC into a vast cartel of raw-material-exporting countries—a Third World bloc, comprising both the affluent oil producers and those without oil. If such a bloc could be forged and maintained, the West-dominated global economic order would be seriously challenged for the first time.

But the Third World today is far from a monolithic bloc, partly because of the residual effects of the past counterrevolutionary policies of the West. Recall that the Shah of Iran owes his throne to the CIA, which engineered the coup that overthrew the nationalist Mossadeq and brought the Shah back from exile. Today the Shah, along with the Saudi ruler, heads the conservative wing of OPEC; the radical wing is led by Libya and Algeria. Likewise, the military dictatorship in Brazil is the strongly supported favorite—if not the creation—of the United States, and today this dictatorship serves as the watchdog of the Latin American status quo. The military dictatorship in Indonesia plays a similar role in Southeast Asia. Thus the Third World today is simultaneously engaged in confrontation with the hitherto dominant industrial powers and locked in an internal struggle over its own identity and future. This internal conflict may be symbolized, at the risk of oversimplification, by the contrast between the Brazilian and Chinese strategies for Third World development. The Brazilian model is being followed, with variations, in Iran, Indonesia, and Nigeria, and the Chinese model in Cuba, North Korea, and Indochina.

The Brazilian solution is adopted by countries seeking to achieve economic growth while preserving their domestic status quo and obtaining the maximum amount of foreign aid available. Foreign governments and multinational corporations generally support such countries, because their conservative policies create what is termed a "congenial climate" for investments and loans. This climate arises from low wage rates set by the government, supine and government-controlled labor unions, lightly regulated access to natural resources, and a wide range of tax inducements and other favorable financial arrangements for foreign capital. Also, the inequitable distribution of purchasing power in such societies generates upper- and middle-class consumer markets that are lucrative for the multinationals. The combination of heavy foreign investments and low labor costs usually ensures rapid exploitation of natural resources and a correspondingly rapid rise in GNP.

This development strategy is always accompanied by a large and increasing disparity in income distribution, and not accidently so, for income inequity is viewed as an essential concomitant of economic growth. "There is likely to be a conflict between rapid growth and equitable distribution of income," argues the American economist Harry Johnson, "and a poor country anxious to develop would probably be well advised not to worry too much about the distribution of income."[7] Likewise, the Pakistani economist Mahbub-ul-Haq states specifically that inequitable income distribution is necessary to facilitate capital saving for investment:

> The underdeveloped countries must consciously accept a philosophy of growth and shelve for the distant future all ideas of equitable distribution and the welfare state. It should be recognized that these are luxuries which only developed countries can afford. . . . Savings

are a function not only of the level of income but also of its distribution. . . . It is clear that distribution of national product should
be such as to favor the saving sectors.[8]

In actual practice, however, this orthodox economic theory has proven
consistently wrong. The end result of the strategy of inequitable distribution of income has not been continued and accelerating economic growth,
with the benefits ultimately trickling down to the masses. The "trickle
down" simply has not materialized; neither has the expected saving of
capital for investment. Thus income disparity has engendered social tension
and political conflict rather than any of the expected benefits—culminating
in the apparent paradox of revolution amid rising GNP.

One reason for this unexpected outcome is that the landlords, merchants, and industrialists favored by the distribution of income have not
invested in the domestic economy as much as expected. Instead, they have
tended to deposit their generous profits in safe foreign banks or to squander
them in conspicuous consumption. Another reason is that the foreign aid
that financed the early stages of economic expansion soon proved to be
an onerous burden, because the terms became less generous and the service
charges piled up to the point of consuming a substantial percentage of the
national income. Foreign aid has also generated inflation pressures, but the
resulting price rises are not matched by corresponding wage increases
because of government restrictions on trade-union activities. Therefore the
mass of the people experience not the trickling down of benefits but the
ravages of an absolute decline in real income. In an age of popular awakening and assertiveness, the juxtaposition of mass misery and provocative
luxury is more likely to culminate in new revolutionary regimes than in
new additions to the ranks of the developed societies.

An early example of a revolution that grew out of conservative development policy was the Baghdad insurrection of July 1958, which literally
exterminated the ruling Hashimite dynasty (see page 48). A later example was the 1968 revolution in Pakistan, where GNP during the preceding decade had increased at a rate of five and one-half percent yearly,
while industry had grown ten percent yearly. But during the same decade
real wages in industry had fallen by at least 25 percent and consumption of
food grains in rural areas had declined by over ten percent.

Today this ominous pattern is being repeated most spectacularly in
Brazil, with its vast continental resources and its military dictatorship at-
tracting enormous amounts of foreign capital by virtue of the congenial
investment conditions that it enforces with ruthless efficiency. Hence the

"Brazilian miracle" of a ten-percent rate of annual economic growth. Again, however, this growth is accompanied by a widening of the gap between rich and poor citizens. The statistics of the soaring GNP and plummeting living standards are drearily familiar. Foreign capital is pouring in from the United States, Europe, and Japan. During the decade between 1963 and 1972 the number of miles of paved highway increased by 153 percent, steel production grew by 153 percent, cement output by 161 percent, and automobile production by 248 percent. Between 1975 and 1980 about 20 billion dollars will be spent in opening up and exploiting the vast mineral resources of the country, and during the same period Brazil is expected to jump from sixteenth to sixth place in world steel production.

What this success story means in terms of everyday living for the mass of Brazilian people has been detailed in the book *From the "Democracy" We Have to the Democracy We Desire* by Senator Andre Franco Montoro, former Minister of Labor and Social Welfare and now a professor of law at the University of São Paulo. During the decade 1965 to 1974, Brazil's GNP rose 56 percent but the real value of the minimum wage dropped 55 percent. Senator Montoro illustrates the resultant decrease in purchasing power by noting that a worker had to put in twice as many hours in 1974 as in 1965 to buy the same basic food supplies. To buy a family's monthly ration of 12 pounds of meat, a poorly paid laborer had to work 65 hours and 57 minutes in March 1974, compared with only 25 hours and 24 minutes in December 1966. According to São Paulo trade-union statistics, the work hours needed to pay for tomatoes and lard almost tripled in the same period, and they doubled for other essentials such as rice, beans, bread, and coffee.

The net result is that Brazil, in the process of becoming the most industrialized nation of Latin America, has also won the dubious distinction of having the lowest average industrial wages. Malnutrition is common. A recent report by the Protection and Research Foundation of São Paulo disclosed that the protein intake of Brazilians was as low as that of Indians and Pakistanis—about 15 grams a day per person, compared with 50 grams in the developed countries. It follows that tuberculosis is widespread in Brazil and that leprosy remains a problem. In the Brazilian Northeast an estimated 90 percent of the population suffers from schistosomiasis; Chagas disease is also common there.[9] Both are carried by tropical parasites. Senator Montoro challenges the government's statements that social services have been improved. He quotes official figures showing that the Ministry of Education's share of the budget dropped from 11.07 percent in 1965 to

4.95 percent in 1974, and that the Ministry of Health's share fell from 4.29 percent in 1966 to .99 percent in 1974.

The dictatorial regime appeared to be relaxing its repressive controls when it allowed the November 1975 congressional elections, the first free electoral contest in 11 years of military rule. But when the democratic opposition unexpectedly won a sweeping triumph, the dictatorship clamped down again, making widespread arrests in order to discourage the democratic opposition, which was preparing for the municipal elections of November 1976. The systematic use of torture as an instrument of national policy has been documented by such reliable organizations as the United States Catholic Conference, the National Conference of Brazilian Bishops, the Vatican, and the World Federation of Trade Unions.[10]

What the "Brazilian miracle" adds up to has been analyzed forthrightly in a declaration signed on May 6, 1973, by three archbishops and ten bishops of the Northeast region. In this 30-page document the ecclesiastics detail the country's unemployment, hunger, illiteracy, and high infant mortality, and brand Brazil's "so-called economic miracle as merely a means to make the rich richer and the poor poorer." They attribute the growing income inequity directly to the subordination of Brazil's human and material resources to the global market economy.

> The social and economic structures in Brazil are built on oppression and injustice that evolve from a situation of a capitalism dependent on the great international centers of power. . . .
> Malnutrition, infant mortality, prostitution, illiteracy, unemployment, cultural and political discrimination, growing imbalance between rich and poor and many other consequences characterize the institutionalized violations in Brazil.
> The need of repression to guarantee the functioning and security of an associated capitalist system shows itself ever more imperious, revealing itself inexorable in closing legislative constitutional institutions and rural and urban workers' unions, depleting student leadership, imposing censorship and measures of persecution of workers, peasants and intellectuals, harassing priests and militant clergy, and assuming the most varied forms of imprisonment, tortures, mutilations and assassinations.

Finally, the eccesiastical leaders warn that "the Church no longer is able to remain inert, waiting passively for the hour of changes. . . . The suppressed masses of workers, peasants and numerous unemployed have taken note of what is going on and are progressively assuming a new liberating conscience." All of which suggests no persuasive reason for assuming that the outcome of the "Brazilian miracle" will be any different from that of the Iraqi or Pakistani "miracles," which were equally touted during their days of glory.[11]

This conclusion is supported by a report on the effects of multinational corporations made public by a committee of the Brazilian Chamber of Deputies and reported in the *Los Angeles Times* on December 1, 1975. The committee consisted of seven members of the government's National Renovating Alliance (ARENA) and six members of the opposition Brazilian Democratic Movement (MDB). The majority ARENA report limited itself largely to reproducing the testimony of witnesses, but the minority MDB report went on to analyze the implications of the testimony. Citing statistics showing that Johnson & Johnson has taken out of Brazil 32 times the amount of capital it has invested, and Esso 25 times, the report states: "It is easy to conclude that, contrary to the official argument, the multinationals have brought about a decapitalization of the national economy."

The MDB report also concludes that the multinationals have accentuated certain distortions that already exist in Brazil's economy, by concentrating on the production of expensive goods such as autos and color television sets instead of seeking to supply the minimum necessities of nutrition, health care, housing, and employment to Brazilians. Referring to repeated assertions by government spokesmen that Brazil has the power to control the multinationals, the committee charges that the government in fact is ignorant even of the process by which many national firms have come under foreign control, and that it therefore lacks the basic information essential for control. Finally, the report concludes that protection of Brazilian national interests requires not only strict regulation of the multinationals but also "an alternative pattern of economic development based on the needs of Brazilians."

The same combination of impressive economic growth and social imbalance prevails in other countries following the Brazilian model. Venezuela, for example, is the world's third largest oil exporter, earning some 10 billion dollars in oil royalties in 1974. "What has happened to the oil money?" asks Sister Aura Delia Goncalez, a Roman Catholic nun who works among the slum dwellers of Caracas. "We have seen nothing good from the petrodollars—only the rise in price of milk and meats, more delinquency, shortages of schools and hospitals."[12] In a nation of 12.2 million people, 2.8 million are unemployed or underemployed, and receive no benefits from the oil revenues.

President Carlos Perez has sought to redistribute the national wealth by launching major development programs in industry and agriculture and by nationalizing basic resources, including American-owned mines and oil fields. The end result is questionable, since Perez' program depends on reform from above rather than mass activation and participation from below. Theoretically, the benefits accruing from the Perez projects should trickle down to the lowest classes, but in a hierarchically organized society, benefits inevitably are sucked sidewise into private channels instead. "Our main bottleneck," explains a government spokesman, "is the lack of administrative capacity. We have brilliant leaders and good workers but the problem is the channels." A skeptical foreign correspondent observes that the Perez development plans "may not have any impact on the slum dwellers, but they have opened up lucrative opportunities to foreign business. Hotels and airlines are crowded with people who want to sell anything from Boeing jets and tanker fleets to Miami real estate."[13] Venezuelan businessmen denounce the government's "socialist tendencies," yet they continue to make 35-percent annual profits and to spend weekends on private yachts or in Miami, while their wives frequent French boutiques and luxury shops on fashionable Abraham Lincoln Avenue.

Meanwhile, half of the 2 million inhabitants of Caracas live in the slums known as *ranchos*. German Carias, a writer and director of public relations for the Central University of Caracas, lived for a time in La Charneca, a slum near the Caracas Hilton. In his book *Habla La Charneca*, he writes:

> The rancho people live like animals. They don't believe in anything because nobody has done anything for them. The ranchos are a breeding place for revolution; the people are hungry, despairing and resentful. . . . [They] are fully aware of the country's oil wealth and they want a share of prosperity. There has been no revolt in the *ranchos* yet because the slum dwellers have not found a leader they believe in. The day they get a leader, they could come down from the hills and take over the city.[14]

The Chinese solution for Third World development is in almost every respect the precise opposite of the Brazilian, advocating (1) revolutionary social change rather than preservation of the status quo and (2) independent development of technology and economy rather than dependence on foreign governments or corporations. These two objectives are deemed interdependent and inseparable. Economic development, according to the Chinese strategy, is unattainable without antecedent social restructuring of a fundamental nature. Foreign aid is acceptable only if domestic resources, both labor and capital, are fully mobilized and utilized. Labor and capital are not being fully used today in most of the Third World, where over one-third of the people are unemployed or underemployed, and where the few industrial plants normally operate at well below capacity because of insufficient purchasing power, a result of income inequality.

The Chinese strategy mobilizes unused labor power for work on rural projects such as roads, dams, wells, irrigation canals, terracing, and reforestation. Although this use of surplus labor has proven enormously successful and productive in China, nothing of comparable magnitude has been achieved in India, Pakistan, or Bangladesh because of the unequal distribution of land in these countries, which deprives the peasants of any incentive for working on projects that under prevailing circumstances would primarily benefit the few large landowners. The Green Revolution, under present landowning arrangements, similarly benefits the landlord oligarchy more than small farmers. In industry, as well, the Chinese have achieved steady and solidly based growth. Their system of worker participation in the making of decisions stimulates worker productivity, and their relative income equality ensures a mass market for their industrial products.

It does not follow that the Chinese completely reject the importation of trade or technology from the outside world. Both, in fact, are actively sought, but only on terms that contribute to the independent development of the national economy rather than its subjection to foreign control. The attainment of China's basic goal of economic independence has been facilitated by China's preceding social revolution. The absence of marked income disparity precludes the formation of an upper- and middle-class consumer market for foreign products, present in many Third World societies that are poorer than China. The great emphasis on urban and rural self-sufficiency has made the Chinese largely independent of outside suppliers for basic necessities and the few semi-luxuries made available to Chinese citizens—watches, radios, cameras, bicycles, sewing machines, and the like. Consequently, when the Chinese turn to Japan for fertilizer plants, or to the United States for planes and oil-drilling equipment, they need not bargain away their control of their agriculture or oil fields or aviation industry.

The significance of the Chinese solution is its role as a developmental model for poor Third World countries. The Chinese strategy—to engage first in social revolution and then in pulling yourself up by your own boot-straps—has a certain appeal for the many Third World lands with archaic institutions and a shortage of almost everything except manpower. In ideological appeal the Chinese are displacing the Russians, whose successful Five Year Plans had been considered a model for underdeveloped countries before World War II. But now, whereas the Soviet Union is a relatively affluent Great Power, the Chinese insistently proclaim their membership in the Third World and repudiate any superpower aspirations. In any case, the Maoist model is being followed, with local variations, in Cambodia and Vietnam; it exercises considerable influence in Mozambique, Guinea-Bissau, and Tanzania; reports indicate that it has had a certain impact even in Ethiopia and Somalia, whose economic backwardness up to now has been matched only by their social stagnation.

The Retarding Lead

Turning from the underdeveloped Third World to the developed First World of Western capitalism and Second World of the Soviet Union and Eastern Europe, we find a situation that is the precise opposite of that of the Third World. Whereas the latter faces the problem of acquiring the capital and technology necessary for economic development, the developed worlds are confronted with the challenge of adapting to human needs the capital and technology they already possess. The developed countries, both the capitalist and the socialist, have evolved certain values and institutions suited to maximizing capital accumulation and technological advance. Their success is reflected in their current status of affluent developedness. But, having attained this status, they now sense that the values and institutions evolved during the process of accumulation have become obstacles to the rational and humane use of that which has been accumulated.

The problem is the Retarding Lead syndrome, which in medieval times hobbled the advanced Chinese and favored the retarded Westerners (see page 6). Today the roles of East and West are reversed. It is the affluent First and Second Worlds that are finding it difficult to abandon or modify ways of thinking and acting that served so well in the past. Their natural reaction to current problems is to apply more of the same—more of the traditional and familiar old solutions. They plan to produce still more, so that the size of the pie will increase; they assume that the relative sizes of the slices for the various classes can remain unchanged. By enlarging the pie, the social and political roles of the classes can continue, and old values and institutions can be maintained.

This plan might be described as the technocratic view of the future, with quantitative growth but without qualitative change—the future as never-ending present. But such a plan simply does not work, either economically or psychologically. Economically, it results in an ever-growing GNP, by which man produces more so that he can consume more so that he can produce more—so that he can eventually suffocate in his own waste. Psychologically, it results in the transformation of man into an insatiable consumption machine, and, as Maslow has noted, man by his very nature cannot remain forever content with this role. He becomes, as noted in Chapters 5 and 6, either like the wealthy residents of Boca Raton, "depressed, psychosomatic, and impotent," or like the Albuquerque commune member who refuses to work 40 hours a week "for someone or something that doesn't give a shit about me so that I can get money to buy things I don't give a shit about owning."

The Retarding Lead effect is clearly evident in the policies and dilemmas of the leading powers of the First and Second Worlds, the United States and the Soviet Union. Of the two the Soviet Union probably suffers more from arteriosclerosis, because it lacks corrective mechanisms. The significant improvement in living standards, combined with the rise of the Soviet Union as a world superpower, has relieved the ruling oligarchy from pressure to modify either their political authoritarianism or their socioeconomic elitism. This hardening of the arteries is illustrated by the case of Andrei Sakharov, who pointed out that Russia not only had failed to overtake the United States in the current Second Industrial Revolution, as Stalin and Khrushchev had boasted it would, but was actually falling further behind (see page 110). Sakharov proposed democratization as the remedy—or, as he put it, "more intelligent use of the brake." But the concept of popular participation in decision making in political and economic matters was too threatening to the status and interests of party functionaries, state bureaucrats, and technical experts. Accordingly, Sakharov, a brilliant academician, was stripped of his honors and positions and cut off from all of his work.

Premier Alexei Kosygin, speaking before a plenum of the Central Committee of the Communist Party on September 27, 1965, diagnosed the Soviet economic difficulties as stemming from the rapid growth of the economy. It had grown too large to be directed efficiently from the center, argued Kosygin, and therefore the way out was to improve management techniques and to rely on the "profit index." As a result, as an article in *Izvestia*, December 1, 1967, observed, "Giving no consideration to market demands, certain factory leaders stop turning out products badly needed by the people . . . for the simple reason that these products make low profits." The alternative possibility of introducing meaningful worker participation was not considered by Kosygin and the other Party leaders. Therefore, the Soviet economy continues to suffer from the effects of a work force that is either uncommitted or actually alienated. Russian newspaper accounts reflect the serious problems of shoddy work, theft of state property, and the world's highest rate of alcoholism.

A recent study of workers in the 18–to–25 age bracket at a large locomotive plant in the Ukraine shows the complete breakdown of "socialist emulation" and "socialist competition"—two surviving institutionalized values designed to stimulate worker participation. Individual workers are singled out as models for others to emulate, and assembly lines, work brigades, and factory shifts vie with one another in "socialist competition." "It exists only on paper," says a lathe worker quoted in the study. "Many people do not even know with whom they are competing." An electrician comments: "On our crew there is no emulation. There is simply a quota that you have to meet." Another worker dismissed the entire motivational system at the locomotive plants as "just fiction." [15]

The symptoms of the Retarding Lead are more glaringly apparent in the open American society, in both domestic and foreign affairs. America has the most powerful military forces ever assembled, an immense and productive economic machine, soaring per capita income, and the largest number of Nobel Prize winners in the various fields of human endeavor. Yet it also suffers from the negative effects of wealth and power. In the economic realm it is burdened with New Deal regulatory agencies that represent the interests they were designed to regulate better than the consumers they supposedly protect, a tax structure used increasingly as a subsidy mechanism in the amount of 92 billion dollars yearly, giant multinational corporations that dominate the economy through their control of raw materials and productive facilities, and key industries that are becoming more concentrated, anticompetitive, and so dependent on military contracts that the entire economy is becoming addicted to military expenditures. One of every five jobs in the United States depends directly or indirectly on the Pentagon, one-half to two-thirds of the engineers and scientists are in military and related technology, and 80 percent of federal research money is devoted to the military arts. America also has teenage drug addicts, price-rigging and bribe-giving business executives, festering and expanding ghettos, a TV "wasteland," a burgeoning crime rate, uncared-for aged, and a deteriorating physical environment.

In foreign affairs, consider the implications of the following account, by President Johnson's press secretary Bill Moyers, of the President's conduct during the Vietnam War:

> Why, then, wasn't he willing to compromise in Vietnam? The irony is, he thought he was. "Well, boys, I've gone the second, third and fourth mile tonight," he said after his Johns Hopkins speech in 1965. He had proposed a multi-billion-dollar rehabilitation program for Indochina, including North Vietnam, and he was convinced that it was a bargain Ho Chi Minh couldn't turn down. Another time he made another offer, in secrecy, and Ho again said no. "I don't understand it," he said with a note of sadness in his voice. "George Meany would've grabbed at a deal like that."
>
> Therein may be the biggest lesson Lyndon Johnson may inadvertently have taught us. We think of ourselves as a broad-minded, good-intentioned, generous people, pursuing worthy goals in a world we assume is aching to copy us. "Surely," the logic goes, "all we have to do is offer them what we would want if we were in their place." . . .
>
> What he had to learn the hard way, and teach us as he went along, was something about the limits of perception.[16]

It is these "limits of perception" that explain the following record on Vietnam:

"The French are going to win. It is a fight that is going to be finished with our help" (Admiral Arthur Radford, Chairman, Joint Chiefs of Staff, 1954).

"Every quantitative measure we have shows we're winning the war" (Robert McNamara, Secretary of Defense, 1962).

"The Vietcong are going to collapse within weeks. Not months, but weeks" (Walt W. Rostow, 1965).

"The enemy has been defeated at every turn" (General William C. Westmoreland, 1968).

"At the moment I do not anticipate the fall of Vietnam. . . . There's an opportunity to salvage the situation by giving the South Vietnamese an opportunity to fight for their freedom" (President Gerald Ford, April 3, 1975).

"Saigon is liberated" (Provisional Revolutionary Government, April 30, 1975).

"Make It Do, Do Without"

The effects of the Retarding Lead can be seen all over the American landscape; Pete Seeger's concrete is visible everywhere. But so is his sprouting green grass—the feature of the American landscape that distinguishes it from the Soviet. In the preceding four chapters we noted the myriad manifestations of this new life in all phases of American society. In addition to those specific efforts toward self-management on a small scale or in individual matters, our time of troubles has engendered, in Western Europe as well as in the United States, many plans for overall social reordering. Their characteristics are as varied as their authors' commitments. The first of the three plans we will examine here is by Dr. Sicco Mansholt, former president of the Common Market Commission, who is apprehensive and soberly concerned with what he considers to be the urgent problem of human survival. Here is an extract of Dr. Mansholt's letter to the Common Market Commission, February 9, 1972:

> More serious are the questions which will soon be presented to us and which are beginning to show more and more clearly. When I say "us" I do not think of Europe, but of the whole of humanity.
>
> These problems concern the following factors, which are the great deciders of the future of humanity:
> —world population growth
> —food production
> —pollution
> —the use of natural resources. . . .
> If Europe follows a well-defined policy, she will be in a better position to impose a similar policy on the rest of the world and notably on the United States and Japan.
> If Europe does not follow a clear policy but follows events and renounces the initiative, I believe that the cause is lost, as in my opinion the United States has not the political force necessary to guide the world towards the solution of this great problem. The United

States is going down-hill and it will be extremely difficult to preserve it from total collapse.

Conclusion: Europe has a mission to accomplish.

(1) Priority for investment in food production.

(2) A great reduction in consumption of material goods per inhabitant, compensated by: social foresight, intellectual expansion, organization of pastimes, recreational activities, etc.

(3) Extension of the life of all domestic goods to prevent waste and the avoidance of production of non-essential goods.

(4) A fight against pollution and exhaustion of primary materials by the reorientation of investment towards recycling, and antipollution measures which will naturally result in a reduction in demand and so of production.

It is obvious that the society of tomorrow could not be directed towards growth, at least in the material field.

To begin with, we must no longer orientate our economic systems toward the maximization of the gross national product. I would suggest the replacement of the former by gross national happiness (it still remains to be seen whether one can quantify happiness).[17]

The second plan, by Robin Clarke, former consultant to UNESCO and editor of *Science Journal,* is expectant, utopian, and couched in terms of self-realization rather than self-preservation.

One might imagine the landscape of the new Utopia looking something like this: a countryside dotted with windmills and solar houses, studded with intensively but organically worked plots of land, food production systems dependent on the integration of many different species, with timber, fish, animals and plants playing mutually dependent roles, with wilderness areas plentifully available where perhaps even our vicious distinction between hunting and domestication was partly broken down; a life style for men and women which involved hard physical work but not over excessively long hours or in a tediously repetitive way; an architecture which sought to free men from external services and which brought them into contact with one another, rather than separated them into cubicles where the goggle box and bed were the only possible diversions; a political system so decentralized and small that individuals—all individuals—could play more than a formal, once-every-five-years role; a philosophy of change that viewed the micro-system as the operative unit; and a city-scape conceived on a human scale and as a centre for recreation.[18]

The third plan, by Marcus Raskin, codirector of the Institute for Policy Studies, advocates a citizens' program for a new America, emanating from grass-roots meetings in which people will test ideas and plans against their own problems and aspirations.

> The Institute for Policy Studies is participating in a citizens' education program in which people across the country develop their own ideas and programs for their city and region. . . . It is likely that this effort will result in new ideas and new levels of participation among people. It is also likely that a new national citizens' program outside the two political parties will emerge through careful work at the local level. . . .
>
> The following . . . presents a sampling of ideas which could be initiated, developed and discussed. . . . The listing is neither exhaustive nor systematic; these proposals are starting points. . . .
>
> Grant low interest loans to farmers, laborers, sharecroppers, to help them in the development of agricultural production, and to refurbish their homes and equipment. Set prices or develop competitive public corporations to sell grain, feed and machinery. . . .
>
> Develop plans for rural reconstruction. Help universities, labor unions, schools of engineering and architecture which will aid any group of 2,000 or more people to build or redevelop a town. Enact a Town Homesteading Act. . . .
>
> Develop community and regional trucking and rail systems and distribution centers (transportation networks) for food and raw materials products. Encourage local markets rather than national and international markets for agricultural products, so that a more natural dietary system will emerge, and so that food value will be measured in terms of nutritional rather than commercial characteristics. . . .
>
> Organize technical assistance teams to help communities start their own enterprises. Encourage the development of worker run enterprises through low interest loans and marketing assistance. Establish public banks governed by local election, to invest only within local communities or blocks. . . .
>
> Oligopolies or "natural" monopolies such as the energy industry, the railroads, the major banks, the airlines, the utilities, the drug industry and other basic industries which are of such concern to people as consumers and workers must now be transformed into systems of public enterprise. Structure must be devised on a local, city and regional basis which will test modes of public participation leading to worker-community-consumer control over basic industry in the economic sphere. . . .

Hold public architectural contests on a city basis for building and refurbishing houses, factories, schools and public squares.

Provide grants to help fund artist-musician communes whose members will work with communities in the development of local, popular culture. Provide grants to start new local newspapers; continue support, regardless of political views, so long as there is a group of 500–1,000 who will read the newspaper.

Forbid commercials on television; create means for public support and public choice on programming. . . .

Encourage cooperation among people within the schools: group examinations, encouragement of cheating (each helping the other). Put science libraries and experimental centers in neighborhoods. Guarantee academic and community teaching jobs to graduates. Establish adult education schools and develop adult labor schools. Encourage research and practical discussions among students on the creation of a new democracy. . . .[19]

These visions of the future are curiously reminiscent of the first Dark Age, in the sense that they suggest a withdrawal or retreat from something glamorous and impressive. But the present retreat is from a precipice or a dead end; it is a withdrawal in order to work out a strategy for survival and to make a fresh start. The new Dark Age, like the original, will not be an age of affluence. The "jet set" celebrities and their playgrounds will become less newsworthy. Supersonic jets and luxury steamers will be remembered as the dinosaurs of a bygone age. Bicycles will become more numerous than autos, even in the America of Henry Ford and General Motors. The old electric trolley will come back in modern streamlined form as the answer to the need for cheap pollution-free mass transit. There might well be a revival of sailing ships, which, making use of modern aerodynamics and light metal alloys, could transport cargoes around the world cleanly and profitably in an era of high fuel costs. If less attention is paid to the "beautiful people," more will be paid to the plain ones organizing the self-sufficient Adams Morgan neighborhood community in Washington, D.C., painstakingly resolving the problems of worker control in Yugoslav factories, working in and managing the successful kibbutzim industries, managing themselves in Chinese communes and factories, and developing the techniques of organic farming and of self-sufficient housing in various countries of the world. In short, there will be a return to the New England adage:

> Use it up
> Wear it out
> Make it do
> Do without

"Drift to Unparalleled Catastrophe"

The new Dark Age will not be a mellow or a comfortable period, especially for those who today enjoy privilege and status. J. B. Priestley, at age 80, contemplating the future from the perspective of his literary career of 60 years, put it candidly and perceptively:

> I should add, without being grandiose about it, that there's a slithering down of civilization. The whole scientific and industrial civilization which began in the 16th century is coming to an end. It won't last. Something will take its place, maybe it will be better. It won't seem better to me.[20]

In late Roman times, writers had similar feelings about a time of transition that, in the words of the historian C. Warren Hollister,

> brought disorganization and savagery, but it also gave Europe the chance for a new beginning, an escape from old customs and lifeless conventions, a release from the stifling prison that the Roman Empire, for most of its inhabitants, had come to be. . . . Life in the post-Roman West was hazardous, ignorant, foul, and deeply insecure, but such was the price of the new beginning. Periods of momentous change are seldom comfortable.[21]

Others have noted the discomfort of such periods. "Pessimism over the future of the world," wrote Alfred North Whitehead in 1925, "comes from a confusion between civilization and security. In the immediate future there will be less security than in the immediate past, less stability. . . . But on the whole, the great ages have been the unstable ages."[22]

It may seem contradictory to consider a "great age" to be one in which its intellectual leaders sense impending doom. Albert Einstein, observing what destructive use was being made of his lifelong work, stated bitterly that if he had his life to live over again he would choose to be a plumber. And on his deathbed he warned: "The unleashed power of the atom has changed everything save our modes of thinking, and thus we drift to un-paralleled catastrophe."

Nuclear holocaust is indeed one of the two ways in which doomsayers foresee the human race making its exit from this planet; the other is ex-tinction of the human species owing to the insufficient time left for man-kind to effect the sociocultural revolution made imperative by the ongoing technological-scientific revolution. The first forecast is a "big bang" theory of the end of mankind; the second is a "slithering down" theory. Perhaps neither is so imminent or unavoidable as it may appear.

The "big bang" is obviously not a remote threat, especially in view of the present proliferation of nuclear weapons. If the end result does prove to be a nuclear war, in the course of which certain countries are subjected to thousands of megatons of nuclear detonations, most scientists agree that, although not all citizens would perish, the traumatic impact on the survivors would be without precedent in history. All or almost all of the large cities would be destroyed; a very large percentage of the total population would be killed; many of the survivors would be burned, maimed, or poisoned by radiation; the necessities of life would be lacking in many regions; and epidemics might follow the destruction of sanitation facilities, adding to the debilitation of a radiation-exposed people. And if several industrialized countries were subjected simultaneously to such nuclear assault, there would be no chance for relief and rehabilitation with outside aid, such as was possible after the two World Wars.

Yet all this does not necessarily mean that the end result of a nuclear holocaust must be the extinction of the human race or its reversion to an-other Stone Age. It might mean, instead, the overnight rise to world leader-ship of the only major society capable of coping with and recuperating from such a trauma—the People's Republic of China. "Dig deep shelters, stock up grain, and keep a cool head" is not merely Mao's injunction; it is a national strategy that has been implemented in both rural and urban areas. Reports from numerous sources indicate the construction in all parts of China of underground shelters, in numbers not approached by any other country. These shelters provide protection against both nuclear and chem-ical weapons and are stocked with food and water; those in urban centers include underground workshops equipped with industrial machinery.

More important is the pervasive communal spirit in China, to which all visitors attest. Organized and habitual mutual aid is the key to surviving nuclear war, but China is the only major civilization that has implemented this custom not in rhetoric but in reality. In contrast, recall the bomb shelters built in the United States a few years ago that were equipped with machine guns to keep less foresightful neighbors away in the event of an atomic attack.

The major difference between the world before a nuclear war and after one might prove to be that, whereas the former is about one-fourth Chinese, the latter might be one-half or three-fourths Chinese. If Christopher Columbus had been Chinese, and the two Americas had been settled by Chinese rather than by Europeans, the world today would already be one-half or three-fourths Chinese. It is ironic that what Columbus gained for the Caucasoid branch of the human race may yet be lost by those Russian and American Caucasoids who choose to "put a cap on the arms race" by increasing the number of nuclear arms.

As for the assumption that human beings are incapable of changing their ways of thinking and acting fast enough to adapt to the new technology, there are at least two reasons for questioning its validity. One is suggested by Thomas S. Kuhn's theory of the structure of scientific revolutions, which is also applicable to social revolutions. Kuhn has shown that jumps in knowledge within one generation—from the Ptolemaic system to the Copernican in astronomy, or from classical to quantum physics—were preceded by an accumulation of anomalies that could not be fitted into the dominant theory despite complicated rationalizations. Such "cognitive dissonance" is finally resolved only when it is simply explained from an entirely different perspective, which resolves the anomalies by restructuring them at a higher level of organization. Modern civilization today is in a state of "cognitive dissonance," with its growing inequities within and among nations, its obliterative weapons, and its environmental deterioration. But these divergences are becoming increasingly intolerable, contradicting the system's own goals and images of itself and resulting in the unrest, alienation, and violence characteristic of our age. Such a crisis can generate a quantum jump in society as well as in science. These jumps have occurred with unforeseen abruptness in the past; the Protestant Reformation and the French Revolution are two cases in point. Comparable jumps can be expected in the near future, generated by the gaps between official creeds and social realities and by the resulting challenge being offered throughout the world to traditional values and institutions.

The other reason for doubting the assumption that mankind cannot change its ways is indicated by the current paradoxical combination of global unity and global diversity. The unity is readily apparent in instant mass-communication media and the space voyages of astronauts and cosmonauts. Equally significant, however, although less obvious, is the unprecedented diversity in social philosophies and institutions. The variety in the Western world ranges from the United States to Sweden, in the Communist world from Yugoslavia to North Korea, and in the underdeveloped world from Bolivia to Tanzania. A significant new social mutation also appears to be emerging in China. In a shrinking world of such diversity, any creative achievement anywhere quickly becomes common knowledge. Sooner or later, enthusiastically or grudgingly, it is studied and discussed and then imitated, adapted, or rejected. The net result is global interaction and cross-fertilization. The law of hybrid vigor operates in the cultural realm as well as the biological.

The Promise of the Coming Dark Age

Kuhn's concept of scientific revolutions and the law of hybrid vigor both suggest that the success and influence of human societies in the future will depend more on their adaptability than on the size of their GNP or the number of their missiles. Adaptability is precisely the chief problem of the affluent First and Second Worlds, laboring under the burden of the Retarding Lead. Jacob Bronowski sensed this dilemma of the developed societies.

> The ascent of man will go on. But do not assume that it will go on carried by Western civilisation as we know it. We are being weighed in the balance at this moment. If we give up, the next step will be taken—but not by us. We have not been given any guarantee that Assyria and Egypt and Rome were not given. We are waiting to be somebody's past too, and not necessarily that of our future. . . . If we do not take the next step in the ascent of man, it will be taken by people elsewhere, in Africa, in China.

Bronowski then reflects poignantly on the prospect of the torch passing to non-Western hands.

> Should I feel that to be sad? No, not in itself. Humanity has a right to change its colour. And yet, wedded as I am to the civilisation that nurtured me, I should feel it to be infinitely sad. I, whom England made, whom it taught its language and its tolerance and excitement in

intellectual pursuits, I should feel it a grave sense of loss (as you would) if a hundred years from now Shakespeare and Newton are the historical fossils in the ascent of man, in the way that Homer and Euclid are.[23]

Bronowski's apprehension that Western man may become the "backward native" of the future will probably prove unwarranted. His concern presupposes that some non-Western people will gain the crushing global hegemony—political, economic, and cultural—enjoyed by the West in modern times. But the tempo of change and the shrinking of the earth into a global village now preclude the gross disparities in levels of development that evolved during millenia of regional isolation, and that existed when Westerners were discovering paleolithic aborigines in Australia and Confucian mandarins in China. Furthermore, the growing mass activation and assertiveness in all societies ensure that the world will never again be dominated by any one country or region. The Vietnam experience offers convincing proof of that proposition. And certainly we will never again witness the internalization of a myth of the superiority of some future *bwana* or *sahib*. More likely than the fossilization of Shakespeare and Newton is the cross-fertilization of Asian and African and European civilizations, with universally beneficial results.

For decades Western scholars have been studying the process of modernization, which is essentially the diffusion of Western values, technology, and political ideas and institutions. But a reverse process is now under way; global interrelationships henceforth will involve a two-way rather than a one-way process. This process is evident in the reflections of the American correspondent Sydney Schanberg, after spending two weeks in the French embassy in Phnom Penh with 800 other foreigners before being evacuated. Schanberg was impressed by the contrast between the foreigners inside the embassy—who were complaining, squabbling, stealing cigarettes, and refusing to shave or cooperate—and the Khmer Rouge soldiers outside the embassy—who were sleeping on the ground and subsisting on rice, salt, and an occasional piece of chicken.

> Why was there not more sharing, more of a community spirit? What made us into such acquisitive, self-protective beings?
> Why did all the Asians live outside, in the heat and rain, while many of the Caucasians, like my group, lived inside, with air-conditioning? We explained it by saying the living arrangements were up to the embassy, but this was clearly not an answer. Was our behavior and our segregation a verdict on our way of life?[24]

A more direct and dramatic example of global cultural interaction is the impact of African resistance movements on Portugal. That country waged colonial wars for decades in order to retain its extensive possessions in Africa. These wars forced the Portuguese dictatorship to devote 40 percent of its budget to military expenditures and to draft one of every four men of military age into the armed forces. The protracted campaigning not only strained the meager resources of Portugal but also won some of the officers over to the revolutionary ideology of the guerrillas they were fighting. Long conversations with their prisoners led them to realize, as they put it, that "Those who benefited from the war were the same financial groups that exploited the people in the metropolis and, comfortably installed in Lisbon and Oporto or abroad, by means of a venal government obliged the Portuguese people to fight in Africa in defense of their immense profits." Thus the colonial experience led to a reappraisal of what was going on at home. "What we saw was that Portugal was itself part of the Third World. Lisbon and Oporto were an illusion, the country within was underdeveloped, with an illiterate and exploited peasantry."[25] Thus revolution in the colonies led directly to revolution in the mother country—to the overthrow of a decades-old Portuguese dictatorship, with repercussions for the Western world that are still far from played out. Whatever the outcome of the Portuguese revolution, it is as significant as it is novel that Admiral Antonio Rosa Coutinho, an influential member of the High Council of the Revolution, should lecture a group of businessmen that "the Armed Forces Movement considers itself a liberation movement like those in Africa, and seeks not only formal independence but total liberation of the people."[26]

Another example of the reversal of the direction of global cultural interaction is to be found in China. That country was the scene of a massive Christian missionary effort during the nineteenth century. Although a significant proportion of the population was never converted, the West nevertheless made important contributions in education, medical services, and, to a lesser degree, religious and philosophical thought. With the Communist revolution after World War II the Christian missionary undertaking came to an end, and Maoist theory and practice began in turn to affect an increasingly divided and uncertain Western world. In October 1974 a group of American scholars held a conference in Washington, D.C., to analyze Maoism as a major new world religion. The Maoist insistence on subordinating self and serving others, according to these scholars, raises the question of whether Christianity and other traditional religions have been "outperformed," and of whether certain aspects of Maoist society may serve as a model for the class-divided Western societies. When asked what Mao "is really trying to do," Norman Webster, Peking correspondent of the *Toronto Globe and Mail*, replied "I believe he's trying to make a Christian out of every person. This is something no one else has ever really tried to do—at least on such an extensive scale."[27] And the *New York Times* correspondent James Reston reported after a visit to China "the tremendous effort to bring out what is best in man, what makes them good, what makes them cooperate with one another and be considerate and not beastly to one another. They are trying that."[28] These statements raise the paradoxical possibility that Maoist China, with its applied Christianity, may leave a deeper imprint on the West today than the West, with its doctrinal Christianity, left on China in the nineteenth century.

Third World influence on the West is also manifest in the profound ethical challenge of the so-called liberation theology. This thinking has been enunciated most clearly by progressive Catholic clergymen in Latin America, especially by the Peruvian theologian Gustavo Gutierrez, whose book *A Theology of Liberation* has been published in English, French, German, Italian, Dutch, and Philippine editions. Interpreting the Bible as a revolutionary book and Jesus as a revolutionary leader, liberation theology demands that the present exploitation of four-fifths of the human family by the remaining one-fifth be ended through rapid social change. It holds that whether this change comes violently or nonviolently depends on the actions of the minority rather than those of the majority, but either way it will come. It asserts that believers in God must be on the side of the oppressed or deny their faith. "It is not a question of admitting or denying a fact which confronts us," says Gutierrez. "Rather, it is a question of which side we are on." But being on the side of the oppressed, insist these theologians, does not mean going to a Third World country or to a black ghetto to "help the people" or to start a revolution. Rather, it means staying in one's established world and working to change by whatever means necessary the power structure, which is responsible for exploitation in the developed world as well as in the underdeveloped. This essentially revolutionary doctrine, although primarily of Third World origin, has won considerable support among Western churchmen, suggesting a parallel in the theological realm to the recent interaction of African revolutionaries and Portuguese army officers in the political realm.

This new two-way interaction between the Western and non-Western worlds can scarcely be viewed as a menace to Western civilization. It represents an infusion of hybrid cultural vigor rather than the eclipse or subordination of the Western world. Perhaps future change will not be Western civilization's transformation into a fossil by developments beyond its control, as Bronowski feared. Rather, we may say that the West was in danger of fossilization, and that the decline has been halted, that revivification has set in, precisely owing to the active participation of *all* peoples of *all* cultures and of *all* social origins.

What we are witnessing today is not the degradation of Western man to the position of "native" but the transcendence of *Homo sapiens* to *Homo humanus*. This was the message of John Maynard Keynes when, in the depth of the Great Depression, he wrote:

> We shall be able to afford to dare to assess the money-motive at its true value. The love of money as a possession . . . will be recognised for what it is, a somewhat disgusting morbidity, one of those semi-criminal, semi-pathological propensities which one hands over with a shudder to the specialists in mental disease. All kinds of social customs and economic practices, affecting the distribution of wealth and of economic rewards and penalties, which we now maintain at all costs, however distasteful and unjust they may be in themselves, because they are tremendously useful in promoting the accumulation of capital, we shall then be free, at last, to discard. . . . We shall once more value ends above means and prefer the good to the useful. We shall honour those who can teach us how to pluck the hour and the day virtuously and well, the delightful people who are capable of taking direct enjoyment in things. . . . But, of course, it will happen gradually, not as a catastrophe. Indeed, it has already begun. [29]

Indeed it has begun, and if we will but open our eyes we can see the green grass sprouting through the concrete. This is the promise of the coming Dark Age.

NOTES

Chapter 1 (Pages 1–13)

1. R. Lopez, *The Birth of Europe* (New York: Evans, 1967), p. 58.
2. Cited by F. W. Walbank, *The Awful Revolution* (Liverpool, England: Liverpool University Press, 1969), pp. 33, 34.
3. A. Lichauco, "The Lichauco Paper: Imperialism in the Philippines," *Monthly Review*, July–August 1973, pp. 12, 109.
4. R. A. Rappaport, "The Flow of Energy in an Agricultural Society," *Scientific American*, September 1971, pp. 130-133.
5. *Newsweek*, January 3, 1969, p. 79.
6. Cited by Lopez, *The Birth of Europe*, p. 25.
7. *New York Times*, January 29, 1968.
8. *Los Angeles Times*, October 24, 1974.
9. *I. F. Stone's Weekly*, July 14, 1969.

Chapter 2 (Pages 14–24)

1. Translation by R. Lopez, *The Birth of Europe* (New York: Evans, 1967), p. 108.
2. *Houses and House-Life of the American Aborigines* (New York, 1881), p. 45.
3. Statement by an Odawa Indian, Wilfred Pelletier, from his collection of essays on education, *This Book Is about Schools*, as cited in the *New York Times*, March 3, 1971.
4. P. Durdin, "From the Space Age to the Tasaday," *New York Times Magazine*, October 8, 1972, p. 15; NBC Report, "The Cave People of the Philippines," October 10, 1972.
5. A. Bandura, *Aggression* (Englewood Cliffs, N. J.: Prentice-Hall, 1973), pp. 113, 322.

6. *Newsweek,* October 17, 1974.
7. Aristotle, *The Politics,* 1253b.
8. A. W. Benn, *The New Politics: A Socialist Reconnaissance* (London: Fabian Tract No. 402, 1970), pp. 9, 10.
9. Cited by D. Lerner, *The Passing of Traditional Society* (New York: Free Press, 1958), p. 214.
10. "God Bless the Grass," words and music by Malvina Reynolds. © Schroder Music Company (ASCAP) 1964. Used by permission. I am indebted to Professor John Platt of the University of Michigan for this reference.

Chapter 3 (Pages 25-55)

1. C. S. Lewis, *The Abolition of Man* (New York: Macmillan, 1947), p. 35.
2. H. Marcuse, *One Dimensional Man* (Boston: Beacon Press, 1964), p. 240.
3. W. Leiss, *The Domination of Nature* (New York: Braziller, 1972), p. 194.
4. Cited by L. Huberman, *We the People,* rev. ed. (New York: Harper, 1947), p. 218.
5. J. M. Blair, *Economic Concentration* (New York: Harcourt Brace Jovanovich, 1972), p. 151.
6. J. K. Page, Jr., and W. Clark, "The New Alchemy: How to Survive in Your Spare Time," *Smithsonian,* February 1975, p. 88.
7. *New York Times,* June 16, 1975.
8. Cited by W. Robbins, *The American Food Scandal* (New York: Morrow, 1974), p. 10.
9. Cited in *Farmworkers in Rural America 1971-1972.* Hearings before the Subcommittee on Children and Youth of the Committee on Labor and Public Welfare, United States Senate, 92nd Congress, January 11, 1972, Part 3A, p. 1156.
10. Cited by J. K. Galbraith, *The Great Crash, 1929* (Boston: Houghton Mifflin, 1955), p. 20.
11. Cited in *Farmworkers in Rural America,* p. 1119.
12. United States Department of Agriculture Economic Research Service, *Farm News Situation,* July 1972, p. 73.
13. Cited in *Farmworkers in Rural America,* p. 1089.
14. J. S. Steinhart and C. E. Steinhart, "Energy Use in the U.S. Food System," *Science,* April 19, 1974, Vol. 184, p. 310.
15. D. Pimentel et al., "Food Production and the Energy Crisis," *Science,* November 2, 1973, Vol. 182, pp. 443-449.
16. Steinhart and Steinhart, "Energy Use," p. 312.

17. B. Commoner, "Energy and Rural People: Address before the National Conference on Rural America, Washington, D.C., April 17, 1975," in *Center for the Biology of Natural Systems* (St. Louis, Mo.: Washington University), p. 21.
18. W. R. Bailey, *The One-Man Farm* (Washington, D.C.: United States Department of Agriculture Economic Research Service, 1973), pp. v, 3.
19. *Farmworkers in Rural America,* pp. 669–670.
20. Commoner, "Energy and Rural People," p. 4.
21. Details in Steinhart and Steinhart, "Energy Use," p. 314.
22. *San Francisco Chronicle,* April 29, 1974.
23. Commoner, "Energy and Rural People," p. 11.
24. *Los Angeles Times,* December 10, 1973.
25. M. Ram, "Les contradictions de la Révolution Verte en Inde," *Le Monde Diplomatique,* October 1974. Cited in *World Hunger: Causes and Remedies: A Transactional Institute Report,* October 1974, pp. 55–56.
26. Cited by J. Omo-Fadaka, "Industrialization and Poverty in the Third World," *Ecologist,* February 1974, p. 61.
27. M. Hoda, in an address to the International Conference on the Indian Government's Document "Approach to the Five Year Plan 1974–79," held at the Imperial College of Science and Technology, London, 1973. Cited by J. Omo-Fadaka, "Industrialization and Poverty," p. 63.
28. *New York Times,* July 14 and 15, 1975.
29. W. E. Smith, "President," *New Yorker,* October 30, 1971, p. 53.
30. *New York Times,* February 4, 1973.
31. Ibid.
32. Cited by J. Omo-Fadaka, "Industrialization and Poverty," p. 62.
33. W. Rich, *Smaller Families through Social and Economic Progress* (Washington, D.C.: Overseas Development Council, 1973), p. 56.
34. This official statement was published in October 1969 in the Communist Party theoretical journal *Hung Chi* and cited in the *New York Times,* October 15, 1969.
35. R. Berger, "Beckoning a New Generation," *Nation,* October 18, 1971, pp. 362–363.
36. *New York Times,* July 23, 1975.
37. R. Alley, "Creative Women," *Broadsheet,* October 1973.

Chapter 4 *(Pages 56–82)*

1. E. Palmore, "Predicting Longevity: A Follow-up Controlling for Age," *Gerontology,* Winter 1969.

2. I. Adelman and C. T. Morris, *Economic Growth and Social Equity in Developing Countries* (Stanford, Calif.: Stanford University Press, 1973), p. 1.

3. *New York Times,* June 25, 1969.

4. Cited by C. G. Benello and D. Roussopoulos, *The Case for Participatory Democracy* (New York: Grossman, 1971), p. 7.

5. *Congressional Record,* April 2, 1973, Series No. S6327.

6. P. Blumberg, *Industrial Democracy: The Sociology of Participation* (New York: Schocken Books, 1969), p. 123.

7. Adelman and Morris, *Economic Growth,* p. 202.

8. *Work in America: Report of a Special Task Force to the Secretary of Health, Education and Welfare* (Cambridge, Mass.: M.I.T. Press, 1973), p. 94.

9. *New York Times,* June 2, 1975.

10. Cited by D. Jenkins, "Beyond Job Enrichment," *Working Papers,* Winter 1975, p. 54.

11. Cited by D. Jenkins, *Job Power* (Garden City, N.Y.: Doubleday, 1973), p. 82.

12. Ibid.

13. *Los Angeles Times,* October 26, 1975.

14. *Wall Street Journal,* February 26, 1973.

15. *San Francisco Chronicle,* November 24, 1972.

16. Ibid., May 22, 1974.

17. *New York Times,* March 19, 1975.

18. *Los Angeles Times,* October 28, 1975.

19. Cited by S. Zukin, *Beyond Marx and Tito: Theory and Practice in Yugoslav Socialism* (Cambridge, England: Cambridge University Press, 1975), p. 162.

20. Ibid., p. 183.

21. J. Zupanov, "Employees' Participation and Social Power in Industry," *First International Conference on Participation and Self-Management, Dubrovnik, Yugoslavia, December 13–17, 1972* (Zagreb, Yugoslavia), Vol. 1, p. 38.

22. Ibid., pp. 38, 39.

23. *Borba,* January 25, 1971. Cited by M. Markovic, *From Affluence to Praxis* (Ann Arbor: University of Michigan Press, 1974), p. 264.

24. Cited by C. Pateman, *Participation and Democratic Theory* (Cambridge, England: Cambridge University Press, 1970), p. 90.

25. J. Goricar, "Workers' Self-Management: Ideal Type—Social Reality," *First International Conference on Participation and Self-Management, Dubrovnik, Yugoslavia, December 13–17, 1972* (Zagreb, Yugoslavia), Vol. 1, p. 31.

26. S. Melman, "Industrial Efficiency under Managerial vs. Cooperative Decision-Making: A Comparative Study of Manufacturing Enterprises in Israel," *Studies in Comparatice Economic Development* (Beverly Hills, Calif.: Sage Publications, 1969).

27. A. Zimbalist, "Workers' Control: Its Structure under Allende," *Monthly Review,* March 1974, pp. 39–42.
28. Cited in "At the Side of the Workers," *Science for the People,* 1973, Vol. 5, No. 6, p. 29.
29. Cited in "Chile: An Unprecedented Situation," *Monthly Review,* February 1973, p. 34.
30. Zimbalist, "Workers' Control," p. 41.
31. A. D. Barnett, *Cadres, Bureaucracy, and Political Power in Communist China* (New York: Columbia University Press, 1967), p. 433.
32. B. M. Richman, "Capitalists and Managers in Communist China," *Harvard Business Review,* January–February 1967, p. 61.
33. L. Kraar, "I Have Seen China," *Fortune,* August 1972, p. 114.
34. S. Topping, *The New York Times Report from China* (New York: Quadrangle, 1971), p. 251.
35. Kraar, "I Have Seen China," p. 114.
36. *New York Times Magazine,* November 26, 1972, p. 101.
37. B. M. Richman, *Industrial Society in Communist China* (New York: Random House, 1969), p. 914.
38. *New York Times,* August 10, 1973.
39. R. Berger, "Beckoning a New Generation," *Nation,* October 18, 1971, p. 362.
40. Cited by Pateman, *Participation and Democratic Theory,* p. 86.
41. Cited by H. I. Hogbin, *Social Change* (London: Watts, 1958), p. 37.
42. M. E. Gettleman and D. Mermelstein, *The Great Society Reader* (New York: Random House, 1967), p. 126.

Chapter 5 *(Pages 83–135)*

1. Cited by C. Pateman, *Participation and Democratic Theory* (Cambridge, England: Cambridge University Press, 1970), p. 5.
2. Ibid., p. 11.
3. A. W. Benn, *The New Politics: A Socialist Reconnaissance* (London: Fabian Tract No. 402), p. 11.
4. *San Francisco Chronicle,* April 21, 1974.
5. L. P. Gerlach, "Fumbling Freely into the Future," *1971 American Anthropological Association Experimental Symposium on Cultural Futurology* (Minneapolis: University of Minnesota, 1971, mimeographed preconference volume), p. G76.
6. A. de Tocqueville, *Democracy in America* (New York: Vintage Books, 1945), p. 259.
7. *New York Times,* January 15, 1971.

8. Ibid., December 17, 1970.
9. *Chicago Sun-Times,* April 27, 1971.
10. Cited by B. A. Stein, "The Centerville Fund, Inc.: A Case Study in Community Economic Control," *Journal of Applied Behavioral Science,* 1973, Vol. 9, Nos. 2 and 3, p. 251.
11. Cited by J. J. Mansbridge, "Town Meeting Democracy," *Working Papers,* 1973, Vol. 1 (Summer), No. 2, p. 7.
12. Stein, "The Centerville Fund," pp. 258–259.
13. Father D. Fisher and Sister Paulette, in *Focus on Neighborhood,* July 25, 1973.
14. Personal communication.
15. J. F. Revel, *Without Marx or Jesus* (Garden City, N.Y.: Doubleday, 1971).
16. *New York Times,* October 4, 1973.
17. Cited in Anthony Lewis' column, *New York Times,* April 15, 1974.
18. *New York Times,* April 9, 1974.
19. *American Families: Trends and Pressures, 1973* (Hearings before the Subcommittee on Children and Youth of the Committee on Labor and Public Welfare, United States Senate, 93rd Congress, First Session, September 24, 1973), pp. 113–114.
20. *Newsweek,* November 10, 1973, p. 48.
21. *New York Times,* December 2, 1972.
22. I. W. Abel, cited by G. Bogdavitch, "Never a Kind Word for Abel," *Nation,* May 7, 1973, p. 591.
23. *Saturday Review World,* April 20, 1974, p. 24.
24. Published in the United States under that title by W. W. Norton, 1968.
25. *New York Times,* January 6, 1973.
26. Ibid., December 23, 1974.
27. *Chicago Daily News,* November 19, 1971.
28. *New York Times,* December 23, 1974.
29. Ibid., March 23, 1974.
30. *Los Angeles Times,* March 19, 1975.
31. N. K. Vien, "The Vietnamese Experience and the Third World," *Bulletin of Concerned Asian Scholars,* September–October 1974, p. 10.
32. *New York Times,* October 3, 1972.
33. B. Davidson, *The Liberation of Guiné* (New York: Penguin Books, 1969), p. 38.
34. Ibid., pp. 88, 89.
35. Ibid., p. 17.
36. Ibid., pp. 126, 127.
37. Ibid., p. 43.
38. Ibid., p. 42.
39. Vien, "The Vietnamese Experience," p. 10.
40. Ibid.

41. *New York Times,* December 14, 1972.
42. Ibid., January 15, 1974.
43. Ibid., February 26, 1974.
44. J. Galtung, "Social Structures, Education Structure and Lifelong Education: The Case of Japan," in *Japan: Reviews of National Politics for Education* (Paris: Organization for Economic Co-operation and Development, 1971), p. 144. Emphasis in original.
45. Cited by M. Meisner, "Leninism and Maoism: Some Populist Perspectives on Marxist-Leninism in China," *China Quarterly,* January–March 1971, p. 18.
46. J. Myrdal and G. Kessle, *China: The Revolution Continued* (New York: Vintage Books, 1972), pp. 20, 129, 130.
47. Cited by J. Gardner, "Political Participation and Chinese Communism," in G. Parry, Ed., *Participation in Politics* (Manchester, England: Manchester University Press, 1972), p. 223.
48. *Peking Review,* September 7, 1973, p. 33.
49. T. I. Emerson, "On Keeping a Revolution," *Nation,* March 29, 1975, p. 371.
50. Melvin Tumin, cited by R. L. Heilbroner, *Between Capitalism and Socialism* (New York: Vintage Books, 1970), p. 110.
51. Cited by K. Mehnert, *China Returns* (New York: Dutton, 1972), p. 173.
52. Cited by Gardner, "Political Participation," p. 223.
53. Cited by B. Schwartz, "Thoughts of Mao Tse-tung," *New York Review of Books,* February 8, 1973, p. 27.
54. R. M. Pfeffer, "Serving the People and Continuing the Revolution," *China Quarterly,* October–December 1972, pp. 622, 623.
55. Schwartz, "Thoughts of Mao," p. 31.

Chapter 6 (Pages 136–163)

1. CBS Television Network, "The Twenty-First Century," May 21, 1967.
2. E. Fromm, *The Revolution of Hope: Toward a Humanized Technology* (New York: Bantam Books, 1968), pp. 39, 40.
3. Cited by G. Lakey, *Strategy for a Living Revolution* (San Francisco: W. H. Freeman and Co., 1973), p. 8.
4. *New York Times,* February 9, 1973.
5. *New York Review of Books,* October 4, 1973, p. 13.
6. *Washington Post,* June 19, 1970.
7. *Working Class Women in a Changing World: A Review of Research Findings* (Chicago: Social Research, Inc., 1973), p. 41.
8. *New York Times,* March 19, 1973.

9. See W. W. Harman, "The New Copernican Revolution," *Stanford Today*, Winter 1969, pp. 6–10; O. W. Markley, "The New Image of Man," *New York Times*, December 16, 1974; and D. S. Elgin, "What Waits across America's Newest Frontier," *Los Angeles Times*, December 19, 1974.

10. *New York Times*, July 6, 1973.

11. R. Skole, "Over Coffee with Olaf Palme," *Nation*, July 6, 1974, pp. 13–15.

12. Cited by W. D. Connor, *Deviance in Soviet Society* (New York: Columbia University Press, 1972), pp. 255, 256.

13. A. Snieckus, "The Soviet Woman Is an Active Creator and Educator," cited by S. M. Lipset, "Social Stratification Research and the Role of Soviet Sociology," in M. Yanowitch and W. A. Fisher, Eds., *Social Stratification and Mobility in the USSR* (White Plains, N.Y.: International Arts and Sciences Press, 1973), p. 266.

14. Cited by E. H. Carr, *1917: Before and After* (New York: Macmillan, 1969), p. 72.

15. Ibid., p. 80.

16. *New York Times*, August 6, 1971.

17. R. A. Medvedey, *Let History Judge* (New York: Knopf, 1971) pp. 539, 540.

18. *New York Times*, January 12, 1974.

19. M. N. Rutkevich and F. R. Filippov, "Social Interchanges," cited in Yanowitch and Fisher, *Social Stratification and Mobility in the USSR*, p. 266.

20. V. Kontorovich, "Sociology and Literature," *Soviet Sociology*, 1968, Vol. 7 (Summer), p. 15. Cited by Lipset, "Social Stratification Research," p. 365.

21. L. I. Sennikova, cited by Lipset, "Social Stratification Research," p. 366.

22. *New York Times*, December 22, 1972.

23. Ibid.

24. *Toronto Globe and Mail*, September 4, 1972.

25. Cited by R. T. deGeorge, *Soviet Ethics and Morality* (Ann Arbor: University of Michigan Press, 1969), p. 106.

26. Ibid. p. 83.

27. *San Francisco Chronicle*, December 29, 1972.

28. Z. A. Medvedev and R. A. Medvedev, *A Question of Madness* (New York: Knopf, 1971), pp. 218, 219.

29. *Los Angeles Times*, November 8, 1975.

30. B. M. Richman, *Industrial Society in Communist China* (New York: Random House, 1969), pp. 224, 225.

31. *New York Times*, May 26, 1975.

32. S. H. L. Wu, "The Changing Peasant Mentality in China: Some Personal Reflections after 27 Years," *Understanding China Newsletter*, November–December 1974, p. 6.

33. S. Schram, *Mao Tse-tung* (New York: Penguin Books, 1966), p. 333.

34. E. Snow, *The Long Revolution* (New York: Random House, 1972), p. 69.

35. K. S. Karol, *The Other Communism* (New York: Hill and Wang, 1967), p. 248.
36. W. Casey, in *Holy Cross Quarterly*, 1975, pp. 5, 9.
37. *New York Times*, September 21, 1974; July 2 and 7, 1975.

Chapter 7 (Pages 164–197)

1. R. Heilbroner, *The Future as History* (New York: Harper, 1959), p. 209.
2. CBS Television Network, October 13, 1970.
3. *New York Times*, September 26, 1974.
4. Cited in A. A. Ekirch, *The Idea of Progress in America, 1815–1860* (New York: Columbia University Press, 1944), p. 32.
5. *New York Times*, July 15, 1975.
6. Letter to the editor, *American Report*.
7. H. G. Johnson, *Money, Trade and Growth* (London: Allen and Unwin, 1962), p. 153. Cited by N. Hamid, "Alternative Development Strategies," *Monthly Review*, October 1974, p. 33.
8. Mahbub-ul-Haq, *The Strategy of Economic Planning* (London: Oxford University Press, 1963), p. 20. Cited by Hamid, "Alternative Development Strategies," p. 33.
9. R. O'Mara, "Brazil: The Booming Despotism," *Nation*, April 27, 1974, p. 517.
10. E. B. Burns, "Brazil since Joao Goulart," *Nation*, April 23, 1973, p. 538.
11. *New York Times*, May 19, 1973.
12. Ibid., May 20, 1975.
13. Ibid.
14. Ibid., March 15, 1974.
15. Ibid., December 2, 1973.
16. Ibid., January 26, 1973.
17. Cited in *Resurgence*, 1972, Vol. 4, No. 2, pp. 30–31.
18. R. Clarke, "Technology for an Alternative Society," *New Scientist*, January 11, 1973.
19. Cited in *American Report*, September 16, 1974. Details available in M. Raskin, *Notes on the Old System* (New York: David McKay, 1974).
20. *New York Times*, April 6, 1974.
21. C. W. Hollister, "Twilight in the West," in L. White, Jr., Ed., *The Transformation of the Roman World* (Berkeley and Los Angeles: University of California Press, 1966), p. 204.
22. A. N. Whitehead, *Science and the Modern World* (New York: New American Library, 1933), pp. 207, 208.

23. J. Bronowski, "The Ascent of Man," British Broadcasting Corporation, 1973, p. 437.
24. *New York Times,* May 9, 1975.
25. K. Maxwell, "The Hidden Revolution in Portugal," *New York Review of Books,* April 17, 1975, pp. 31, 32.
26. *New York Times,* June 30, 1975.
27. Cited by J. F. Melby, "Maoism as a World Force," *Annals of the American Academy of Political and Social Science,* July 1972, p. 27.
28. CBS Television Network, "Reston on China: A Conversation with Eric Sevareid," August 31, 1971.
29. J. M. Keynes, *Essays in Persuasion* (New York: Harcourt, 1932), pp. 371–373.

INDEX